Science & Technology Education Library

VOLUME 34

SCOPE

The book series *Science & Technology Education Library* provides a publication forum
for scholarship in science and technology education. It aims to publish innovative books
which are at the forefront of the field. Monographs as well as collections of papers will
be published.

For other titles published in this series, go to
www.springer.com/series/6512

Researching Design Learning

Issues and Findings from Two Decades of Research and Development

By

RICHARD KIMBELL

Goldsmiths, University of London, UK

and

KAY STABLES

Goldsmiths, University of London, UK

 Springer

Authors
Prof. Richard Kimbell
1 Jesses Lane
Guildford, Surrey
Burrows Cross House
Gomshall GU5 9QF
United Kingdom

Prof. Kay Stables
28 Goldington St.
London NW1 1UE
United Kingdom

ISBN: 978-1-4020-9054-7   e-ISBN: 978-1-4020-5115-9

Library of Congress Control Number: 2008934468

Printed on acid-free paper

9 8 7 6 5 4 3 2 1

springer.com

To Harriet, Tony and the families

We promise not to write another one. Not for a while anyway.

Contents

Foreword

A book on technology education research, written by Richard Kimbell and Kay Stables is one of those books that need no recommendation for those who know the field. Their work is internationally known for its quality. Their names are the first to pop up when one organises a conference on technology education and seeks for keynote presenters in a conference section on assessment. For people in technology education the combination of Kimbell and Stables is almost synonymous with Goldsmiths College. Any College can hardly wish itself better ambassadors to establish a reputation for the institute than these two colleagues.

Having written that, what else is there to be written about this book? It offers exactly what one would expect of these authors: a thorough and well-written survey of all the different aspects of technology education research. It presents both a sound philosophical underpinning for what should be researched and how it should be researched, as well as a rich variety of examples taken directly from the practice of the authors and their colleagues. Even though this latter element does give this book a distinct UK flavour, the book deserves to have a place in the 'must read' literature for technology education internationally.

The authors are primarily known for their work on assessment. The scope of the book is wider ('research' in general) and comprises also teaching and learning. Still I believe that it is justified to take the term 'assessment' to be a key term here. The strength of what the authors have done is that they have taken a wide view on assessment. To do proper assessment, one needs to do research on it, and even consider assessment itself to be a form of research. To do proper assessment, one has to see it in relation with teaching and learning. Writing about assessment in an isolated way does not make much sense. Doing that was perhaps the biggest mistakes of the early days in technology education. One of the merits of this book is that it positions assessment in a broader context. Assessment is more than finding out what mark pupils should be awarded.

It is not easy to find proper ways to understand and assess the full complexity of what goes on in technology education lessons and projects. But the Goldsmiths contribution to finding the answer, or rather to finding answers, is substantial, and it is a good thing that now they are all documented here in this book.

From the above it may be evident that I warmly recommend this book to those who are involved in technology education as well as those whose interests include the wider fields of learning through design not just in assessment but also in policy making, curriculum development, teaching or educating teachers.

Eindhoven, July 2007
Marc J. de Vries

Preface

Kay Stables and Richard Kimbell started working together on research projects at Goldsmiths College in January 1986. Richard was a lecturer and Kay was newly appointed after completing her MA at the Royal College of Art. In the intervening years (filled with wars, pestilence, Chernobyl, national curriculum, Margaret Thatcher and 11 Secretaries of State for Education) Kay's hair has gone grey, and Richard's has just gone. Now, both of us are professors in the University.

Amongst all the national and international turmoil, not least in the education world, there have been some fixed points around which we have sought to organise our professional activities over those 20+ years. At the top of this list is a set of beliefs and values about **learning** and **teaching**, **designing** and **design & technology**. And progressively, as we explored the world of **research**, there is a set of beliefs and values about that too. They have been like lodestones holding us on course through some very choppy waters. It is these positions of principle that we have tried to articulate in Part One of this book.

In Part Two, we offer a straightforward (though heavily abbreviated) descriptive account of 20 of the research projects that we have undertaken. To make them more manageable we have organised them into four cognate groupings, concerning assessment, fundamental research, public policy and curricular initiatives, though in reality many of the projects could arguably be located in more than one of these groups.

In Part Three, we attempt to draw together what we have learned through the process of conducting these projects.

Over the last decade we have supervised many research students who are now rightly proud owners of their doctoral degrees – though interestingly neither of us has one. But an almost inevitable part of the training for these students has been their immersion in one or more of our projects, and the detailed scrutiny and analysis of many more. They tell us that from this induction process they have learnt a lot about how to do research, about research design, instrument design, analysis techniques and much more. It may be somewhat late in the day, but we decided that there might be a wider audience out there who might similarly gain benefit from our work. So – 2 years ago – we set about designing it.

Whilst the majority of our work has been designed to support design & technology as a curriculum discipline, this is not always the case (particularly the projects discussed in Chapter 8). We recognise that the current formulation of design & technology is – in any case – merely a transitory phenomenon. It was significantly different 10 years ago and in another 10 years it may be completely different again. But there are things about it that will remain. At its core is the concept of design-based learning and we would like to believe that this will outlive any specific manifestation of the subject. Accordingly, we have titled the book *Researching Design Learning*, deliberately using this broader, more inclusive label.

It is also important to acknowledge that much of our work has been in the UK context – though not always conducted in the UK. We recognise the confusion that sometimes encumbers this shorthand label, and when we talk of the National Curriculum we mean the England and Wales curriculum – Scotland and Northern Ireland have their own versions. However, we believe that our research approaches have application to **any** curriculum and learning setting – not just those concerned with design-based learning.

We hope that readers will derive some interest and enlightenment from this very brief account of our research over the last 20+ years. We would also be pleased to hear from any readers who have a view about it.

Richard Kimbell and Kay Stables
Goldsmiths, University of London, UK
2007

Acknowledgements

This book is based on the research we have conducted for more than 20+ years. That work could not have gone ahead without the whole-hearted professionalism of all the members of the research teams that we assembled for the projects. Some individuals have been at the heart of many of our projects, and none more than Soo Miller and Ruth Wright, to whom we are deeply indebted. We would also like to thank:

Mike Fletcher, who first helped us to understand statistics

Tony Lawler, for his 'pictures' of designing, both as artwork and metaphor

Maggie Rogers, for being our guide to understanding young learners

John Saxton, whose understanding of design & technology is unrivalled

Gerry Turtle, whose meticulous organisation created the Technology Education Research Unit (TERU) research archive

Roy Vickery, for good-humouredly keeping the accounts straight

Tony Wheeler, for enthusiastically bombarding us with new ideas and technologies.

We are grateful to all the others who have played key roles in our projects over the years:

Jenny Bain, Tom Baird, Tom Balchin, Graham Brown-Martin, Paul Clewes, Jo Compton, Jules Davidoff, Karim Derrick, Ali Farrell, Françiose Fokias, Richard Green, Paddy O'Hagan, Wesley Hamilton, Jo Hayes, Linz Hayes, Clare Kelly, Sandie Kendall, Terry Liddament, Di Lockyer, Pat Mahoney, Susan McLaren, Olefile Molwane, Sue Moore, Chloe Nast, Sandra Parker, Jim Patterson, David Perry, Debbie Roberson, Juliet Sprake, Tristram Shepard, Will Wharfe, Gillian Whitehouse, Ian Williams, Andrew Wozniak and Sangbong Yi.

A significant proportion of our work has been undertaken in schools, and it would not have been possible without the enthusiastic support of the teachers and the young people who have so willingly subjected themselves to our activities. We are continually delighted by their imagination and capabilities, and are grateful for their cooperation.

We are also indebted to the students and staff of the Design and Educational Studies Departments at Goldsmiths, and particularly to the research students whose regular critical appraisals of our work keep us on our toes. In the wider design & technology world, we are aware of the string of thinkers who have contributed so much to our understanding: Ken Baynes, John Eggleston, Peter Green, George Hicks, Mike Ive, David Layton, Vic Kelly and Roy Richards being at the head of a long list.

Finally, we would like to express our appreciation to the 'blind' reviewers who obviously spent a great deal of time and care in reading and commenting on the original manuscript. Their comments were pertinent, encouraging and very helpful to us in honing the final version. If we ever find out who they are, we will buy them a beer.

Introduction

THE STORY OF TERU

Why you might find this chapter interesting

In this chapter we summarise the entire body of work that we have undertaken in the Technology Education Research Unit (TERU) at Goldsmiths. It spans a period in more than 20 years and we have structured the story so as to be broadly chronological. Interestingly this chronology also reflects a series of shifts in the nature of the work, originating in research concerning assessment and moving progressively through phases of fundamental research, public policy and curricular initiatives before returning once again to assessment priorities. We have mapped this chronology in the graphic that introduces Part Two of the book (see page 66).

***

1.   TERU AND PERFORMANCE ASSESSMENT

In 1984, the UK Department of Education & Science announced design & technology as a new field of enquiry to be tackled by its research branch, the Assessment of Performance Unit (APU). Established in 1975, the APU's prime task was surveying and monitoring levels of achievement in schools. By the time the design & technology contract was issued, it had conducted extensive surveys in mathematics, English, science and modern languages, typically at ages 8, 11 and 15. Much had been discovered about what learners could be expected to achieve in these subjects at those ages. Progressively, however, a change of focus was detectable in the conduct of those surveys. APU began to focus less on mere monitoring, and more on providing support for curriculum development.

Early APU surveys were seen largely as providing data about what learners could or could not do – and how this changed over time. In curricular terms APU was distinctly non-interventionist. Progressively however, the concern became to understand why learners performed in the ways they did; teasing out learning blocks and helping teachers to enhance learning. APU was increasingly becoming a force for curriculum development. (Kimbell et al., 1991, p. 11)

With the 1984 announcement that APU wished to survey design & technology, tenders were invited. The contract to undertake the research was won by Goldsmiths.

The proposal enabled a research team to be created in the design & technology department at Goldsmiths. This team was directed to Professor Vic Kelly (a curriculum specialist) and the research was coordinated by Richard Kimbell (a lecturer in design & technology). At the launch of the project, the team additionally comprised Kay Stables (a specialist textiles teacher), John Saxton and Jim Patterson (both craft, design & technology teachers). Other appointments were made during the subsequent 5 years.

Our approach to this first research project – and the major issues that arose within it – is explained in detail in Chapter 5. Suffice it to say here that over the following 5 years this research team developed a quite new approach to performance assessment in design & technology. We found new ways to describe the domains of performance and developed approaches for supporting and enriching learners' performance. We developed this approach into 26 tests that we took into 700 schools across England, Wales and Northern Ireland, and in total we assessed the performance of approximately 10,000 learners. The resulting performance data were analysed from many perspectives, and the final report contained national performance levels analysed in relation to gender, ability, and the curriculum that had been experienced by the learners. We also revealed generalised features of design & technology activities that have serious effects on performance levels, such as the nature of tasks and their contextual setting as well as the structures of activity through which learners tackle those tasks. The full research report was published in 1991 (Kimbell et al., 1991).

But before then, in 1989, other research ventures were appearing on the horizon – not least concerning the planned implementation of design & technology in the National Curriculum. With the imminent prospect of a number of new research and development projects coming into the Design Department at Goldsmiths, in 1990 Richard created TERU – the Technology Education Research Unit, as a Unit within which we could draw together all these research and development activities in support of design & technology in schools.

On the strength of *APU Design & Technology*, we acquired three new projects – two of which centred upon approaches to the performance assessment of learners in design & technology classrooms, workshops and studios. Specifically, we were invited to create prototype tests for National Curriculum design & technology – at age 14 (1989–1992) and at age 7 (1990–1992). Both these projects took further the models of research that had been originated within *APU Design & Technology*; the age 14 project being directed by Jim Patterson, and the age 7 project by Kay.

Richard directed the third project – developing curriculum support materials for design & technology for the newly created National Curriculum Council – alongside the preparations for publication of the *APU Design & Technology* report.

2.   THE NEED FOR FUNDAMENTAL RESEARCH

APU Design & Technology had been the first large-scale research to be undertaken in design & technology. The subject itself was a new concept – drawn together through a series of curriculum initiatives that gradually coalesced into design & technology in the late 1980s. Plenty of curriculum development projects had taken place in these evolutionary years, but nothing of a fundamental nature to enable the design & technology community to create the conceptual underpinning that is necessary for real understanding of a subject. Design & technology – at this time – was best described as 'what was done' by a group of practitioners who shared a set of ideals about teaching and learning in workshop and studio settings.

In our own national context, these ideals and practices had been rationalised (in 1985) as part of the revision of 16+ examinations. Prior to this point, there had been a twin system of qualifications at 16+; the General Certificate of Education (GCE), for the 'top' 25% of ability of the population, and the Certificate of Secondary Education (CSE) for the rest. In 1985 these two systems were merged into the General Certificate of Secondary Education (GCSE) and the opportunity was also taken to consolidate and update the content of the subjects to be examined. Two of those GCSE subjects, Craft Design & Technology (work in wood, metals and plastics, graphics and technological systems) and Home Economics (work in food, textiles, child development and home management) were the core of what was subsequently to become design & technology.

In both groupings, the role of **designing** was accentuated, and this subsequently became the organising feature that dominated design & technology when it was launched as a 'new' subject as part of the first England and Wales National Curriculum. This new subject drew from all its founding formulations, most notably Craft Design & Technology and Home Economics, but there was at least as much doubt and confusion about its composition and practices as there was clarity and light. The formulation of National Curriculum Programmes of Study and Attainment Targets – built around designing and making – forced the amalgamation of these two groupings into design & technology as it now (broadly) exists. The disparate traditions and practices created enormous tensions within design & technology. The situation cried out for some fundamental research that could build a conceptual framework to make sense of the beast that had been created.

In 1991, Richard applied to the Economic and Social Research Council (ESRC) for a grant to fund a project to explore – and seek to understand – the practices that proliferated at that point. In 1992, the ESRC approved the award and a new 2-year project was launched within TERU: *Understanding Technological Approaches* to teaching and learning in the curriculum.

In this project we explored in detail real-time projects in design & technology at every school year from Year 1 to Year 11 in the new National Curriculum (i.e. with learners from age 5 to 16) in every area of design & technology. The approach was broadly to **observe** projects from start to finish – usually 3–4 hours with Years 1 and 2, but as long as 48 hours with Year 11. The observations were built around a common framework – enabling us to make direct connections between the approaches to designing and making across this complete age range.

Analysing these detailed observations (taken over 2 years) enabled us to characterise approaches to design & technology teaching & learning, and describe it in ways that had hitherto not been possible. We published this work in 'Understanding Practice in Design & Technology' (Kimbell et al., 1996).

3.   THE DEMANDS OF PUBLIC POLICY

By the mid-1990s design & technology had become a fixed point on the educational landscape. Having escaped from the obscurity imposed by its fractured history, design & technology – as a single entity – began to assert itself into areas of public life. All kinds of issues began to emerge with interested professional bodies, not least with the UK Design & Engineering Councils, both organisations with certain responsibilities for managing, promoting or regulating their professions who also have a brief to inform and educate the general public about their activities. Particular interest in design & technology is related to:

- Its role as a university entrance qualification
- Its employment value for school leavers
- Its role as an economic driver in a knowledge-economy
- The challenge of recruiting and training teachers

From 1995, we were approached on a range of these issues to run projects that could illuminate areas of public policy. The first of these arose through the Design Council, building case studies of 'good practice' so as to exemplify what was meant by design & technology. However, the bodies for these public policy projects were typically **less** concerned with developing good practice in schools, and more concerned with understanding the distinctive contribution that design & technology could make in areas of public and professional life. Their priority was to seek **conceptual** clarity about the subject rather than to support the development of practice in schools.

We presented a case to the Design Council, that **designing** is a distinctive way of thinking, and they awarded us a grant for a 2-year project exploring exactly that territory. The project *Decisions by Design* (1995–1997) explored the power of designerly thinking for those who are not (and do not intend to become) designers. How is design thinking similar to and different from 'ordinary' thinking? What is its distinctive character? The successful conclusion of this project led to further projects in the general area of transferable design skills for employment. The first, *Design Skills for Work* (1997–1999), addressed the general question 'what are designers good at, if they are not being designers?' This was followed by a project exploring the attitudes of design students towards a career in teaching – *Attitudes of Potential Teachers of Design & Technology* (1999–2000).

At the same time the Engineering Council – interested in routes from school into engineering – was concerned to explore the role of mathematics in design & technology. The serious drop-off of candidates coming forward with pure and applied mathematics and physics, along with the increasing awareness of the engineering nature of some design & technology, had encouraged some universities to seek students who had successfully completed design & technology Advanced Level examination courses. The project *Technological Maths* – seeking to identify the nature and extent of the mathematics in design & technology – ran in TERU from 1996–1997. A second project for the Engineering Council – *Design & Technology in a Knowledge Economy* (2000–2001) – aimed to locate design & technology within the wider debate about the need for curriculum change to support future knowledge economies.

Towards the end of the 1990s, the National Curriculum formulation of design & technology had worked its way through the entire school population, primary and secondary. It had evolved through two official versions (1990 and 1995, and the 2000 version was looming) as well as a number of unofficial ones, inspired by particular interest groups. A centre of gravity had emerged for the subject, consolidating into forms of classroom and workshop practice that were more commonly understood and accepted. So changes at this point were destined to be less sweeping and more incremental – tweaking the formula rather than slinging it out the window.

So the need for evidence about the performance of particular approaches to learning and teaching within this curriculum became ever more necessary and in TERU we became involved in all kinds of evaluative projects – seeking to understand and make evident the particular strengths and weaknesses of this or that curriculum initiative or approach.

4.   EVALUATING CURRICULAR INITIATIVES

Ironically, the first of these evaluation exercises was for a foreign government. The presence of design & technology in the UK had for some years been exerting an influence on the international scene, and the consolidated form of National Curriculum design & technology had been influential, especially in the English-speaking world where UK journals and conference speakers were available.

It was the new Mandela administration in South Africa that invited TERU to undertake its first evaluation of a curriculum initiative, funded by the Department for International Development (DFID). In the North West Province – centred on Mafikeng – the provincial curriculum team, in association with a non-governmental organisation (NGO), had undertaken a pilot study to introduce a technology education curriculum for learners in their final 2 years of schooling. The scale of the challenge of undertaking this curriculum in rural schools in South Africa is difficult to imagine in more 'developed' countries:

- Schools with minimal facilities and (sometimes) no electricity
- Involving teachers from subject backgrounds as diverse as geography and Afrikaans
- Traveling huge distances to attend training sessions
- Training for a curriculum that was dramatically different from former (craft) practice
- Resources brought into the schools by van across huge distances
- With the curriculum expert (the van driver) visiting perhaps twice a year

Our evaluation of the curriculum and of the Province's procedures for developing and disseminating it became part of the wider South Africa education debate when technology was absorbed into their national curriculum framework.

Other evaluation projects followed; for London's Design Museum, exploring the effects of their educational outreach programmes; for the Design & Technology Teachers' Association (DATA), evaluating the impact of Pro-DESKTOP computer aided design software; for the National Endowment for Science Technology and the Arts (NESTA), developing a new **systems and control** curriculum with LEGO soft and hardware; for Middlesbrough Local Education Authority (LEA), evaluating literacy developments through design & technology in primary schools; and for the BBC, evaluating their *Roboteers in Residence* programme that brought expert roboteers into schools to work with learners developing robots for a BBC TV programme.

5.   THE NEW MILLENNIUM

In 2000, a number of related events took place that shaped the activities of TERU over the following 5 years. The latest version of the National Curriculum (NC2000) was launched, with some amendments to the Programmes of Study and the Attainment Target. Most critically, however, it included for the first time a statement about the importance of design & technology in the curriculum. It may seem odd that such a 'vision statement' should not be published until a decade after the original launch of design & technology in the 1990 National Curriculum. The recognition of this need for a clear statement of intent was reflected right across the curriculum – from all subjects – and these statements were drafted with expert subject groups in 1999 as cornerstones for the launch of the fully revised curriculum.

However, the issue ran deeper for those of us concerned with learning through design. The tortuous history of design & technology, and the rapid evolutionary steps that it had progressed through in the decade immediately prior to the establishment of the National Curriculum in 1990, all contributed to the recognition – in the UK Government Department for Education & Employment; in DATA (the Design and Technology Association), the subject's professional Association; and in Higher Education and teacher education establishments – that the newborn baby would need careful nurturing in the immediate years ahead. Accordingly, the Department for Education & Employment established a Design & Technology Strategy Group to oversee these years and to bring forward recommendations for the immediate future.

One of the earliest tasks undertaken by this group was to analyse the internal coherence of design & technology as presented in its revised version, and specifically in relation to the 'fit' between the newly created vision statement and the Programmes of Study and the Attainment Target, both of which had evolved through three versions of the National Curriculum. Some discrepancies became apparent. Among these was the recognition that whilst the vision accentuated the importance of developing learners' creativity and innovation, and significantly through the vehicle of teamwork, teachers – particularly through the assessment criteria for the GCSE examinations – were not required to acknowledge or reward these qualities.

In the light of these mismatches, TERU was commissioned to undertake a project to reinvigorate the creative heart of designing and develop approaches to the assessment of design & technology that would reward teamwork and innovation.

6.   PERFORMANCE ASSESSMENT AND INNOVATION

In January 2003, we launched the project *Assessing Design Innovation* and in many ways this drew TERU back to its origins in the Assessment of Performance Unit in the mid-1980s. We were back to exploring approaches to performance assessment in design & technology, but with the additional requirement that the approaches we developed should be focused on supporting teamwork and enhancing learner innovation.

But by now we had a great deal more experience of research and development approaches. We were able to draw on the wide range of techniques that we have developed in our earlier work:

- Exploring the nature of design & technology
- Supporting the development of public policy
- Evaluating curriculum initiatives

Over 2 years from January 2003 to December 2004 we worked with a small number of LEAs and schools across the country, and produced models for assessing design innovation that were subsequently not only reported to the (now renamed) Department for Education and Skills and its curriculum and assessment 'watchdog' the Qualifications and Curriculum Authority, but were also shared with the General Certificate of Secondary Education Awarding Bodies. One of the immediate outcomes of this project was the development by one of these awarding bodies of a new form of syllabus and examination based on the approach we had developed in the project.

In the process of developing our approach to assessment in this project, we explored a range of new technologies to see how they might be helpful. Among these technologies were the use of digital cameras to record learners' emerging work, and of some simple computer aided design interfaces to support their ideation. It became apparent to us that these digital technologies offered the potential radically to transform the assessment process, and we proposed to Qualifications and Curriculum Authority and the Department for Education and Skills that these technologies should be the explicit focus of a research and development project. This proposal came simultaneously with the challenge to the examination Awarding Bodies to accept design & technology assessment portfolios on disk – i.e. digitally. This was – at one level – merely a natural evolution of design & technology, but – at another level – a serious challenge to the established assessment procedures of the Qualifications and Curriculum Authority.

In the light of all these pressures, our proposal was accepted and project *e-scape* is currently underway. The project will run to 2009 and will result in digitally based portfolio assessments for design & technology, findings for the first two phases of this being included in later sections of this book. In the third (and final) phase exploratory steps will be undertaken to examine the implications and possibilities for replicating *e-scape* approaches into the assessment of learner performance in other subjects, in the first instance geography and science.

Stepping outside the boundaries of design & technology was also a feature of a further performance assessment project that we undertook in parallel with *Assessing Design Innovation*. This project, commissioned by the Royal Society for the Arts (RSA), was aimed at exploring approaches to assessing generic competences such as teamworking, systematic thinking and managing risk that were being developed through a further RSA project 'Opening Minds: Education for the 21st Century' (Bayliss, 1999). The TERU project, *Researching Assessment Approaches*, was conducted during 2002–2003. Meanwhile, the initial *Assessing Design Innovation* project materials were being utilised in collaborative work (not reported in this book) with the University of Strathclyde (McLaren et al., 2006) and the Stockholm Institute of Education (Skogh, 2005).

7. THE EMERGING STORY OF TERU

The major blocks of research and development outlined here, that we have undertaken within TERU over the last 20 years, were not consciously planned out from the start. But neither were they arbitrarily taken on.

The APU starting point in 1985 was unexpected, and was undertaken with more enthusiasm for design & technology than expertise in assessment research. We have progressively acquired that expertise. But after that first project for APU, the priorities for our subsequent work have reflected the concerns of a new subject emerging into the spotlight of National Curriculum from the relative obscurity of a collection of historical and typically unregarded and undervalued subjects.

One of the biggest difficulties for the new fledgling design & technology was that there was almost nothing in the way of research upon which to base decisions about curriculum, or pedagogy, or assessment. Practice in schools therefore emerged on the basis of hunches and best guesses and things that had worked in the past. There was painfully little foundation on which to build a coherent and progressive vision of design & technology.

> Design & Technology lacks a research base in pupils understanding and learning such as is available in the cases of mathematics and science. (DES/WO, 1988b, p. 7)

> Craft Design & Technology stands out as the most under researched area of the curriculum. The literature of the subject barely exists. (Penfold, 1988, preface p. ix)

TERU was established in response to these challenging observations. Moreover, it was founded on the belief that learning in and through design & technology has some features that make it unusual in the curriculum, and that enable it to contribute positively and uniquely to the education of young people. The research and development that we have undertaken has been informed by this belief and has sought to throw light onto the traditions and practices of teaching and learning in design & technology workshops, studios and classrooms.

This book tells the story of this research and of the issues and themes that have intertwined through the projects and formed the understandings that we now hold. In what immediately follows we lay down the theoretical and conceptual underpinnings for what have been major threads throughout the work: our standpoints on **capability**, on **learning and teaching**, on **assessing performance** and on the **methodological** priorities that inform our approach to research.

OUR PHILOSOPHICAL POSITION

In Part One, we outline the **beliefs** and **values** that formed the starting points for our research endeavours. In the mid-1980s we were essentially a team of experienced teachers with views about the nature of being human; of what it means to learn; and of what is uniquely offered to those two concerns by learning through design activity.

These beliefs exerted an enormous influence on our practices; an influence that has become ever more apparent to us as we have undertaken the projects. So much so that – in order fully to appreciate the projects – it seems appropriate that we should lay out here these beliefs and values for inspection and analysis. They amount to a conceptual lens through which we view and act on the educational world. We have organised it through four themes:

- Capability
- Learning and teaching
- Assessment
- Research

Chapter 1

CAPABILITY
A philosophical position

Why you might find this chapter interesting

*In this chapter we focus attention on what – for us – is the central goal of education. Whilst some might prioritise knowledge, understanding and scholarship as the cornerstones that mark out the 'educated' person, we hold a somewhat different view. We prefer a view of education that celebrates qualities that empower people to make a difference in the world. Developing learners' **capability** therefore seems to us a more important goal.*

We discuss the roots of this capability in humans and locate design & technology capability within a wider 'capability' debate in education. We challenge the argument that capability-based learning should be informed by extrinsic motives such as employability, since we see it rather as a fundamental entitlement for all learners. We use some of the differences between UK and USA priorities in technology education to highlight the core issues and conclude with a discussion of (a celebration of) the critical role of uncertainty to this view of education.

***

We began our research in the mid-1980s with a pre-existing mindset about capability. It was never explicitly stated, and certainly it was never written down, but it was present – tacitly – in every team discussion that took place in those early formative years struggling with the *APU Design & Technology* project. We were essentially a team of experienced teachers with implicitly held views about the nature of being human; of what it means to learn; and of what is uniquely offered to those two concerns by learning through design activity.

1.   CREATIVE HUMANKIND

With the clear vision that hindsight enables, it would probably have been very helpful if we had attempted to write down exactly what we thought we meant by design & technology capability, but being by instinct designers, we attempted rather to draw and model it. Subsequently, we found our concrete thoughts were put neatly into words by Bronowski when he was describing the uniqueness of humankind.

> Among the multitude of animals that scamper, fly, burrow and swim around us, man is the only one who is not locked into his environment. His imagination, his reason, his emotional subtlety and toughness make it possible for him not to accept the environment but to change it. (Bronowski, 1973, p. 19)
>
> Man is not the most majestic of the creatures. But he has what no other animal possesses, a jigsaw of faculties, which alone, over three thousand million years of life, make him creative. (Ibid. p. 42)
>
> And (this) derive(s) from ... the ability to visualise the future, to foresee what may happen and plan to anticipate it, and to represent it to ourselves as images that we project and move about inside our head. (Ibid. p. 56)

Bronowski's focus here on creativity, as a unique quality in humankind, has subsequently been expressed by others, including Csikszentmihalyi.

> Creativity is a central source of meaning in our lives for several reasons. ... First, most of the things that are interesting, important and *human* are the results of creativity. We share 98% of our makeup with chimpanzees. What makes us different – our language, values, artistic expression, scientific understanding, and technology – is the result of individual ingenuity that was recognised, rewarded and transmitted through learning. Without creativity, it would be difficult indeed to distinguish humans from apes. (Csikszentmihalyi, 1996, p. 2)

This view is also supported by Nelson and Stolterman (2003) who view design as being an entirely natural part of human behaviour that is engaged in at some level by practically all humans everyday of their lives. The way we intentionally act on our world through design is at the heart of human progress. As they point out:

> Humans did not discover fire – they designed it. The wheel was not something our ancestors merely stumbled over in a stroke of good luck; it, too, was designed. (Nelson & Stolterman, 2003, p. 9)

2. IMAGING AND MODELLING

In our position paper for *APU Design & Technology* (Kelly et al., 1987) we focused on the creative process that Bronowski describes as 'the ability to visualise the future, to foresee what may happen and plan to anticipate it, and to represent it to ourselves as images that we project and move about inside our head' placing at its heart the ability to 'image' and 'model'. In the 1987 paper, we cited Kosslyn's work on imaging (Kosslyn, 1979) and Bruce Archer's characterisation of the internalisation of this process as using 'the mind's eye' (Archer, 1980). We have continued to recognise the significance of the ability to image and model, particularly their **dynamic** nature, caught well in the words of Eisner.

> There is a difference between recalled images and their imaginative transformation. Were we limited to the recall of the images we had once experienced, cultural development would be in trouble. Imagination gives us the images of the possible that provide a platform for seeing the actual, and by seeing the actual freshly, we can do something about creating what lies beyond it. Imagination, fed by the sensory features of experience, is expressed in the arts through the image. The image, the central term of imagination, is qualitative in character. We do indeed see in our mind's eye. (Eisner, 2002, p. 4)

Even in the early days of our discussions we took a broad view of imaging, linking it to the way in which we draw on all our senses in this process, as reflected here by Eisner.

> Our conceptual life operates in each of the sensory modalities and in their combination. We not only can generate in the mind's eye a visual image; we can see that image even while hearing music 'around' it. We can taste a banana without actually tasting it. We can envision an opera without actually seeing or hearing it. (Ibid. p. 22)

This cognitive process is complemented by the more concrete imaging and modelling – using words, images three dimensional models and so on, in a process that we might call 'designing' and it has been our belief from the outset of all our research that this process lies at the heart of design & technology capability. In the 1987 paper, we gave form to our ideas about designing, expressing them through a model showing thought and action in an iterative and interactive relationship. It encapsulated for us a way of structuring the processes that are involved in taking an idea from its first hazy conception through to becoming a working reality. In articulating our view, we were explicitly avoiding what, at the time, were more common linear or cyclical models of designing. We believed that any designing process was driven by the development of the idea and that taking an initial spark of a hazy conception forward involved a range of sub-processes such as making judgements, finding out new information, articulating the form of the idea, solving problems and so on. But we believed that these subprocesses could not be prescribed in advance, they needed to be engaged in responsively, led by the demands in the task and the idea itself. By the end of *APU Design & Technology* the model had developed to take the form it has subsequently become commonly known in, and we reproduce it in Figure 1-1.

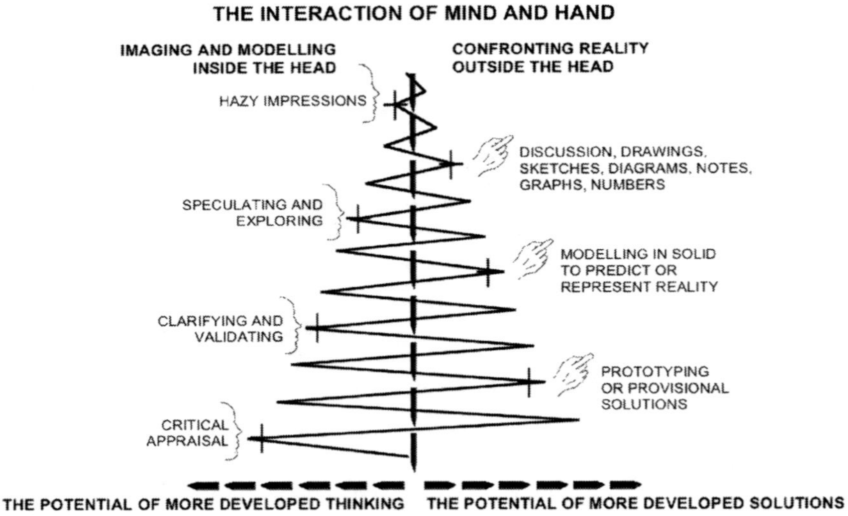

THE INTERACTION OF MIND AND HAND

| IMAGING AND MODELLING INSIDE THE HEAD | CONFRONTING REALITY OUTSIDE THE HEAD |

HAZY IMPRESSIONS

DISCUSSION, DRAWINGS, SKETCHES, DIAGRAMS, NOTES, GRAPHS, NUMBERS

SPECULATING AND EXPLORING

MODELLING IN SOLID TO PREDICT OR REPRESENT REALITY

CLARIFYING AND VALIDATING

PROTOTYPING OR PROVISIONAL SOLUTIONS

CRITICAL APPRAISAL

THE POTENTIAL OF MORE DEVELOPED THINKING   THE POTENTIAL OF MORE DEVELOPED SOLUTIONS

Figure 1-1. The APU design & technology model

In articulating 'designing' in this way we were also, in effect, giving form to our view of designerly thinking – that this too is **idea-driven** and progresses through an iteration between thought and action. In making a link between designing and designerly thinking we were also stepping into the territory of cognition and learning and it has been our view from the outset that engaging in the designerly thinking promoted by our responsive, iterative view of designing has immense potential for learning. Oxman (2001) presents a similar perspective in her plea for a shift in design education (in her case at higher education level) away from emphasising the products of designing and towards the cognitive properties of design learning. As with our model, she stresses the importance of visual representation and reasoning and not only identifies the critical nature of imaging and cognitive modelling for developing designerly thinking, but also makes the link (with particular reference to Papert, 1991) to knowledge, and designerly ways of knowing.

> Through constructing representations of design thinking the student gradually becomes richer in his ability to think in designerly ways. This contributes to an understanding of cognitive processes, which are characteristics of design, or as Papert has stated, this form of education contributes to 'knowing rather than to knowledge'. (Oxman, 2001, p. 282)

The link between designing, knowledge and knowing is one we pick up later in this chapter as we consider in more detail the place of knowledge within our view of designing processes.

Our view of process was influenced by those from within design education (e.g. Archer, 1980; Archer et al., 1976; Design Council, 1980; Roberts, 1979) and from the world of designing (e.g. Darke, 1979) and at the time that we were first developing our model, the importance of imaging and modelling ideas was also being recognised by those initiating the original design & technology National Curriculum. In 1988, the National Curriculum Design and Technology Working Party produced their Interim Report, laying down the rationale for design & technology's development as a National Curriculum subject, stressing the significance of imaging and modelling ideas.

> In so far as the cognitive processes involved in design and technology are understood today, there is a further characteristic, which merits attention. As opposed to scientists, who are concerned to explore and understand what is, designers and technologists are concerned with what might be, the conception and realisation of 'the form of things unknown'. In describing their work, they talk of 'seeing with the mind's eye'. This is literally a visionary act, a mode of thought which is non-verbal and which has been a characteristic of design and technology throughout its history. ... Imaging finds its representation in drawings, diagrams, plans, models, prototypes and computer displays and simulations, before its eventual realisation in a product, which may be an artifact, system or environment. It is a distinctive aspect of the creative thinking of designers and technologists, different from and complementary to verbal modes. Its development should be an important aim of design and technology education in all schools. (DES/WO, 1988b, pp. 4–5)

3.   OUR STARTING POINT WITH *CAPABILITY*

From the outset it has been our view that this process of imaging and modelling is central to the development of capability and in stating this we wish to be clear about our use of the label **capability** and the difference between it and other related words like competence, knowledge or skill. By capability we mean **the power to produce an effect** – a change and hopefully an improvement. In the context of design & technology capability, this is refined somewhat to being **the power to produce change and improvement in the made world**.

This is very different from our view of competence, skill, or knowledge. One can be competent or skilful in all kinds of things, such as soldering or drawing, and one could equally be knowledgeable about (e.g.) forces or materials. These may be thought of as 'inputs' to capability. It would be difficult to be capable without a good collection of competences, skills and knowledge resources. These provide **capacity** but on their own they are not enough. Capability involves additionally the ability to make good choices about what to do (e.g. what skills to deploy) and when.

Design & technology capability is **procedural** and in an educational setting can enable learners to organise and manage themselves through a project. Capability is evident in the way learners shape and direct their work and in the collective bag of decisions and actions that allow the learner to emerge at the end of a project with a prototype solution to the task. Whilst knowledge, skills and competences can be disaggregated from any task and examined separately, capability cannot. Capability is the ability to pursue the task with imagination and rigour, and to draw it to a resolution that makes a difference/improves the made world. Whilst knowledge and skills can be seen as 'inputs', capability can only be seen in terms of procedures (the task in action) and outcomes (did I do the right things; did it work?). This is why design & technology is so rich in opportunities for learners to analyse themselves and their practice. Only through such self-critical analysis and reflection can they improve.

The idea of capability as conscious human action is articulated in Black and Harrison's *In place of Confusion* (1985) – a position paper that they were writing at the same time that we were seeking to clarify our own position for *APU Design & Technology*. They also make the important link between the process of taking action and the resources that one draws on in the process.

This interaction between the processes of innovative activity and the resources being called upon is itself one of the key elements of successful human capability. It is a continuous engagement and negotiation between ideas and facts, guesswork and logic, judgments and concepts, determination and skills. (Black & Harrison, 1985, p. 6)

Embedded in the concept of capability is that of **potential** – and here again we find reference to the uniqueness of humankind – that capability is both developed and demonstrated by the human **motivation** to change and improve.

4. A WIDER CAPABILITY DEBATE

The debate about capability is not exclusively within the field of design & technology. The notion of capability as dynamic and proactive and relating to what people **can do** had been developed by the UK RSA into an 'Education for Capability' project which was initiated as a reaction against a view of education as scholarship. This was expressed in the project's Manifesto, created in 1979, in the following way.

Young people in secondary or higher education increasingly specialize, and do so too often in ways that mean that they are taught to practice only the skills of scholarship and science. They acquire knowledge of particular subjects, but are not equipped to use the knowledge in ways that are relevant to the world outside the education system.

This imbalance is harmful to individuals, to industry and to society. (Cited in Burgess, 1986, p. ix)

Put simply:

Capability involves not only thinking and analysing but also the ability to make and to do – and the ability to do what you say you will do. (Nuttgens, 1986, p. 31)

In the mid-1980s, as we were seeking to give form to our ideas about design a technology capability, Sir Toby Weaver (former Deputy Secretary at the Department for Education and Science and architect of the English polytechnic system) presented his view of 'Education for What' within the context of this wider education for capability debate.

It may be the prejudice of an administrator, but there seems to me to be a vital attribute whose development ranks too low among the educator's major aims. I am thinking of a person's general capacity to manage his own life, to cope with his environment, to profit from experience, to master what used to be called the art of living, to reach sensible decisions and to act on them. To call this quality 'gumption' or 'nous' is to incur the charge of vulgarity; to call it 'wisdom' verges on the high-faluting; to call it 'lifemanship' lacks seriousness. May I settle for Capability as the nearest I can get to describing the ability to apply one's general stock of knowledge and manifold of skills, as Bacon put it, for the benefit and use of men? (Weaver, 1986, p. 55)

Weaver goes on to emphasise the importance of an action perspective.

I should like to see a substantial shift in the centre of gravity from passive absorption of culture to the active development of creativity and communion. (Ibid, p. 57)

5.   CAPABILITY AS 'FUNCTIONINGS'

While our focus is specifically with design & technology, our view of both the motivation and the potential of capability sits comfortably with the model of capability promoted by the Nobel Prize-winning economist Amartya Sen whose 'capabilities approach' has been adopted by groups as diverse as environmentalists, health professionals and social scientists. Sen's view is that the well-being of a person is dependent on an interrelated set of what he terms 'functionings' that are made up of what people can **be** and what they can **do**. (Sen, 1992) These functionings range from what are seen as elementary or fundamental functionings like being well nourished and well sheltered to more complex functionings such as having self-respect or taking part in community. Capability is expressed in terms of the capability to function and is importantly linked to the freedom to achieve functions. Sen sees capability as an active force in which conscious choice is operating – he contrasts, for example, a person starving because they have no food with a person starving because of a decision to fast. As an economist with a strong interest in human rights, Sen is fundamentally concerned with equality. For him, 'well-being' – for an individual or for society – is achieved through the capability to function, which in turn is related to 'the person's freedom to choose from possible livings' (Sen, 1992, p. 40). This is contrasted with a view of equality that is about the provision of resources to meet a person's needs – that is seen as a more passive 'welfarist' approach.

Needs is a more passive concept than 'capability' and it is arguable that the perspective of positive freedom links naturally with capabilities (what can the person do?) rather than with the fulfillment of their needs (what can be done for the person?). (Sen, 1984, p. 514)

Putting Sen's more general concept into the context of design & technology we are presenting capability as proactive choice to achieve functionings that result in improvement in the made world. From an educational perspective it is about enabling learners to have the confidence, competence and motivation to choose to **be** the person to take on the design & technology challenge and **do effective and appropriate things** to address that challenge.

6.   CAPABILITY AND INSTRUMENTALITY?

However, there is an interesting tension in some of the literature surrounding capability not least in terms of the often oversimplified debate about the purpose of education (is it to be educational or instrumental?). Some advocates of capability-based education present scholarship, knowledge and its acquisition in negative terms, and in so doing, the concept of a liberal education (with its philosophical founding fathers, Plato, Matthew Arnold, et al.) is challenged. An extreme testimony of this view projects capability as a quasi-industrial imperative.

> Our education fails to provide the right quantities, and the right balance of the appropriately skilled personnel we need for industrial capability. Secondly the general ethos and thrust of British education are, if anything, hostile to industry and careers in industry. ... At present, therefore, we are *not* educating for capability and we are paying the price for it in chronic industrial unsuccess. (Barnet, 1986, p. 12)

We do not accept or agree with this instrumental interpretation of capability in education. We take the view that design & technology capability should be an entitlement for **all** learners, so that all may partake in the creative activities that distinguish humankind from the rest of the animal world. If subsequently some then choose to engage with industrial pursuits, that is their right and their choice.

Interestingly, this inclusive view of capability was expressed by Malcolm Shirley, the Director General of the Engineering Council, writing the Foreword to *Design and technology in a knowledge economy* (Kimbell & Perry, 2001). The foreword represents a strong endorsement of the concept of design & technology capability.

> A report 'The Universe of Engineering' published by the Royal Academy of Engineering last year, drew attention to the pervasive nature of engineering in the economy and society....The report stressed the importance of engineering process, which had received less consideration than engineering knowledge over the years. In describing engineering process, it used very similar terms to those used here to describe design and technology. ... The two papers make it clear why design and

technology has to be important for all those concerned with engineering. As this paper makes clear, however, design and technology is about far more than career preparation. More than any other area of the curriculum, it is about capability for all. (Shirley, in Kimbell & Perry, 2001, p. 1)

7.   TRANSATLANTIC DISSONANCE

Our beliefs about capability, tacit in the early days of the APU project, are fundamental to the culture of design & technology that has evolved most notably in England and Wales. In focusing so explicitly on capability we are promoting a different rationale to the way technology education is developing in other cultures where the focus is not on **capability** but on technological **literacy**. Identifying the fundamental difference between the two further qualifies our own position. This difference can be seen in comparisons between curriculum statements from England and from the USA. The design & technology curriculum documentation for England is prefaced with a statement about 'The importance of design and technology' that places great emphasis on capability – on the learner's ability to operate as a design and technologist.

> Design and technology prepares pupils to participate in tomorrow's rapidly changing technologies. They learn to think and intervene creatively to improve quality of life. The subject calls for pupils to become autonomous and creative problem solvers, as individuals and members of a team. They must look for needs, wants and opportunities and respond to them by developing a range of ideas and making products and systems. They combine practical skills with an understanding of aesthetics, social and environmental issues, function and industrial practices. As they do so, they reflect on and evaluate present and past design and technology, its uses and effects. Through design and technology, all pupils can become discriminating and informed users of products, and become innovators. (DfEE/QCA, 1999, p. 15)

This contrasts with the USA emphasis on technological **literacy**, focusing on **understanding** and **using** technology, as highlighted by the following extract from the documentation developed by the Technology for All Americans Project, guiding individual states on their development of technological education.

> Technology Content Standards is designed as a guide for educating students in developing technological literacy. Technological literacy is the ability to use, manage, assess and understand technology. A technologically literate person understands, in increasingly sophisticated

ways that evolve over time, what technology is, how it is created and how it shapes society, and in turn is shaped by society. ... A technologically literate person will be comfortable with and objective about technology, neither scared of it nor infatuated with it. (ITEA, 2000, pp. 9–10)

This position is further qualified by the National Academy of Engineering's report 'Technically Speaking: Why all Americans need to **know more about** technology' (our emphasis) which presents technological literacy in the following way.

Technological literacy encompasses three interdependent dimensions – knowledge, ways of thinking and acting, and capabilities. ...the goal of technological literacy is to provide people with the tools to participate intelligently and thoughtfully in the world around them. (Pearson & Young, 2002, p. 3)

The passage goes on to explain that 'ways of thinking and acting' relates to asking questions, seeking information and making decisions and 'capabilities' are exemplified by being able to use computers, fix simple mechanical or technological problems at home or work and apply basic mathematical concepts to make informed judgements about technology. While we recognise and respect this approach for its potential to make for well informed, critical users and consumers of technology, it is not the active, interventionist 'doing' and 'being' a design and technologist emphasised by the concept of capability we believe in and have subscribed to through our research.

This somewhat different view of the world is echoed in the different mindset that is brought to assessment in the USA. A study recently completed by the US National Academy of Engineering and National Research Council (Garmire & Pearson, 2006), clearly identified these differences.

The British design & technology curriculum centres on doing 'authentic' design tasks, activities that represent a believable and meaningful challenge. From an assessment standpoint, performance ... is of primary interest. Specific knowledge ... capabilities ...ways of thinking ... decision-making are relevant only in so far as they advance a student's design work. However there is considerable interest in how students *use* their knowledge, recognise when they are missing key information and how skillfully they gather new data ...

In contrast in the United States, curriculum in technology, as in most subjects, is centred on the acquisition of specific knowledge and skills. ... Assessments are based mostly on content standards, which represent expert judgements about the most important knowledge and skills for students to master.

The committee found a great deal to commend the British approach to assessing design-related thinking. For one thing, the design centred method much more closely mimics the process of technology development in the real world and seems likely to promote higher order thinking... The idea that design always involves some degree of uncertainty and that no human designed product is without shortcomings are more likely to be understood at a deeper level by someone who is engaged in an authentic design challenge than by someone who has not'. (Garmire & Pearson, 2006, pp. 107–110)

8.   THE IMPORTANCE OF UNCERTAINTY

The notion of uncertainty in designing, identified by Garmire and Pearson, is another significant dimension in our view of developing capability. It is quite possible – in fact it is quite common – for learners to be competent, skilful and knowledgeable but not capable; for capability is quite a tricky thing to develop. Whilst skills can be deliberately taught, capability is a much more subtle phenomenon that can only be acquired through experience of different kinds of designing. It involves building up a repertoire of approaches (which to an extent can be taught) but then knowing which to deploy at the right time and in the right way. It involves knowing how to act (what to do next) when you do not know the answer.

For a learner, not knowing the 'answer' could be aligned with their lack of experience, but in fact is much more fundamentally aligned with the **indeterminacy** of design challenges where there is no single 'right' answer or solution, no fixed field of knowledge to be drawn on. This has led to designing being characterised as an activity fraught with 'wicked problems'– a term coined by Horst Rittel, and referring generally to the 'social reality' of designing in which there are 'no definitive conditions or limits'. (Buchanan, 1995, p. 15)

Inevitably therefore, being a capable design & technologist means being able to operate within this soup of indeterminacy and, while experienced designers have a whole repertoire of previous experience or 'precedent' to draw on (Lawson, 2004), a good programme of learning and teaching in design & technology prepares learners to deal with this uncertainty. This is precisely the point that Hicks (1983) was making at the time of the launch of the *APU* project

Teaching facts is one thing; teaching pupils in such a way that they can apply facts is another, but providing learning opportunities which encourage pupils to use information naturally when handling uncertainty, in a manner which results in capability, is a challenge of a different kind. (Hicks, 1983, p. 1)

This sentiment is echoed in the more general view of capability promoted through the Higher Education for Capability project (which was spawned by the original RSA initiative):

Capability is not just about skills and knowledge. Taking effective and appropriate action within unfamiliar and changing circumstances involves judgements, values, the self-confidence to take risks and a commitment to learn from experience. (Stephenson, 1992, p. 2)

For a professional designer, operating in a context of uncertainty represents the status quo, as can be seen from the wry remark of the engineering designer Ted Happold who claimed:

I really have, perhaps, one real talent; that is that I don't mind at all living in the area of total uncertainty. (Cross, 1990, p. 130 quoting Davies, 1985)

For the novice designer there is huge learning potential in such situations that have much in common with Vygotsky's articulation of how learning takes place in this area of uncertainty, which he famously labelled the 'Zone of Proximal Development'. Teachers have a key role in supporting learners when they are operating beyond their previously experienced limits, but it cannot be in terms of telling them what to do. As soon as teachers resort to that – which is frequently the easiest thing to do – they deny to the learners the opportunity to extend themselves as they grapple with their uncertainty.

9.   UNCERTAINTY AND THE NEED TO KNOW

This uncertainty zone is rich in learning potential, and we have sought to exploit it in several ways, not least through our explicit treatment of 'the need to know'. As learners tackle tasks in design & technology the things they will need to know in order to deal with them are difficult to predict in advance of getting into the activity. When a new breed of Advanced level design & technology examination syllabuses was being drafted, the examination awarding bodies commissioned a report on how they might tackle the problem of specifying the knowledge and skills within the subject. The resulting report (Threlfall, 1980) pointed out that the knowledge and skills required in a task, arise from the task as a solution develops.

Subsequently, the Department of Education and Science (DES) produced its booklet 'Understanding design & technology', in which the very same view was explicitly expressed.

> The designer does not need to know all about everything so much as to know what to find out, what form the knowledge should take, and what depth of knowledge is required for a particular purpose. (DES, 1981. p. 5)

So when Hicks – the senior Her Majesty's Inspector at the DES – made his comments about handling uncertainty, he was reflecting a view that was not only widely accepted amongst designers, but also with the policy makers. Our response to this, in assessment terms, was to say that we would like to know whether learners were able to identify these areas of uncertainty. Thus was born the idea of challenging learners – at points through the activity – to identify what things they would like/need to **know more about** in order to make progress. Their responses told us a good deal about their awareness of their position within the task, and their grip on the range of things that might be useful to them. But it also told us more than that, for – from the learner's point of view – there are risks in the process. Not only were we asking them to tackle a task in which there were significant areas of uncertainty, but also, moreover, we were asking them (requiring them) to be explicit about what they did not know – and what they might need to find out more about. It is easy to see how learners might be a bit cagey about this if they see themselves in an assessment setting. It is hardly normal to advertise one's shortcomings whilst being assessed.

So capability is made up of more than just intellectual and physical components. There is a strong emotional strand that contributes to the whole. The **confidence** to lay out one's thinking and to take risks with ideas, as well as the confidence to admit to uncertainty about elements of it, is all part of the mix of capability. Bronowski describes it as 'imagination, … reason, … emotional subtlety and toughness'.

By the mid-1980s, the practice of design & technology teaching was becoming more widespread, and the emergence of the GCSE in 1985 – drawing both from the academic assessment tradition of the GCE and the practical tradition of the CSE – provided an opportunity to consolidate good practice. It also provided the spur to launch *APU Design & Technology* that year.

But when the APU team came together we were more confident about the **concept** of design & technology capability, than we were about the **practice** of design & technology teaching. The concept was not explicitly written down but it was collectively and tacitly held. Our position on the **practice** of design & technology teaching was that it too often failed to live up to the challenge on the concept. We had all experienced the methodological treadmill of teaching a design process step by step (brief, investigation, ideas, etc.) and had all reacted against it. What McCormick et al. (1994) were later to describe as the 'ritual' of marching learners through a routinised design process was deeply unsatisfactory. By contrast, the concept of procedural capability seemed entirely right. So we began to seek ways to describe the capability in a different way.

In articulating our view of capability we have strayed into the territory of how this view relates to learning – **developing** capability and **exercising** capability being closely entwined. We now turn to focus more explicitly on the learning dimension, how it is informed by, and informs on, our understanding of capability.

Chapter 2

LEARNING AND TEACHING
A philosophical position

Why you might find this chapter interesting

Our position on **capability** *as the key goal of education, which we described in Chapter 1, carries with it some inevitable consequences for learning and teaching, and we examine these in this chapter. We describe the need for learning to be active and task-centred, recognising the individuality of learners. One of the more tricky issues to emerge from these priorities concerns the role of knowledge. If learning is task-focused and individualised, how is this to be reconciled with notions of pre-existing high-status bodies of knowledge? What is technological knowledge and how does it operate as learners undertake tasks? We explore the concept of learners' 'need-to-know' and the pedagogic imperatives that are entailed for teachers seeking to manage it. And this inevitably raises the issue of progression and what it means to become progressively more capable.*

***

In the same way that – at the start of *APU Design & Technology* in 1985 – we held implicit views about capability in design & technology, we also held views about learning and teaching. And central to this was our belief in a view of learning as active.

1.   LEARNING THROUGH ACTIVITIES

The first manifestations of what was to become design & technology was beginning to emerge in the curriculum in the early 1960s and at that time it was not usual to think about curriculum subjects in terms of activity. Typically, 'subjects' were seen more as bodies of knowledge with discrete associated procedures. But equally in the early 1960s there were rustlings of discontent in the undergrowth. Crowther (1959) had castigated teachers and schools for the barren-ness of the learning landscape, and warned of the waste that resulted. His report was even more pointed since his brief had been to report on the education of 15–18-year-olds; i.e. sixth form students in (predominantly) Grammar (academically selective) schools. Why, he asked, is it that so many of our intelligent youngsters lose their intellectual curiosity before they have exhausted their capacity to learn? (Crowther, 1959)

Crowther was convinced that it was more to do with the diet of force-fed-facts, mindless-memorising and dull-drill than with anything to do with the capacities and potentialities of young people. Crowther's report required us to consider an 'alternative road' to learning that was premised on **activities** and **problem solving**. His contribution has been widely acknowledged as one of the levers that began to move the curriculum towards a view of active learning. Specifically in our story, his work inspired a Schools' Council (the main 1970s UK Government-funded curriculum development agency) research and development project that began to move one branch of science education towards **science and technology**, which in turn became absorbed into the wider concept of design & technology. With Crowther's influence operating at one end of the schooling continuum, Plowden (1967) chipped in at the other end. Her report on 'play' as a vehicle for learning in the early years of schooling had profound effects on primary education for decades. And we do well to recall that designing has been described by Papanek as 'goal directed play' (Papanek, 1995, p. 7)

Through a combination of these influences – and a lot of outstanding development projects from the School's Council (established in 1970) – the mood music in schools was shifting in dramatic ways in the decade from the mid-1960s to the mid-1970s. In design & technology it became common-place to talk about 'projects' or 'activities'. The purpose behind the activity, however, was frequently disputed, and particularly in the context of whether its focus was to be educational or instrumental.

2.   INTRINSIC AND/OR INSTRUMENTAL?

In Chapter 1, we drew attention to the way in which the concept of capability had been caught up in this debate. Extreme concepts of a liberal education (focusing on intrinsic values) can readily be characterised as having a concern with academic scholarship disassociated from any real-world application. At the other extreme, some see education as failing unless it equips young people with skills needed directly for industry. The history of design & technology in schools provides it with both liberal and vocational roots; what Hirst describes as a 'double purpose'.

> [T]he aim of the study of a discipline in liberal education is not that of its study in a specialist or technical course. The first is concerned with developing a person's ways of understanding experience, the others are concerned with mastering the details of knowledge, how it is established, and the use of it in other enterprises, particularly those of a practical nature. ... But the two purposes are quite distinct and there is no reason to suppose that by aiming at one the other can automatically be achieved as well. (Hirst, 1974, p. 48)

Theodore Lewis, commenting on the dual roots and purpose of technology education in the USA, provides a picture of the healthy 'crossing of borders' between the two purposes, seeing it as more to do with the 'stance' of the teacher (or curriculum) than content – knowledge and skills being seen as 'neutral' (Lewis, 1996). From our point of view, this distinction is helpful – not least because it devalues neither position. But our view of capability, much like Sen's, places human, not industrial, development as the **primary** motive.

Many of our starting points for developing approaches to learning and teaching are derived by extension from our view of capability. As an example, if one believes – as we do – that capability involves (amongst many other things) coping with uncertainty, then **teaching** for capability must allow uncertainty into the agenda. Common sense might suggest that with very inexperienced learners we might set tasks that involve a **limited amount** of uncertainty. But as learners get more experienced, tasks might extend and deepen these levels of uncertainty.

3.   TASK-CENTRED LEARNING

But even to say this is to reveal a deeper philosophical starting point that is again implied in the concept of capability. We believe that learning for capability in design & technology should typically be **task-centred** in the sense that learners are expected to take a task from a starting point (which may be of many kinds) to a resolution that involves a change/improvement in the made world. We also believe it should be **issues-rich** as it is the range and depth of issues available for the learner to contend with that gives meaning and authenticity to the task, contextualises and situates the learning, and provides scope for the learner to take ownership of the task.

This task-centred, issues-rich view makes the learner an **active participant** in the process. In so doing, we are committed to a view of the teacher as being more a **guide** than an **instructor**. Teaching is therefore more about helping learners to **find their way** through a task rather then telling them what to do. The 'guide on the side' more than the 'sage on the stage'. There are of course many different ways of being a guide, and equally many different kinds of tasks that might need to be negotiated by learners, and some of this will be fleshed out later in this section. For now however it is enough to establish in principle the task-centred nature of the activity and the collaborative guide-like nature of teaching.

Teaching in this view is co-experiential; we experience the task together. As teachers, we attempt to help learners to see what has not been seen before; to try what has not been tried before; so as to enrich their strategy-bank and deepen their sensitivity to such tasks in the future. We engage in all kinds of artifice; creating environments, playing roles, developing concept models, concocting idea factories; and all with the aim of helping learners to see how they might extend their ideas and their approaches. If we manage to help them to improve their ideas; then that is a success. But if they additionally can see the value of the strategy that we used to help them (if they can see through the artifice), then the value is ten times greater, since it will have an afterlife well beyond the details of the project.

This view of the activity accentuates the central goal of developing the personal capability of learners to cope with the challenges in the task, whatever the task may be. The teacher/guide is there to support that process. Again, common sense might suggest that with very inexperienced learners, the guiding might need to be more proactive and intensive, whilst with experienced learners it might be less intrusive. The ultimate position, towards which both learners and teachers should strive, is learner autonomy. As this point is reached, learners are able to negotiate their tasks independently and pursue them imaginatively and rigorously without external direction, using resources appropriately.

4.   LEARNERS AS INDIVIDUALS

Since we take the view that learners should be active participants in their own learning, we have also to acknowledge that learners are individuals with many differences. Some will be strong visualisers whilst other will be strong verbalisers; some will tend towards the analytic, while others accentuate the intuitive. Because of our views about capability, task centred learning, and active participation by learners, we acknowledge – indeed we celebrate – the fact that these individual differences will have an impact on the ways in which learners tackle tasks and the kinds of results they strive for and find acceptable. We are therefore drawn towards Gardner's view (1983) of multifaceted intelligence. Equally, we accept that this will inevitably mean that as learners work through a task they will tend to see some forms of response as more appropriate than others and some kinds of outcomes as more important than others. But there are limits to our flexibility in this matter. For example, if we were to accept that an individual might be a stronger visualiser than a verbaliser, this does not allow the teacher to shrug off responsibility for developing in that learner the key verbal elements of capability, particularly as we acknowledge that both visualising and verbalising play crucial roles in designing. Rather it says something about how the teacher might go about doing it. Our position might be summarised as 'working on weaknesses by playing from strengths'. We recognise the complexity of the role the teacher must play in this situation, as characterised in Kimbell and Perry.

> We can properly argue that design and technology can be made to appeal to learners who approach it from very different starting points. As when playing the organ, the teacher can pull out different stops for different learners – emphasising this or that approach – essentially customising it to the requirements of individuals. (Kimbell and Perry, 2001, p. 12)

Whilst we acknowledge and celebrate difference, we also hold to the core requirements that follow from our view of capability. Learners – being individuals – will see the task differently, will value the various parts of it differently, will undertake their designing with different strengths and weaknesses, will prioritise the range of possible outcomes differently. This learner-individualism is inevitable and appropriate. It also helps to clarify the role of the teacher, which is to broaden the individuals' repertoire; to enrich their comfort zone; to enlarge the scope of their vision; to challenge them to grow.

5. THE CONSEQUENCES FOR ASSESSMENT

If we allow this, we must also accept that learners will be drawn towards the display of different kinds of excellence, and this has profound implications for anyone concerned with assessment. Our view of capability leads us towards a view of assessment that is concerned primarily with learners' **performance**; their ability to pursue a task and draw it to a satisfactory conclusion that creates change in the made world. But this has to be squared with our view of individual difference; celebrating the different approaches that might be demonstrated by a range of learners. In short, we consider that there are many ways of being good in design & technology. We are in a world in which two very different pieces of work could be awarded the same marks. Moreover – despite having the same mark – the **reasons** for awarding the mark to the two pieces might be very different. We delve deeper into this matter in the following chapter.

6.   THE POSITION OF KNOWLEDGE AND SKILLS

We have already made it clear to the reader that we do not see the teacher as primarily a transmitter of bodies of knowledge and skill, but rather a 'coach' in the tricky arts of pursuing tasks effectively. This view of teaching arises from our procedural view of capability, and it also leads us to a pragmatic and predatory view about the role of knowledge and skills. We operate in what Schön describes as the messy 'indeterminate zones of practice', full of complexity, uncertainty and value conflict (Schön, 1987, p. 6). This characterisation was picked up in 1988 by the Design and Technology National Curriculum Working Group, in laying out design & technology's crucial role in the curriculum as

> capability to operate effectively and creatively in the made world. The goal is increased 'competence in the indeterminate zones of practice'. (DES/WO, 1988b, p. 3)

In this messy territory, we are very much in sympathy with Waks (2001) when he links Schön's notion of 'knowledge-in-action' to Polanyi's (1958) 'tacit' knowledge and, emphasising situated learning and 'apprenticeship' (see Rogoff, 1990), suggests that 'to design is to discover a framework of meaning in an indeterminate situation through practical operations in the situation' (Waks, 2001, p. 44). Finally, our use of the term **predatory** in this context is merely to assert that when engaged in such tasks, **any** knowledge (or skills) may be hijacked for our purposes. All knowledge has the potential to be design & technology knowledge. Whilst the disciplines of science or history might feel confident of drawing boundaries around what is and what is not scientific or historical knowledge, no such boundary can be drawn around design & technology, which we have described elsewhere as 'a restive and itinerant non-discipline' (Kimbell & Perry, 2001, p.19).

Herschbach (1995) provides a rationale for this, focusing on the way technological knowledge is intrinsically bound up with human activity.

> Technological knowledge arises from, and is embedded in, human activity, in contrast to scientific knowledge, for example, which is an expression of the physical world and its phenomena. ... It is through activity that technological knowledge is defined; it is activity which establishes and

orders the framework within which technological knowledge is generated and used. (Herschbach, 1995, pp. 32–33)

Nelson and Stolterman (2003) develop the idea further, by applauding the disciplines of science, economics and so on for their impressive wealth and depth of knowledge, but conclude that, being bound up in inquiry rather than praxis, can only contribute to the 'management of human affairs' (p. 2) whereas design can draw on this knowledge in order to make 'the world to be what we would like it to be'. (Ibid.)

In considering the way knowledge should be situated in the design & technology National Curriculum, the Design and Technology National Curriculum Working Group made distinctions about the **types** of knowledge that are at the core of design & technology.

Distinctions are sometimes drawn between

'Knowing that' and 'knowing how'

'Propositional knowledge' and 'action knowledge'

Homo sapien (man the understander) and *Homo faber* (man the maker')

Whilst it would be misleading to imply that the components in these polarities are mutually independent, it is the second in each pair which is indicative of what is distinctive about an education in design & technology. (DES/WO, 1988b, pp. 3–4)

In the design & technology classroom, if any piece of knowledge relates to my task and might be useful, then it's mine. In this situation it is important for teachers to engage in the process of supporting learners to identify and draw on new areas of knowledge and use them 'in action' in a design & technology task. This will locate the new knowledge to be understood by the learner as design & technology knowledge – and then to be available in their repertoire to be drawn on in future. Christiaans and Venselaar refer to this in the following terms:

the encoded and retrieved design-relevant knowledge, and the strategies that are used to organise and control this knowledge. (Christiaans and Venselaar, 2005, p. 219)

The educational value that we believe can be realised through this process is underscored by Herschbach:

Technological knowledge, then, is more than a compendium of information to be transferred to the student; it is more than various facts, laws, theories, concepts and general information proffered to students. Technical knowledge is dynamic, and meaning is constructed and reconstructed as individuals grapple with the use of knowledge, whether it be conceptual, analytical or manipulative. Generalizations, theories, principles, technical maxims and procedures take on meaning as they are applied to practical applications. Activity helps make explicit to the learner how knowledge is generated, communicated and used to analyze and solve technological problems. Then again, knowledge becomes intelligible through activity as it is categorized, classified and given form; through technological activity students are helped to perceive, understand, and assign meaning. Effective instruction, in other words, includes the distinct ways through which technological knowledge is generated, used, assigned meaning, and reconstructed. (Herschbach, 1995, p. 39)

In learning and teaching situations, knowledge is a resource, a means to an end, not an end in itself – again a point made by the Design and Technology National Curriculum Working Group.

[T]he main outcome of pupils' design and technological activity should be capability in the realms of practical action. In achieving this, pupils will, of course, acquire and use knowledge of different kinds – 'knowing that', 'knowing about' and 'knowing how' – but this will always be a means to an end, rather than an end in itself. (DES/WO, 1988b, pp. 25–26)

They go on to point out:

What is crucial here is that knowledge is not possessed only in propositional form ('knowing that'), but that it becomes active by being integrated into the imagining, decision making, modelling, making, evaluating and other processes which constitute design and technological activity. Understanding (in the sense of the ability to use and apply knowledge in different situations), rather than knowledge (with its connotation of inert information), describes better what is important for design and technology. (Ibid. p. 30)

7.   THE 'NEED TO KNOW'

Accordingly, since our earliest *APU Design & Technology* position paper (Kelly et al., 1987) we have held a 'need to know' approach that seems to us to have immense learning potential.

It is necessary first to recognise that pupils' existing experience provides them with a platform of substance which they are able to bring to bear on the tasks. ... At the start of an activity ... it is not only possible, but also essential, that pupils are able to function effectively without all the detailed knowledge and skills upon which a developed solution would depend, but effective functioning requires that pupils have the ability and willingness to seek out appropriate knowledge and apply it.

It is the process of speculating about possibilities that begins to reveal to pupils the relevance and potential application of their existing repertoire of knowledge and skill. More importantly however, it begins to clarify what they need in order to develop their solution further. The recognition that new knowledge and skills are needed in order to continue is provoked by the questions that arise in their speculations, and the crucial role of the teacher at this point is in helping pupils to recognise and address these questions. (Kelly et al., 1987, p. 19–20)

We also provided the example of the possible 'needs to know' of a learner designing a bike repair stand, reproduced here in Figure 2-1 and it is interesting to reconsider this example in terms of the way it draws on both conceptual knowledge (e.g. 'how can I make it adjustable/collapsible?') and procedural knowledge (e.g. 'how can I best test my idea?') and raises a further question about the level of understanding of any particular area of knowledge being drawn on. McCormick (1999a) refers to the importance of linking procedural and conceptual knowledge in order to create effective action and this example provides a good illustration of the point.

Figure 2-1. The 'need to know'. (From Kelly et al., 1987 p. 19.)

Concurrent with the start of *APU Design & Technology*, Black and Harrison were laying down their framework for developing technological capability. They highlight the need for 'a sound base of knowledge and both intellectual and physical skills appropriate to the job in hand'. (Black and

Harrison, 1985, p. 5). They saw this base as providing the 'resources' to be drawn on in innovative activity. We would agree with the need for such resources, our belief having always been that new resources are most effectively acquired on and through the task in hand – hence our highlighting of the importance of the need to know. McCormick, in reviewing the early days of a National Curriculum that is capability focused, identified the lack of a clear focus and understanding for the place of knowledge in the equation.

> The role of using 'knowledge' has always been present in ideas of capability, but its relationship to process is ill-defined as is how knowledge is used in action. (McCormick, 1999a, p. 5)

The dilemma of how and when to introduce new knowledge has been one that has plagued educationalist for years. LaPorte sums up the dilemma nicely.

> How do we make decisions about the proper proportion of time we spend on developing requisite procedural and theoretical knowledge on the one hand, and engagement in actually solving the problem on the other? As educators in this field we are constantly making these decisions, but upon what basis? (LaPorte, 2004, p. 5)

This issue has frequently appeared in the literature in terms of the relationship between 'content' and 'process'. Lewis (1999) makes a case for them to be viewed 'not dichotomously, but rather symbiotically' (p. 45). His rationale for doing this lies in the way they 'play out' in good technology classrooms.

> Come Monday morning in technology education classrooms, teachers and their students meet once more to enact the subject. The better teachers make arrangements to allow for the varying interests and abilities of their charges. And once classes got going, the onlooker sees a hive of activity. In this milieu we find the essence of the subject. Content and processes are important of course, but they are not kept in separate compartments. Rather, these teachers see the subject as a whole. (Lewis, 1999, p. 56)

At the heart of this issue there is a choice to be made, and the choice we make will depend upon the values we hold. Our position on this is clear. Wherever and whenever possible, we believe that knowledge and skills should be **sought out** by learners rather than **force-fed** by teachers. We hold this position for two reasons. First it derives directly from our view of the development of **autonomous capability** in learners – as opposed to dependency on the teacher. Second it acts as a thought-requiring antidote to a view of curriculum as predefined content (e.g. about mechanisms or nutrition or whatever). If the content of curriculum is predefined, the **tasks** that we set for learners all too easily become mere vehicles to 'carry' the content. In the process, they become meaningless non-tasks that learners readily see straight through. When tasks are used in this way – as a motivational spoon of sugar to sweeten the force-fed pill of content – we should not be surprised when learners reject them.

8. CONTENT, PROCESS AND PEDAGOGY

In recent years, in the UK, a number of strategies have been promoted to deal with this matter. From the Nuffield design & technology project (www.nuffieldcurriculumcentre.org/) we have seen 'resource tasks' (to teach stuff) and 'capability tasks' (for learners to demonstrate the application of that stuff). The National Curriculum framework prefers the labels 'focused practical tasks' and 'design and make assignments'.

Since the emergence of this formulation, the early years of secondary school design & technology (age 11–14 years) have typically been reduced to a sad procession of non-tasks being presented to learners under the guise of 'focused practical tasks'. These tasks are typically very thinly disguised instructional units in which the very idea of learners grappling with the 'need-to-know' is laughable. They do not 'need to know' anything because the teacher instructs them in everything they might need to know. And inevitably, one of the characteristic features of the design & technology environment with this age group is the queue of learners waiting for the teacher to tell them what to do next. Such programmes stifle imagination and replace it with dependency. This is not a new insight. Nearly a century ago John Dewey was making this same point in his treatise on How We Think, originally published in 1910.

> The practical problem of the teacher is to preserve a balance between so little showing and telling as to fail to stimulate reflection and so much as to choke thought. (Dewey, 1991, p. 207)

So … do you believe it is more effective to teach knowledge (or skill) in advance of it being required or at the point at which it is required? We acknowledge that an answer to this question carries with it pedagogic and classroom management issues. But our position remains clear. We have already nailed our colours to the mast of designing – of imaging and modelling – and, again from the 1987 position paper, we make a direct link between engaging in this process and learning.

The 'need to know' is the bridge which gives pupils access into the universe of external knowledge and skills, and motivates them to proceed beyond their existing capabilities and resources.

In this way the progressive nature of imaging and modelling engages pupils with the need to acquire, at appropriate levels, new usable knowledge and skills. The knowledge required is that which the pupil identifies as necessary for the task; it cannot, therefore, be predetermined. (Kelly et al., 1987, p. 20)

In referring to design learning amongst professional designers, Eastman (2001) also focuses on the strong relationship between the nature of imaging and modelling and the way in which a designer's knowledge is used. He usefully subdivides this knowledge into four categories (factual, informal, procedural and experiential) and proposes that there is a process of manipulation, of 'generate-and-test', in which a designer's pre-existing knowledge is brought to bear on a design task, which in turn is the spur to seeking new knowledge and hence new learning. This perspective resonates with the iterative *APU Design and Technology* model (see page 16 and page 75) and highlights the way the model, when linked to the way knowledge is used and acquired in the service of designing, is as much a model of learning as it is of designing. Just in the way that the Design and Technology National Curriculum Working Group referred to knowledge as being a means to aid practical action, so the process can be seen as a means to an end of developing capability – or as Williams (2000) put it, to achieve the goals of

becoming independent problem solvers, becoming creative and reflective, and becoming critical and expressive. (Williams, 2000, p. 52)

9. , LEVELS OF KNOWLEDGE

While for some purposes detailed, in-depth knowledge is required (e.g. mechanisms that allow for the adjustability of the bike stand), it does not follow that all knowledge is required in depth. Indeed at certain stages in the process of designing and making detailed knowledge can be a positive hindrance, enabling learners to get 'bogged down' in too much detail.

Part of our attachment to a 'need to know' approach is bound up in our belief that progress is not always dependent on detailed knowledge. In the original *APU Design & Technology* assessment framework we developed an approach to mapping the level of knowledge being applied at any point in a task, using the descriptors of **black box, street level** and **working knowledge**:

- Black box – I do not know how it (e.g. a torch) works, but I know it does.
- Street level – common knowledge **on the street** (I know the torch has batteries, a bulb and a switch and that they are somehow connected).
- Working knowledge – I know enough to manipulate/modify the product (I can rewire the torch to make it behave differently).

We took the view that the level being evidenced should be appropriate to the stage of development of an idea.

> Quality extension of knowledge and skills includes: operating at a level appropriate to the stage in designing – black box may be appropriate when preliminary ideas are flowing in a divergent way, but working knowledge will be necessary when the detail of the designing and making is being considered. (Kimbell et al., 1996, p. 75)

McCormick deals with a similar idea when he makes a plea for the recognition in teaching and learning situations of **qualitative** and procedural knowledge that comes from the 'real worlds' of everyday life and expert practitioners. (McCormick, 1999b) Amongst the examples of qualitative reasoning he uses, he draws on a coaching video for snooker players, the language of which he describes as being

> quite unlike that of physics, and in particular the discussion of how to hit the ball and the resulting effect is carried out entirely in qualitative terms. For example … the clock positions used to describe where to hit the cue ball … hit the ball at six o'clock [at the bottom] to get bottom spin. (McCormick, 1999b, p. 114)

In fact there is a good deal of similarity between the 'qualitative reasoning' he describes as being used by experts and the types of 'need to know' we were mapping in the APU project. Embedded in both is the importance of familiarity, relevance and timeliness and an understanding of using knowledge as a resource. There are times when too much knowledge can be a bad thing – when the knowledge gets in the way of idea generation. Knowing how something has been done in the past can act as a block to fresh ideas and approaches. For young learners this often appears in the guise of a stereotypical response to a task and so the challenge for the teacher becomes to create a context and task that allows learners to bring prior experience and knowledge but to have to adapt or transform it in the new situation. For experienced designers the problem can be more acute, and they need to learn to 'consciously not-know' – a concept expressed by Nelson and Stolterman (2003) in the following way.

> The interesting thing about design knowledge is that it emerges from a conscious not-knowing. By this we mean that design knowledge – while using reason (conscious knowledge), intuition (hardwired, unconscious

knowledge) and imagination (subconscious knowledge) as constituent elements – requires an initial state of intelligent ignorance. This state is very much like the Taoist 'empty mind' or the Buddhist 'new mind'. It is the quality of mind that is present during play, when it is important to be completely open to what is emergent in the moment, rather than being preoccupied with past experience, or anticipating a future event. (Nelson & Stolterman, 2003, p. 44)

10.   PROGRESSION IN LEARNING

Whether we are talking about the development of the learner's procedural or conceptual understandings, or more generally about the development of their capability, a further aspect of our beliefs about learning and teaching is how we view progression in learning. The prevailing paradigm (we might term it **mechanical**) holds that younger (less knowledgeable/experienced) learners will be engaged in different tasks from older (more knowledgeable/-experienced) learners. Moreover, their conduct of those tasks will involve them in different kinds of activity. There is however an alternative paradigm (we might call it **organic**) that holds that learner activity (e.g. in design & technology) should be the same at any age – and the differences emerge merely in the quality and depth of the **outcomes** from that activity and the **understandings** that they demonstrate. This paradigm derives from a philosophy that was articulated elegantly by Bruner:

Any idea or problem or body of knowledge can be presented in a form simple enough so that any particular learner can understand it in a recognizable form. (Bruner, 1966, p. 44)

Generally (though not exclusively), the National Curriculum for design & technology took this latter organic view. Whatever the age of learners, they will be involved in trying to understand the task; in developing some design proposals (through imaging and modelling); in planning and making their outcome; and then in reviewing it against the requirements that arose through their initial understanding of the task. The difference is that as learners get more capable they are more able to develop and exploit their ideas in more complex and sophisticated ways.

Progression is about un-pealing progressive layers of meaning and consequence; like peeling an onion. Whilst a 6 yr old can see that a product needs to be safe, a 12 year old might additionally be able to identify a range of risks (fire/cuts/swallowing etc) and make proposals to counteract them. A 16 yr old might then be expected to unpick the safety legislation that surrounds a product and interpret it through their designing. (Kimbell, 1994, p. 190)

But there is something a bit counter-intuitive about this organic paradigm, and it was too easy for the writers of the National Curriculum attainment levels to fall into the rather more common-sense mechanical paradigm of assuming that different levels of performance involve learners doing different things. This was seen to be particularly the case in areas of intellectual challenge, such as the identification and detailing of the task. We showed however that – contrary to expectation – very young learners were quite able to identify tasks for themselves.

> It is clear that where six year olds have the opportunity to explore and become familiar with a context, situation or set of circumstances, they can identify their own purpose and intentions in a design and technological task. Where the child has identified purpose, the task is pursued rigorously and thoughtfully. (Stables, 1992a, p. 377)

A second problem with the mechanical paradigm concerns the concept of 'knowing' – 'I knew this, then I knew that, but now I know this'. But progression in knowing is just as likely to involve a recognition of ignorance (Witte et al., 1989) or of 'un-knowing'. Munn's research explored the subjective experiences of pre-school emergent readers who, the more they realised what was involved in reading, the less they were likely to consider they could do it. (Munn, 1995). It would seem that progress is more about recognising what you **do not** know, than what you **do** know. So we are drawn back to the importance of the 'need to know' at the same time recognising that this can be unsettling.

> While an understanding of what it is that one doesn't know is an essential pre-requisite to learning, it is vital for children's confidence in their own learning that they are not overwhelmed by this feeling of not knowing. (Munn, 1995, p. 112)

There is a clear role here for the teacher in managing the situation – and once again we would refer to the importance of new learning taking place in a supported way, as expressed in Vygotsky's Zone of Proximal Development (1978). What is also happening with Munn's emergent readers is that those who are recognising that they cannot yet read are becoming meta-cognitive about their ability, raising further important messages for learning and teaching. This focus on self-awareness of learners is also the subject of Oxman's concerns with design learning of postgraduate students – while the age group and level of experience is entirely difference to the subjects of Munn's research, there are similar messages about progression to be extracted. Oxman's research (2001) explores models through which design students can explicitly track their own design thinking – and, while in the process they may not become a better 'maker of designs', their understanding, knowledge and designerly thinking skills will improve.

Encouraging and supporting a learner's reflection on their own learning, or what Glaser terms self-regulatory ability (Glaser, 1992) is a critical component in the potential for the learning to be useful in future tasks or challenges whatever the age or level of experience of the learner involved. As we have pointed out elsewhere

> As children are encouraged to think back over their work and turn tacit concrete operations into explicit understandings, they can make them more robust and more transferable to new situations. (Kimbell et al., 1996, p. 82)

We have laid out here the views and values that inform our approach to learning and teaching. Inevitably they also underpin much of what we believe to be important educationally when considering assessment and it is to this topic that we now turn.

Chapter 3

ASSESSMENT
A philosophical position

Why you might find this chapter interesting

Just as our arguments in Chapter 1 had consequences for Chapter 2, so too do those two chapters have consequences for Chapter 3. If education is to be centred on developing capability, and if this is to be developed through task-focused and individualised activities in which learners themselves contribute to the articulation of what counts as knowledge, then the consequences for assessment are profound.

We outline the case for authentic performance assessment in which knowledge is seen as a resource for action rather than as an end in itself. We explore the challenge of making learners' capability evident, and some of the interrelationships that exist between assessment and learning. Finally, we examine some important distinctions that inform our view of assessment; between judging and mapping; between norms and criteria; between 'better/worse' and just 'different'.

***

We have described our views of capability and of learning in design & technology, and how these emerged from our philosophical starting points with the *APU Design & Technology* project in 1985. The challenge here is to outline in a similar way our philosophical starting points with assessment. As with learning, it is important to start by considering what we see as the primary purpose of assessment and this takes us, once again, into the tricky terrain of intrinsic and instrumental motivations.

1.   A SKETCHY HISTORY

Historically, the drive for assessment came from an instrumental route, initially, in the UK, to introduce more meritocratic procedures for entry to the military, universities and civil service and then, as a way of establishing standards, as exit exams. (MacLeod, 1982). Whilst some major assessment initiatives originated in the 19th century, it was the first half of the 20th century that saw the addition of 'intelligence' testing and (particularly in the USA) multiple choice tests, designed to provide summative information to aid decisions about further educational destinations or options in the employment market (Black, 1998). As practicing teachers, we were first involved in the assessment game in the 1970s and in the following two decades witnessed a shift in emphasis towards a view of assessment that was more closely aligned with learning:

- Introduction of the CSE with its emphasis on coursework assessment as providing a better indication of what learners were actually capable of doing
- Development of criterion-based assessment of the GCSE, indicating a move away from purely normative approaches for explicit selection purposes
- Introduction of the National Curriculum as an entitlement for all children aged 5–16, in which the rhetoric focused on more intrinsic aims, as outlined by the Task Group on Assessment and Testing

    Promoting children's learning is a principal aim of schools. Assessment lies at the heart of this process. (DES/WO, 1988a, para 3)

- Emphasis on key skills and transferability highlighted originally through the developments in vocational education leading to the General National Vocational Qualification (GNVQ).

2.   PURPOSES FOR ASSESSMENT

This very sketchy and selective history contextualises our own starting point – as a team of practitioners who had been engaged with the 'grass roots' end of this shift. With our beliefs in capability and learning, we welcomed this more educational direction, placing the child – the learner – at the centre of the process. This is not to deny that the label 'assessment' is used appropriately in different ways, and for different purposes, typically:

- 'Formative' – to support learners in making progress during a programme of study

- 'Summative' – to award grades and certificates at the end of a programme of study
- 'Evaluative' – to support judgements about the quality of a programme of study

Nor is it to deny the importance of these different purposes in supporting learning. Over the 20+ years of our work in TERU, we have undertaken projects that involved all of these purposes, but we have always taken a particular view about what it is appropriate to assess and how it might be done. We recognise the huge variety of assessment techniques that are available, from short, sharp, multiple-choice tests, through timed written examinations, to extended personal project work. Sometimes the focus of assessment might be on conceptual knowledge, sometimes on analysing and ordering information, sometimes on developing arguments, and sometimes on solving problems. Within this range of possibilities, our view of design & technology capability draws us towards some of these techniques and repels us from others.

3.   PRIORITISING 'PERFORMANCE'

Of the many priorities that we might hold concerning the assessment challenge, ours has always been to find ways of assessing the **performance** of learners in design & technology. Given a description of what design & technology capability entails (see Chapter 1) our priority has been to find ways of assessing how well learners are able to demonstrate this capability. Since design & technology is an activity that is premised on bringing about change in the made world, then common sense suggests that the best way of assessing learners' capability in design & technology is to put them into an activity and see how well they can do it.

This is performance assessment. It takes as its starting point the description of capability, and embodies it in a 'real' task; real in the sense that the activity represents a believable, authentic design & technology challenge. We then assess how well learners manage themselves through the task and how successfully they manage to resolve it. This approach is often described in the literature as 'authentic' assessment:

> Assessment is authentic when we directly examine student performance on worthy intellectual tasks. Traditional assessment, by contrast, relies on indirect or proxy 'items' ... from which we think valid inferences can be made about the student's performance at those valued challenges. (Wiggins, 1990, p. 1)

The 'proxy' measures that Wiggins refers to might include all kinds of 'bits' of design & technology, each of which could become the focus of assessment, including the following:

- Design & technological knowledge about
  - Mechanical/electrical systems
  - History of technology
  - Design theories/movements
- Design & technological skills
  - Drawing and representation skills
  - Tool and materials skills (soldering)
- Subsets of design & technology activity/process
  - Product analysis
  - Market research

An analysis of the last 20 years of design & technology assessment in England and Wales (from public examinations) would render all kinds of examples from this list. In order to have any faith in such assessments, one would have to assume that the measures derived from these assessments could usefully inform us about learners' design & technology capability. They would be what Wiggins describes as 'proxy' measures.

Our problem with this approach is that we do not believe that it is worthwhile to test learners' ability to recall a technological body of knowledge, for example about electrical flow in a circuit, or structural integrity in a framework. Nor would we waste time in setting abstracted tests of skills, such as soldering or drawing. In part, this is for the pragmatic reason that the range of things that one might need to know or be able to do in design & technology is **so vast**, that any selection for testing purposes would be arbitrary in the extreme and therefore highly likely to render a false reading of the 'capability' of the learner. But beyond this pragmatic judgement there is also a point of principle. Since the range of knowledge and skills that might be important to the pursuit of a design & technology task is potentially so vast (see our discussion of 'predatory' in Chapter 3), it is important that learners develop a particular view of knowledge and skills and how to acquire them. They need to see knowledge and skills as **resources for action** rather than as ends in themselves. The arbitrary collection of bits and pieces of predefined knowledge and skills for the purposes of assessment, sets up false attitudes towards knowledge and skills and runs counter to our philosophy of design & technology.

Moreover, this argument goes a step further. If there is a universe of knowledge and skills 'out there' that might at some point become useful to the learner in pursuing a task, the most critical capability is to be able to get hold of it as and when it is needed. The inevitable consequence for assessment is that rather than testing learners' ability to 'hold' certain bits of knowledge and skill we need to assess their ability to access it appropriately at the right depth and in the right form. Since the depth and form required will be contingent on the task that is being pursued, then our assessment of learners' ability to access it must similarly be made within the framework of the task being pursued. A further point to consider here is the relationship between learning and assessment – if we believe that the acquisition of knowledge and skills should be on a 'need to know' basis, deriving from and embedded in well-contextualised, authentic design & technology tasks, it follows that to be an appropriate and 'fair' test, the assessment should be undertaken in a parallel setting. So, again we are back to the inevitability of analysing how learners pursue authentic design & technology tasks both to assess their generalised ability to do so and to assess their ability to deal with the challenge of knowledge and skills that arise through the task.

From the start of our activities in TERU we have taken this position. In the mid-1980s for the *APU Design & Technology* project we developed specific parts of our assessment activities to explore how learners dealt with the 'need to know' when pursuing their activity. Did they acknowledge it at all? Did they recognise the breadth of the knowledge that might be used to enrich their work? Did they have an approach to help them gather it appropriately?

4.   PROMOTING EVIDENCE OF CAPABILITY

This approach is illustrative of a wider strategy underpinning our work. We take the view that capability in design & technology – the big picture – is comprised of a mass of interrelated qualities that can be itemised; an example being the ability to draw upon task-related knowledge as necessary. It is necessary to be clear about these qualities before embarking on any assessment, and to that end, our assessment exercises typically start with the creation of an assessment framework that lays out the qualities with which we are concerned. Thereafter we consider the kinds of subactivities that might authentically be embedded into the overall activity in such a way as to throw up **evidence** of these qualities. In short, we seek to build a convincing overall design & technology activity by weaving together a set of subactivities that could reasonably be expected to promote the evidence that we seek in order to make judgements of learners' capability.

> [B]ecause design and technological activity is so integrative, the approach to the assessment of pupils' performance in this area should ideally be holistic, that is to say, based on the detailed and systematic observation of pupils' work throughout a design and technological task

from the recognition of need or opportunity to appraisal of the product. (DES/WO, 1988b, p. 12)

Taking the effort to present an assessment activity that is integrative, also necessarily assumes a process of making judgements that respects the integrity of an inevitably complex, disordered range of evidence. While it would be more straightforward from a manageability viewpoint if an assessment activity compartmentalises evidence in the way that a traditional test might do, this flies in the face of our belief about the nature of both designing and capability. Therefore, we have consistently developed, employed and shared approaches that maintain the integrity of the activity. Interestingly, one of the by-products of this approach has been that teachers who have witnessed the use of our assessment activities, have typically sought to acquire and replicate them not because they want to use them for testing, but because they see them as good, capability-building activities.

This has not compromised the explicit assessment focus of our activities. Indeed we typically insert all kinds of devices and prompts to provoke certain types of responses from learners, which in turn provide evidence of capability. We do this especially where it helps capture evidence that would otherwise have been intangible or ephemeral. But what we have resisted is the distortion of activities for assessment purposes. The activity structure must – above all else – be an authentic and valid representation of design & technology. Learners must be able to develop their ideas responsively, driven by design intentions and in the process leaving behind a trace of where they have been. This trace enables us to gather insights into what those intentions were and how they shaped the emerging solution.

5.   ASSESSMENT FOR LEARNING

Quite apart from the authentic assessment value that flows from this approach, there is huge learning potential. In conventional project-work settings in schools, the evidence of the many different qualities of capability tend to arise in unpredictable and often unplanned ways, and the evidence is typically jumbled up in the learner's project folder. Moreover, the creation of the folder is typically strung out over an extended timespan. In this setting it is hard for teachers to focus learners' attention on particular qualities – and therefore it is hard for learners to appreciate what they consist of.

By contrast, our approach has been explicitly to target these qualities of capability, weaving a specific set of requirements into the activity that can be made obvious to both the learner and teacher. As a result, we frequently find ourselves in discussion with teachers who come to see the activity differently – developing a more clinical appreciation of what the qualities involved are and how they might be evidenced. At the same time, learners appreciate the explicitness with which we describe what we mean by being **capable**. It is important to us that any assessment activity should also be a learning activity, and ideally this should be for teachers as well as learners.

It follows from this learning-driven view of assessment that we do not see our assessment activities as things that can be 'passed' and 'failed'. Rather they are activities that learners can do more or less well, or differently, and – critically – that they are capable of getting better at. Performance assessment of this kind helps learners improve their performance, and helps teachers support them. Taking this view has caused us to consider the way our approach to assessment sits with the notions of 'passing' and 'failing' and therefore the concept of achievement as opposed to attainment – the latter term being used quite explicitly within the formal assessment culture introduced by the National Curriculum. It has always been our belief that all humans – and therefore by definition all learners, have potential design & technological capability, whether or not they have been through an explicit schooling experience that aims to develop that potential. We are not here declaring a belief in the aptitude testing of Eysenck (e.g. 1976) or Jensen (e.g. 1981) – quite the opposite. The assessment activities we have structured over the years anticipate some level of achievement by all who undertake them – indeed we have consciously structured them to be motivational and achievable, even by those with no formal curricular experience in this area. We have aimed to make them positive (and, potentially, learning) experiences through which attainment can be viewed and, in the hands of class teachers, more general achievements can also be valued. This latter point was illustrated nicely for us in early trials for *APU Design & Technology*, when a teacher looked through the work of a class of 15-year-olds and commented that one learner, with a reading age of eight, had written more in the 2 hours of this assessment activity than he had written in the whole of the last school term. An achievement in itself, in addition to the specifics of design & technology capability that he was able to display during the activity.

These views about an appropriate formulation for assessment activities in design & technology arise initially from our view of capability and what counts as an authentic way of getting evidence of it. This starting point has subsequently been fleshed out in a series of assessment projects that have enabled us progressively to understand how we might do it. But this is only half of the problem. It is one thing to create an authentic design & technology activity to draw out evidence of the capability of learners. It is another thing altogether to develop an assessment procedure so that two assessors, looking at the same piece of work, make the same judgement about the level of capability on display. How should we approach this challenge? Again our starting point derives from our view of capability.

6.   MAKING ASSESSMENT JUDGEMENTS

There are lots of ways of tackling a task and some will be better than others given the context and other details. Imagine for example the very limited task of serving hot baked beans. One might use a can opener, remove the top and then stand the can in the ashes beside the campfire. Or the beans might be dispensed into a ceramic bowl and put in a microwave cooker. One might put them into a saucepan and use a gas hob, or even mix them up with mashed potato and stick them in as slow oven. Each of these approaches would do the job, but judgements about better/worse approaches depend upon contextual and other features in the task.

To make a judgement about how well the task has been done, it requires the assessor to see the specifics of any approach **in the context of the task as a whole**. This realisation – drawn from exploratory work in the *APU Design & Technology* project – drew us to an approach to assessment that starts with taking in **the big picture** of what learners are trying to do, and only thereafter digging down into the detail of the procedural strategies, conceptual knowledge and practical skills they are choosing to deploy. We do not start by assessing the detail and then try to 'add up' the overall result. We make an overall judgement and then drill down into it to tease out its constituent parts. (For a more detailed discussion of the relationship between atomistic and holistic assessment see Kimbell, 1997, pp. 38–39.)

There is a further important consequence of this approach. The beans example demonstrates four different sources of heat; campfire, microwave, hob, oven. If, for reasons of context and task, the campfire is chosen, what can the assessor judge about the learner's knowledge of or skill in using a microwave? Nothing. If the learner chooses not to use it, the assessor has no way of knowing whether the learner could have done so, had she needed to.

When engaged in performance assessment in design & technology it is impossible to predict exactly what learners will choose to do, so the assessment framework cannot specify – in advance – particular bodies of knowledge or skill. The assessment framework may reasonably ask 'how effectively is the learner able to develop their ideas'. But it cannot ask 'how well can the learner sketch/draw ideas in three-dimensions (3D)'. Since ideas might be developed in many different ways, the assessment cannot – authentically – demand one particular method.

7.   ASSESSING AND MAPPING

We might however be interested in the question of whether drawing skills are related to good performance in developing ideas. This explains the dual approach that we have typically adopted to square this circle. We make **assessment judgements** about the ability of learners to develop their ideas, and we **map** the knowledge and skills that they use to do it. The mapping process is not judgemental, but merely descriptive. Subsequent analysis of performance data then allows us to examine the connections (if there are any) between the individual maps that learners generate, and their levels of performance.

So once again we find ourselves facing the individuality of performance in design & technology. We are in a world in which two very different pieces of work could be awarded the same marks because our approach to assessment does not require us to force all learners through an identical set of practices. Rather we are able to celebrate the differences that might be demonstrated whilst assessing against a common framework of capability.

8.   NORMS AND CRITERIA

It might be assumed from this focus on the individual that we would wholeheartedly endorse the gradual move away from normative forms of assessment towards notions of criterion-referenced assessment. However, while we would support the egalitarian principle behind this move, we recognise (along with others) the oversimplification of the reality of professional judgements that it assumes, as if assessments could be made in such a 'pure', isolated and decontextualised way. This is an issue raised by Tufnell in discussing the development of assessment activities for the National Curriculum, who cites the common-sense reality expressed by Angoff:

> [I]f you scratch a criterion-referenced interpretation, you will very likely find a norm-referenced set of assumptions underneath. (Angoff, 1974, p. 13)

Further problems arise if one takes the more organic view of progression we presented in the previous chapter, also discussed by Tufnell in respect of the levels of attainment defined through the National Curriculum.

> The adoption of a multi-level scale of achievement was an ambitious enterprise. Such scales established sets of explicit criteria defining progress for pupils from 5 to 16. ... As design and technology capability defined a process, the assumption was that each level described a more complex and

sophisticated activity that required the employment of more demanding skills and greater depth of subject knowledge. The complexity of defining these criteria so that they were applicable to pupils over their eleven years of schooling and could be interpreted consistently by teachers was underestimated. (Tufnell, 2000, pp. 105–106)

The issue of how a particular criterion is interpreted has been very important to us in pursuing research in assessment, as we have inevitably been concerned with the reliability and the validity of judgements being made. To assume (in the way that early versions of National Curriculum design & technology did) that a criterion can stand on its own in providing the basis for reliable and objective judgement is frankly naive. This point can be illustrated well from an example used elsewhere (Kimbell, 1997) that identifies the dilemma faced by teachers (and others) making such judgements, in this instance in relation to a statement that required pupils be able to 'use specialist modelling techniques to develop design proposals'.

How do we calibrate the achievement threshold for such a statement? At what level of capability does a 'no' become a 'yes'? Does it refer to a 5-year-old squeezing out some Plasticene, or to an 8-year-old experimenting with a Lego mechanism, or to a 15-year-old modelling in a computer-aided design system? (Kimbell, 1997, p. 24)

Ironically, the calibration job becomes a little easier when we know that this is a 'level 6 statement' – because we start to bring normative judgements to bear on it. Clearly, criterion referencing is neither a precise science nor a complete, unproblematic solution.

9.   FOCUSING ON INDIVIDUALS

For these reason, in creating structures for locating evidence demonstrated, we have sought to **characterise**, rather than **define** what evidence would look like at any particular level. We then exemplify this in the context of whole pieces of work. Thus, by definition, we 'norm' the evidence by situating it in a particular context, from which generalisations about the nature of the evidence and the capability it elucidates can be shared and understood. While our focus has been predominantly on making assessment judgements in a research context, the resources developed for this purpose allow teachers to understand better the nature of capability. They are then well placed, when working with an individual learner, to use these understandings not normatively, but ipsatively, transforming assessment **of** learning into assessment **for** learning.

Ipsative assessment is assessment of a pupil not against norms (based on the performance of his/her peers) or against criteria (derived from particular conceptions of subjects and/or of education) but against his/her own previous levels of attainment and performance. In short, it is linked to a view of education as individual development (Kelly, 1992, p. 12)

With the views we hold about an individualist, developmental approach to assessment, comes our view of each learner as special and different. We do not believe that there is a single way of being 'good' at design & technology, and accordingly our approach has been to diagnose and understand the range of ways in which learners demonstrate their capability. And we try to do it in such a way that learners and teachers can become aware of their idiosyncratic strengths and weaknesses, once again focusing on assessment **for** learning.

In the end it all comes down to this. Our view of assessment in design & technology has emerged as a natural extension of our view of capability in design & technology, and of how that capability can be fostered. In the projects that are described in Part Two, our beliefs will be illuminated as our approaches are fleshed out. But the challenge of this book is to present our approaches as researchers. How have we adopted and developed research approaches that sit comfortably with our beliefs about capability and learning? How have we utilised these approaches in ways that enable us to gain deeper understandings – about capability, learning and research itself? It is to our position as researchers that we now turn.

Chapter 4

RESEARCH
A philosophical position

Why you might find this chapter interesting

Our standpoint on research is rather more difficult to articulate in terms of our position when we first set out on the research journey with APU design & technology. For in truth we had – at that time – very limited experience of anything that might be described as research methodology, and yet we had won the contract in direct competition with many experienced research groups. Our approach was to see the APU research task as a design task, with all the concomitant 'needs-to-know' that flow from the positions we have articulated in the preceding chapters. And we designed our way through it.

In this chapter we relive some of the debates that enabled us to shape our position on research, using these to orientate ourselves with the research literature and with the pre-existing research traditions of the Assessment of Performance Unit. We emerge with a position that could barely be described as a paradigm, but that was – at the time – sufficiently clear to enable us to undertake the task and draw it to a successful conclusion.

***

We began our research careers with *APU Design & Technology*; with shared but tacit beliefs and practitioner skills from the classroom. In retrospect it is astonishing that the DES accepted our APU research proposal, since we had no established expertise in assessment research. We cut our teeth on that first project. Faced with the need to climb a steep research learning curve, and with our practitioner backgrounds, we explored a rich and scary terrain of methodologies and techniques, led instinctively by our beliefs about capability and learning, and being drawn towards approaches that seemed (intuitively) to fit with the task in hand. Where appropriate we relied on tried and tested approaches to such matters as survey design and compiling case records, but equally the open vista of opportunities encouraged us to create some entirely new tools; not least the process-rich activities for assessing design and technological performance 'on task' that proved, in retrospect, to be the hallmark of the project.

At that stage we had no explicit thoughts about the 'paradigm' we occupied and, indeed, were intrigued when others viewed our approach and attempted to label it for us – notably as a 'curriculum' model of research. It was as our research experience, expertise and repertoire grew that we ourselves began to see an alignment with certain research approaches, although never finding a particular 'camp' with which we were entirely comfortable. Two of our critical concerns illustrate our emerging position and provide an illuminative backcloth to our conceptual framework for research, and what might loosely be termed our 'paradigm'.

1.   DESIGNING AS THINKING

First there is the intimate association between **designing** processes and more generalised **thinking** processes.

> Design discourse seems to trade in various oppositions, such as design as an abstract reasoning or thinking process opposed to design as an embodied activity dependent upon tools and media (Coyne et al., 2002, p. 269)

We explored the tricky territory that surrounds the question 'when is design & technology not design & technology?' Designing something like an umbrella clearly counts as the former. But what about designing a play? Are characters like materials? Is a plot like a mechanism? Playwrights are creative thinkers who start with some raw 'material' and fashion new 'products'. But is it design & technology? We arrived at a conclusion that highlighted the importance of creative thinking in terms of the 'made world' of objects, systems and environments. But we recognised that this was neither a watertight definition nor an entirely convincing way of distinguishing between design & technology thinking and other, wider forms of creative thinking.

Much of our subsequent work has been concerned with this interesting area and one of the projects that we report in Part Two was specifically designed to enquire into this connection and equally into the disconnection. What is unique about design thinking? Whilst that project did enable us to identify some distinctive features of what we might term 'designerly thinking', it is hard to claim that more generalised thinking processes might not in some cases, and with some people, and in some circumstances, contain these distinctive elements.

2.   RESEARCH AS A DESIGN TASK

The second matter, inspired in part by the first, is the association between **designing** processes and **researching** processes. In many of the research tasks we have been involved in, we have been struck by the parallels between what we were seeking to do as researchers, and what we also do as designers. In many cases there is a client – whose needs/interests drive the research brief. To that extent both kinds of activity are task-focused. Moreover, the research task is frequently a 'wicked' one (Buchanan, 1995) in which the real issues are deeply intertwined, or lie hidden until you have dug away much of the overburden of detritus. Frequently we find ourselves developing new tools to generate some leverage on these intractable issues. The development and trialling of such tools is itself a design-like challenge that moves through many iteration of ideas, models and prototypes.

As we begin to see the piles of data that emerge from the research activities, we again behave as designers. We begin to model scenarios that enable us to explore patterns and make sense of these data. What if we look at it this way? Or that way? What if we sequenced the analysis differently? What would happen if we prioritised this over that? And so on. All these 'what if' questions are as critical to making sense of research data as they are to designers in developing new products, systems, ideas or environments. Finally, as some answers begin to offer themselves up to the research questions that we have set ourselves, we model yet again. Only this time we reverse model. In seeking to make recommendations to improve the current status of things, we speculate on (i.e. we model) how things might be different if we changed element x or y. It is more 'what if' modelling. Just as new design solutions tend to throw up new problems and opportunities for further design briefs, so too with research outcomes. The answers to research questions are just as likely to result in the posing of more questions.

All in all, research is a very designerly kind of activity. Maybe that is why we enjoy it.

This relationship was explored by Gill Hope, a former TERU research student, who investigated prevailing research approaches to situate her own. She compared deterministic approaches that line up a plan of action in advance of embarking on research with her own more iterative approach that involved a certain amount of forward planning that was then modified and changed as the process unfolded. She coined the phrases 'design-before-you-start' and 'design-as-you-go' and subsequently 'research-before-you-start' and 'research-as-you-go' to characterise the prescriptive versus responsive nature of these approaches (Hope, 2004a). While we recognise the management advantages provided by the more prescriptive approach, the second has more in keeping with the reality of tackling a design (or research) task. Iterative, responsive, 'designerly' ways of approaching research seemed right to us; seemed to enable common-sense starting points and allow rigorous methodologies to be progressively constructed and articulated. It has been interesting to read subsequently that a similar approach has drawn groups of researchers from other disciplinary backgrounds to embrace these ideas through a 'design experiments' research approach (Kelly, 2003), adopted and adapted from design engineering.

> Just as the design activity for an artifact, intervention or initiative is a creative process so too is the ensuing research process. As a result it is difficult to provide a detailed outline of the procedures one must follow to do a design experiment. (Gorard and Taylor, 2004, p. 108)

When considering what specific research methodologies should be utilised, Design Experiments researchers see research as an iterative process in which 'fitness for purpose' and methodological freedom are critical rules of engagement. The importance they place on this is derived from the complexity they see in the research endeavour, and this has resonance with what we have identified above as the 'wicked problems' of research. In recognising this complexity, they indicate what some might see as the methodological weakness of their 'design experiments' research, which we (incidentally) see more as strengths.

> Although the design experiment may be beneficial and appropriate in several areas of educational enquiry, adopting this approach is currently not a straightforward matter. Design experiments are messier than traditional experiments, because they monitor many dependent variables, characterise the situation ethnographically, revise the procedures at will, allow participants to interact, develop profiles rather than hypotheses, involve users and participants in the design, and generate copious amounts of data of various sorts. They tend to involve the following characteristics:
>
> • design activity – focus on process and product;
> • transportation – focus on design and outcome;
> • academic scholarship and scientific enquiry;
> • multiple datasets and multiple research methods;
> • a central role for users (e.g. practitioners and policy-makers);
> • evaluation;
> • design-based model building. (Gorard and Taylor, 2004, p. 103)

'Design experiments' research, in line with our own, is eclectic in relation to methods, willingly combining qualitative and quantitative approaches, in a way that Gorard and Taylor identify as pragmatic. However, where their view of pragmatism extends to seeing ideology as an obstacle to research, we would have more sympathy with the view expressed by Freebody who, as an avowed cultural scientist, sees no problem in combining different methods of research, as long as they are employed within, in his terms, shared understandings of cultural practice, where the use of different methodologies

> are purposeful ... in terms of the histories of their development as ways of knowing about educational activities and, more broadly, about cultural practice. (Freebody, 2003, pp. 51–52)

So while we recognise the imperative to be pragmatic, we would not see this as being at the expense of our own ideological stance and culture as design & technology educators. Rather we see ourselves as research 'free spirits', driven by the 'need to know' and using, exploiting or creating methodologies that sit within our belief systems and that allow us, using the words of Freebody, to '"re-see the everyday" and go beyond "re-enamel[ing] ... the pre-known and pre-evaluated"'. (Ibid. p. 42)

3.   CREATIVE, PRAGMATIC MULTIMETHODS

We could not claim to have been aware of all these subtleties when we launched *APU Design & Technology* at the outset of our research activities in TERU, but we were aware of the complexities that it might involve, and we were deeply unconvinced by the prevailing research ethic in the Assessment of Performance Unit itself, that prioritised a singular, and particularly scientific/quantitative approach. In reporting that first project we were clear on our own, differing, position, stating:

> There is no single, all-embracing approach to research in education. There are many approaches – indeed new approaches are constantly emerging as researchers tackle different kinds of problems and devise strategies to suit them. And so it is necessary not only to select the approach that is most suitable for any particular research undertaking, but also to demonstrate why it is more suitable than other approaches that might have been chosen. (Kimbell et al., 1991, p. 11)

This project had provided us with the very real opportunities of exploring this position first hand:

> The features of the research design which was developed to meet these complexities (in the brief) are of interest not only within the context of this project but also in relation to educational research in general. For they pointed the team towards a humanistic rather than a purely scientific research paradigm, towards analysis as much as quantification and towards

judgmental forms of monitoring rather than attempts simply at measurement. (Ibid. p. 13)

Recognition of complexity, as stated here, should not be seen as implying that we throw all our eggs in one paradigmatic basket rather than another. In fact we are not persuaded by the frequently polarised – and therefore unhelpful – debate about 'positivism' on one hand and 'interpretive' approaches on the other. It is a false dichotomy, since, as Davis observes,

> the most 'participant' of ethnographers tend to use a rigour in their data collection and reporting which is a legacy of positivist approaches. (Davis, 2001, p. 111)

We would go further than this and suggest that this rigour is not merely a 'legacy', implying some kind of un-thought-out hangover, but it is rather a deliberate decision. To be meaningful, data needs to be managed with discipline, but this does not imply **positivist** tendencies, but rather **intelligent** ones. The differences lie more in the tricky question of what will count as data.

The diversity and multifaceted natures of designing, teaching & learning that we find ourselves researching suggests to us the value of flexibility and pragmatism in developing a research design. We therefore 'reject dichotomous thinking on pragmatic grounds' (Schwandt, 1994, p. 131) and are drawn towards 'a general methodology that is grounded in data systematically gathered and analysed' (Strauss & Corbin, 1994, p. 273). More than that however, we believe that 'sources of data traditionally rejected as having bias (anecdotes, opinions, subjective judgments, etc.) can be legitimately used to enrich theory' (Pessant & McMahon, 1979, p. 21). Indeed, the range of data provided through multiple methods enables a variety of viewpoints to be provided, which, as Eisner has pointed out, increases the potential for understanding:

> Because I am a conceptual pluralist, I believe it is important from an epistemological perspective for scholars to have available to them different methods for the study of education. Different methods make different forms of understanding possible. Hence, I am seeking neither a new hegemony nor a new orthodoxy, but rather the expansion of the utensils in our methodological pantry. (Eisner, 1993, pp. 54–55)

As we interweave qualitative with quantitative approaches (using observation, interview, discourse analysis, group debate, photo-montage, questionnaire, structured activity, and many more techniques of data collection and presentation) we recognise the need to avoid 'eclectic laziness' (Powney & Watts, 1987). It could be argued that we lean towards grounded theory, and might be called relativists, but the labels are unimportant. We use a multiplicity of approaches, as designers use tools. We develop new approaches (and tools) when we find that existing ones do not do what we need them to do.

Whilst our approach might seem cavalier, it is not sloppy. If we are dealing in numbers (e.g. with a questionnaire), then we recognise the need to deal with them properly. Samples need to be carefully designed and justified; return rates are important; and the analysis of resulting data must be undertaken with due regard for established statistical procedures. On the other hand, if we are in a classroom, acting as participant observers of learning and teaching activities, then our data collection has to be undertaken with due regard for ethnographic procedures, e.g. in ensuring anonymity, making sure everyone knows what we are doing, and allowing participants an authentic voice. As Freebody points out, the quality of the research is not dependent on the method itself, but on the way the method is employed.

> The fundamental ways to enhance reliability and validity are the same for ethnographic research as they are for any other kind – through ensuring the clarity and accuracy of the representations of: the context of the research; the statement of the problem to be investigated; the ways in which the researcher gained access to the data; the assumptions of the participants; and the understandings on the site about the researcher's role as researcher. (Freebody, 2003, p. 77)

This multiplicity of approaches typically has allowed us to triangulate one set of data against another, towards the aim of greater validity. We often use numbers (e.g. from questionnaire analysis) to spot trends or tendencies in the data. We then use more qualitative data to put flesh on the bones of the trends – bringing them to life through examples, stories and case studies. We see no contradiction in this. We regard it merely as pragmatic research practice, undertaken intelligently, within the context of the values and beliefs we hold about capability, learning and teaching design & technology.

We have sought in this part of the book to lay bare our educational and research convictions which, taken together, provide the conceptual framework within which we have always operated and continue to operate. We now move to the 'meat' in the sandwich; to telling the abbreviated stories of the twenty research projects through which we have developed our repertoire and our understandings.

We begin, inevitably, with a more detailed account of that first venture, *APU Design & Technology.*

THE PROJECTS

In our original plans for this book, the accounts of the Projects (what is now Part Two) represented a far greater proportion of the whole than it does now. But as we wrote the accounts of the projects, it became evident that we needed Parts One and Three to make sense of the story. As these grew in significance, the accounts themselves were edited ever more tightly. There is a limit to this process however since Part Two still has an important role. Because the plain truth is that these projects have been the rootstock through which we have grown our understanding about research. We started with a set of beliefs and understandings (about learning and assessment and so on) and – through a 20+ year struggle with the projects described here – we have progressively come to understand the business of research.

For readers to be able to see these projects as our learning vehicle, there must be enough of the substance of the projects to make sense of them. They are, in a sense, an inventory. The TERU stock. Stylistically, what follows in Part Two is very different from Parts One and Three. In constructing the accounts of the projects, it would have been inefficient for us to describe everything about all of them – since there would be much repetition. So we have chosen rather to tell some of the critical parts of each story. We have concentrated more on the differences than the similarities; sometimes focusing on research design problems; sometimes on data collection; sometimes on analysis; and sometimes on presentation.

We apologise in advance if the brevity of some of these accounts occasionally undermines the story of the project. It has been a very difficult balance to strike, but we hope that there is sufficient meat in each account for the central messages to become apparent to readers.

So whilst Part One was concerned primarily with our philosophical starting points, in Part Two we provide a series of vignettes of the 20 *projects* that have occupied our time over the last 20+ years. It opens with an account of our first research venture in the mid-1980s for the Assessment of Performance Unit and thereafter we have clustered the projects into four cognate groupings:

- Assessment
- Fundamental research
- Public policy
- Evaluating curricular initiatives

The following timeline provides an overview of what happened when.

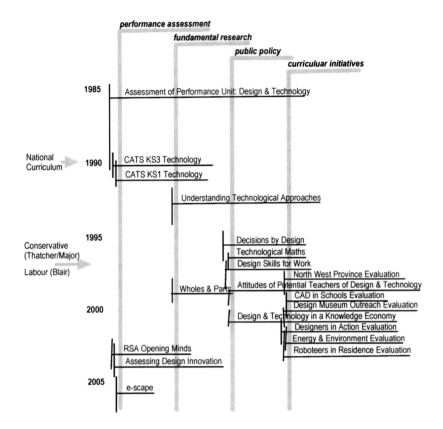

TERU Projects timeline

Chapter 5

APU DESIGN & TECHNOLOGY

Why you might find this project interesting

This chapter marks the origins of our research activities in TERU, and the challenge was enormous. The well established 'light sampling' methodology of the Assessment of Performance Unit (like the National Assessment of Educational Progress [NAEP] in the USA) required two conditions that – on the face of it – ran counter to all the traditions of assessment in design & technology.

- *Test time was limited to 1 hour, whilst normal 'authentic' design projects typically stretch over days, weeks and months.*
- *We were never to see the teachers or the learners. The tests were to be packaged so that they could be sent by post to randomly selected schools, unpacked by the teacher, and administered 'cold' to a randomly selected group of learners.*

*Despite these challenging conditions, we were determined NOT to create just another written test. We would create test **activities**. Meaningful designing activities that would probe the **capability** of learners.*

  We describe here how – over 5 years – we developed the instruments, conducted pilot and national surveys, trained assessors, analysed learner performance against variables (such as gender and curriculum experience) and created the first comprehensive database of learner capability in design & technology. And in the process we reconceptualised the nature of performance and modeled the impact of learning and teaching.

***

1.   INTRODUCTION

This chapter draws heavily from the text and the images in the final report that we prepared at the conclusion of the *APU Design & Technology* project (Kimbell et al., 1991). The last copies of that report have long since been distributed, and because we continue to receive requests for it, we are in the process of recreating it in pdf format on the TERU web site. What follows in this chapter might be seen as some of the edited highlights of that report.

2.   CONTEXT

The Assessment of Performance Unit was a research arm of the DES, and it was established in 1975 to survey and monitor levels of achievement in schools. In the decade to 1985 there was a gradual shift from monitoring, towards supporting curriculum development through an increasing focus on understanding what enhanced or blocked learning – and it was in this climate that *APU Design & Technology* was launched.

The case for an APU survey in Technology was first proposed in 1979 and in 1980 the DES created a Working Party to consider the assessment of design and technological abilities. In 1981, it published a discussion document 'Understanding Design and Technology' (Assessment of Performance Unit, 1981). The group had been set three interrelated tasks:

- Identifying those aspects of an understanding of both design & technology most likely to be reflected in primary and secondary schools
- Considering when and where abilities in design & technology appear in the school curriculum
- Suggesting how these aspects of learners' development might be assessed

In addressing these tasks, the group defined design & technology in terms of skills, knowledge and values. It identified four constituent categories of skills (investigation, invention, implementation and evaluation) and saw knowledge lying in three groups of technological concepts (control, energy and materials). It drew attention to four areas within which values might be assessed (technical, economic, aesthetic and moral). It made two additional points in relation to assessment in this area.

First, the acquisition of an understanding of design & technology **by** a child, and the detection of that understanding **in** a child, are contingent on the child's engagement in purposeful and comprehensive activity.

Second, the Working Group stressed that design & technology is both subject-based and cross-curricular. It does not stem from a single area of the school curriculum. The group pointed out that it may therefore not be as easy for schools to assess learners' performance in this field as in mathematics or foreign language.

The group concluded that further investigation would be necessary and announced that, as a first stage, a survey had been commissioned by the DES 'to determine how, when and where the abilities listed ... appear in the average school curriculum'. That survey was undertaken by the National Centre for School Technology at Trent Polytechnic and the report of that survey was published in 1983, reasserting the definition of technological capability.

> Technological capability is the capacity to take action to master the physical world and increase the quality of life by employing the problem-solving skills, certain knowledge about energy, materials and methods of control, and the ability to make value judgments. (Assessment of Performance Unit, 1983, Part I, p. 2)

Starting from this concept of technological capability the Trent research team explored three issues.

- How is this capability fostered – by what teaching method?
- When does the teaching occur – at what age?
- Where is this capability fostered – in which school subjects?

Its findings led to the view that all school subjects contributed to some degree to the development of all the twelve competencies listed, but that teachers from a much smaller number of subjects claimed to foster the practical skills and other abilities needed for tackling problems, applying knowledge and making value judgements, in a way which might be useful in technological situations.

The survey identified three different levels of technological education:

- Creation of a general **awareness** of technology, arising throughout the curriculum
- Acquisition of applicable **skills** and **knowledge** and the ability to make **value judgements**, which occurs in a limited range of subject
- Experience of **tackling and solving** real technological problems, which occurs almost exclusively in the subjects of Technology and of Craft, Design and Technology'. (Assessment of Performance Unit, 1983, synopsis p. 2)

It also noted that in the schools' context of 1983 all three levels of technological education were more likely to occur at age 14–16 than at any other and it therefore recommended that monitoring should focus, in the first instance, on the 14–16 age range. It should also take account of all three of the levels of technological education it had identified, and measurement of performance at each of these levels should be correlated with studies of school conditions, learners' curricula, and teaching methods employed. It was in response to these recommendations that *APU Design & Technology* was established – the recommendations constituting the main elements of its research brief.

3.   BRIEF

The brief referred to the evolutionary state of design & technology at that time, with elements of the evolving subject appearing (particularly) in Art and Design, Craft Design & Technology, Home Economics, and Science and Technology and drew attention to the recent work on the GCSE criteria for those subjects.

The research brief set out several principles to guide the assessment programme. These included:

- Development of criterion-based assessment instruments which would measure particular aspects of competence and enable several levels of performance in each particular aspect to be described
- Assessment of attitudes and value-judgements as well as knowledge and practical strategies
- Holistic as well as analytical treatment of learners' performance – the central feature to be assessed being the capacity to bring together appropriate skills, values and knowledge in the process of coming to grips with some of the problems of living in and exerting influence upon the made world
- Collection of data relating to curriculum content and other conditions in which learners' learning takes place, as well as the usual range of school-based variables collected by all Assessment of Performance Unit projects

The research brief was distributed for competitive tender, and the project was subsequently awarded to Goldsmiths, University of London.

4.   METHODOLOGY

Given the brief, we faced challenges of a conceptual as well as of an empirical kind. As we identified in Chapter 4, this pointed us towards **humanistic** approaches and to forms of monitoring that went beyond simple measurement. They also necessitated the development of assessment instruments that would facilitate and support these forms of research.The monitoring was to be **cross-curricular,** in that it was to embrace all learners, regardless of whether their curricula had or had not included elements of those 'subjects' identified as specifically concerned to promote design & technology capability. Its focus had to be **procedural,** since the definition of design & technological capability that we inherited was couched in procedural terms. It had to seek to identify **holistic** capability, since, as earlier studies had indicated, design & technology activity requires an appropriate interaction of skills, knowledge and values, and cannot be assessed appropriately by any process of merely aggregating discrete levels of performance in these areas. Consequently, it needed to transcend performance and seek further evidence of the **intellectual processes** that underlie or accompany such performance. It also had to operate in an area of the curriculum in which a range of quite different practices and philosophies could be discerned, and at a time when those practices and philosophies were themselves undergoing rapid and significant changes. This meant that the very concept of design & technological capability had itself to be recognised as **problematic.**

4.1   Research Design

The development of an appropriate research design began from this last consideration, the problematic nature of design & technological capability. We recognised that we could not set out to monitor design & technological capability without first establishing what it is, or, more accurately, without making quite clear and public the definition we had adopted. We thus addressed our first attention to elucidating and justifying that definition. In developing it, we built on the views that had emerged from the research and discussions that had preceded the establishment of the project. To make public the stance that we adopted, a position paper was published, 'Design and Technological Activity: A Framework for Assessment' (Kelly et al., 1987).

We also recognised the need for this definition to be seen as developmental so as not itself to become a straitjacket. Rather, it needed to be accepted as problematic and itself a subject for research. What was required was a definition sharp enough to make possible the development of test instruments, but at the same time sufficiently flexible to accommodate those changes in both the practice and the concept of education in design & technology that occurred throughout the life of the project.

Our research design therefore addressed conceptual as well as empirical questions. It aimed to advance our thinking as well as our practice. Our task was to explore the continually evolving concept of design & technological capability, to assess the extent of its incidence in the 15-year-old population and to identify factors that might either promote or inhibit its development. This exploration had to be undertaken in a manner which would support rather than retard the continuing development of this curriculum area and which would feed and enhance teachers' conceptual understanding as well as their technical competence.

Finally, the requirement that the project collect 'data relating to curriculum content and other conditions under which learners' learning takes place' made this an exercise in curriculum research and evaluation as well as the assessment of learner performance. The nature of the curriculum we had been invited to evaluate made it necessary to adopt formative as well as summative approaches to its evaluation.

4.2   Describing Design & Technology

In the 1987 position paper, we analysed a range of models that were – at that time – being used to explain the processes involved in design & technology. These ranged from simple linear models (Figure 5-1) to cyclical and even interactive cyclical models (Figure 5-3); and they expressed the design 'steps' in various levels of detail (Figure 5-2).

Figure 5-1. A linear model of designing – anonymous and ubiquitous

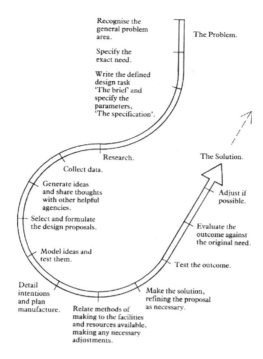

Figure 5-2. An HMI version of 'the design loop' (DES/HMI, 1987, p. 10)

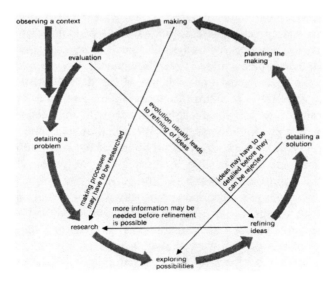

Figure 5-3. A cyclical/interactive model. (From Secondary Examinations Council, 1985, p. 10.)

Innumerable variants of this basic idea can be found in the literature and gradually, as teachers became more experienced at working with them, the models were themselves refined. We recognised however that all these models were based on an analysis of the **behaviours** that were seen to be appropriate for designers at particular points in the designing activity. As we pointed out, we were concerned to transcend such behavioural accounts and seek to understand the **intellectual processes** that underlie, or accompany, such performance.

Accordingly we were dissatisfied with these behavioural descriptions of what learners do when they tackle a task. The models had been helpful guides to the sorts of activity that might go on in design & technology, but they had equally been dangerous in prescribing 'stages' of the process that need to be 'done' by learners.

We attempted to create a different way of looking at design & technology. We rejected the idea of describing the activity in terms of the **behaviours** that are seen to be staging posts in the process, or in terms of the **products** that result from it. Instead we concentrated on the thinking and decision-making processes that are manifested in those behaviours and that result in those products. We were more interested in **why** and **how** learners chose to do things than in **what** it was they chose to do. The learner's thoughts and intentions were the key drivers for our way of describing design & technology activity.

We gradually came to see the essence of design & technology as being the interaction of mind and hand – inside and outside the head. It involves **more** than conceptual understanding – but is dependent upon it, and it involves **more** than practical skill – but again is dependent upon it. In design & technology, ideas conceived in the mind need to be expressed in concrete form before they can be examined to see how useful they are.

The act of expression is a crucial part of the development of thinking. Without such expression it is almost impossible for an idea to move very far forward because few people are able to cope with that degree of mental imaging. It is like playing mental chess. We can all manage the first move or two – but trying to hold in our mind an image of the board after 20 moves (and countermoves) is impossible for most of us. With the chessboard in front of us (as a concrete expression of the current state of our thinking) we can achieve a far more cunning and sophisticated level of thinking.

So too with design ideas – the concrete expression of them not only clarifies them for us, but also enables us to confront the details and consequences of the ideas in ways that are simply not possible with internal images. Cognitive modelling by itself – manipulating ideas purely in the mind's eye – has severe limitations when it comes to complex ideas or patterns. It is through externalised modelling techniques that such complex ideas can be expressed and clarified, thus supporting the next stage of cognitive modelling. These ideas informed the model of designing we developed through *APU Design & Technology*, which we have described earlier in our discussion of capability (see Chapter 1). We crystallised this idea visually (repeated here as Figure 5-4) and in the following statement from the final report of the project.

It is our contention that this inter-relationship between modelling ideas in the mind, and modelling ideas in reality is the cornerstone of capability in design and technology. (Kimbell et al. 1991, p. 21)

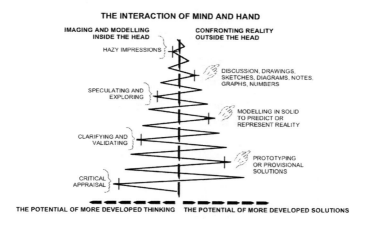

Figure 5-4. The APU Design & Technology model of process

Choosing the most appropriate form of modelling involves thinking not only about what the idea is that needs to be expressed, but equally about how the modelling is supposed to help. **Discussion** (verbal modelling) may be the best way to start. It is very quick and it helps people to get a grip on some of the big issues and difficulties that might need to be tackled. But discussion alone does not allow us to get into the detail that may be required. Accordingly, different types of modelling are needed that may be **diagrammatic**, or **computer simulated, graphic or 3D** that enable fine detail to be explored and resolved.

This view of the design and development activity had important consequences for our view of constructing assessment tasks.

4.3   Test Development

We took the view that we should not be interested in conceptual understanding for itself, or in the decontextualised display of any particular communication skill but rather in the extent to which learners can **use** their understandings and skills when they are tackling real tasks.

Capability in design & technology involves the active, **purposeful deployment** of understandings and skills – not just their passive demonstration. Isolated tests of knowledge and skills were therefore quite inappropriate and we had to look toward the development of test tasks that could give us a measure of active capability.

This idea, when applied to our model of the activity meant that we had to consider a completely different way of looking at tests; one that would maintain the integrity of the imaging and modelling (inside/outside, conceptual/expressive) processes.

4.3.1   Assessing Intellectual Processes

One of the most intractable difficulties with which we were grappling was that processes (as opposed to products) are difficult to assess because you cannot see them. They are a bit like the wind: you cannot see it but you can see its results. Similarly you cannot really **see investigating** or **evaluating**, but you can see the results of good (or poor) investigating and evaluating and you can observe the associated **behaviours**.

But before we can assess the effectiveness of any piece of behaviour we need to know the **intention** that the learner has in doing it. Without that, our assessment must of necessity be based on guesswork – and that will not do. Accordingly, any assessment of intellectual processes (rather than knowledge or skills) must be conditional upon our ability to get inside the learner's mind and share their intentions.

Some of our most interesting work resulted from this realisation of the central importance of learner intention and we developed a number of strategies to encourage learners to make their intentions explicit.

4.3.2   Assessing and Mapping

We were also drawn to a distinction between those things that should properly be assessed (i.e. how **well** a learner does something) and those things that it is not appropriate to assess but very important to map. For example, when tackling a task to do with using wind energy to power a bird scarer for a domestic garden, some learners developed mechanical systems whilst others developed electronic systems or visual systems. It matters little what system they used so long as they could develop it to the point where it had a reasonable chance of working. Nevertheless it was interesting to us to map the **content** of the responses whilst assessing the **quality** of them. One important reason for such mapping is that it can be very illuminative to examine what content areas learners felt it important or appropriate to use and which they felt at home with when tackling their tasks.

4.3.3   Three Kinds of Tests

For the reasons outlined above, we were committed to an active, task-centred approach to assessing design & technology, which under any normal circumstances could be expected to take days (if not weeks and months) rather than hours. The 'light-sampling' principles that quite properly underlay APU monitoring gave us access to a 2% sample of the 15-year-old cohort – approximately 10,000 learners in 700 schools. However, we were under strict instructions (from the DES) to monopolise **the very minimum of time** for any one learner, and after a good deal of negotiation, we agreed to a normal maximum test time of 90 min.

In devising the assessment instruments we were guided by two key factors. First, it was necessary to build assessment devices that were genuinely design & technology, i.e. that integrate all aspects of capability and allow holistic assessments to be made. Second, these assessments had to be based as much on value judgements as on scientific measurement.

Addressing these problems led us to develop three approaches to assessment:

- Case records of **Extended Project Work** in which fieldworkers conducted individual interviews with learners, collecting detailed information throughout their General Certificate for Secondary Education project work to build into case records of individual learner performance. In this strategy the emphasis was on collecting illuminative rather than statistically reliable data. Because the **whole project** was scrutinised, all aspect of performance could be monitored and assessed.
- **Ninety minute focused tests** where learners completed two structured tasks from different contexts or themes, working with restricted resources in a specially designed learner response booklet. Because of the degree of external control exerted, and the large numbers of learners involved in them, this element of the survey provided the most statistically reliable data. However, because of the short time allowed, each task only examined certain aspects of capability.
- **Modelling tests** in which the 90 min focused tasks were resourced with extra time (half day), a range of soft and rigid modelling materials and the opportunity for learners to collaborate and discuss their emerging

ideas. These tests were a hybrid between the other two, and while they had strong elements of control within them, they allowed for learner interaction. They were run by trained administrators who provided additional illuminative material, giving a balance between the first two test types.

Whilst the development of the case records involved a great deal of detailed data collection, the approach was essentially conventional, involving interview and photography techniques and some observation of practice. By contrast, the 90 min focused tests took the form of a new approach to assessment – that of performance based, or authentic assessment. There had been some development of this approach to assessment in other areas of the curriculum, for example, in science (Shavelson et al., 1991; Johnson, 1989), but the approach was completely new in the research world of design & technology education and it is worth some discussion of their development.

4.3.4   Developing the 90 min Test Activities

The whole of the learner sample would be undertaking these tests, and nothing in our collective experience gave us any confidence that it was possible to develop activity-based design & technology assessment in such a short time. Moreover, to add to the difficulties, the tests had to be delivered through the post to a school. A teacher was required merely to open the package, take out the test, administer it to a randomly selected group of 15-year-old learners, repackage the work and send it back to us.

The idea of a design team
It was clear from the outset that it would be impossible to set worthwhile design tasks and expect all learners to tackle them from start to finish. A period of 90 min is just not enough. Accordingly, we settled on the idea of segmenting the activity so as to expose or highlight a different phase in each of four different test forms:

- Starting points
- Early ideas
- Developing solutions
- Evaluating products

We were therefore asking learners to undertake **part** of a design task, and to make sense of that we created the notion of a **design team** – the work of the individual being **part** of the team's response.

So, in 'starting points', the learner had to take the task from the very start – the brief – to make sense of it all and establish some idea starting points which could be handed over for others in the team to develop. In 'early ideas', the learner would then not only get the task brief, but also some starting points that had been developed by the notional team, the individual task being to develop some early ideas towards a concept model of a solution, which could be passed back to the team to develop. The 'developing solutions' test took this a stage further. Not only did learners get the task details, but were also presented with a 'concept model' of a solution that has been developed by members of their notional team. Their task was to refine and develop this concept model so that it would work well. In 'evaluating products', the learner was presented with a range of solutions to a task (developed by the notional team), and has to undertake a critical appraisal of them and engage in some refining redesign of the selected best option.

We were asking learners to suspend reality to engage in this process. It was clear to them and to their teachers that there was not really a design team. It was a device to make meaningful the scant 90 min engagement with the task. Early trials suggested that both learners and teachers could see the value of the team concept, and so it proved in the main survey.

Getting started – the context videos
In general, getting started on a project is always a difficult stage, because it involves so many unknowns. Ideas are often hazy, the design needs are not fully understood and no obvious starting point or route is clearly marked out. If this is true generally, we knew that it would be even more difficult in a 90 min test activity.

The literature – and our experience – pointed to the importance of **contextualising** the task. We created a set of short (6 min) videos in which we captured the essence of the setting for each task. As an example, with a task about children and safety, we set the scene for the learners of a range of situations in which children might be at risk – on roads, near water, in kitchens, near sharp tools and boiling liquids. Into this scene we then set a particular need or design task – the need to make a child visible at dusk or a way of making irons and ironing boards safer. In presenting tasks in this way we made the first step towards clarifying the issues that were crucial within the task, and had suggested (implicitly through the questions we raised) some potential lines of development. The value of embedding activities in contexts in this way is that it enables the learner to see the wider picture; their designing is not taking place in isolation from their own lives or the lives of others. The approach made sense to us as educators and, while we were not aware of it at the time, has much in common with the 'anchored instruction' approach being developed largely in the USA at a similar point in time, where there was a parallel concern to situate and contextualise learning in the 'real world' (Cognition and Technology Group at Vanderbilt, 1990).

For **our** assessment purposes we identified three broad **contexts** with two **themes** in each. After several trials, we finally settled on a series of six video programmes, each standardised in particular ways but dealing with a different set of issues:

- 'Products and systems for people' considered the needs of two different sets of clients. The first video in this context – 'Is it all child's play?' looked at the learning needs of children. The second – 'everyday problems for the elderly' – focused on the increasing difficulties experienced by elderly people when shopping, storing and preparing food.
- 'Products and systems for the environment' took two contrasting environments; the first video considering public (indoor) spaces – 'looking at post offices', the second – 'growing places' considering private (outdoor) spaces such as back yards and gardens.
- 'Products and systems for industry' focused on two different sorts of production situations. One video showed a small-scale 'mini enterprise' setting – 'the packaging business'. The other was explicitly concerned with mass production – 'quantity with quality'.

Taken together we believed (when we set them up in 1987) that they represented a wide and appropriate range of settings for tasks in design & technology and it is interesting to note how they foreshadowed the first (1990) National Curriculum classifications of 'artefacts, systems and environments'. Interestingly, the reactions from teachers administering the tests were most encouraging.

> Video an excellent start and stimulus. ... Good video – clear exposition of issues. ... Excellent 'feed in' input and re-cap of main points at the end. ... Interesting, kept their attention. Good connection between the real world and what can be achieved in school. (Administrators' comments database, school Nos. 0091, 3011, 0526, 8757)

'Picking up the baton': the concept models

Giving learners a part-task is easy enough if the part they are tackling is the start of the task – a 'starting points' test. But if they were to be given a 'developing solutions' test, how do you drop learners into the middle of a development task without them first clarifying the task and generating some initial thinking? Since the notional team had developed some starting points and early ideas, we had to find a way of presenting the 'good ideas' from the team for the learners then to pursue.

Figure 5-5. The 'concept model' for developing a leaflet dispenser

We presented these 'good ideas' to the learners either as graphic or as concrete 'concept models'. For example, in 'looking at post offices' the learners were given the task of organising the distribution of the mass of leaflets (for pension, /driving licence, /TV licence, etc.) that are typically found in post offices. In the 'developing solutions' test the idea from the design team was based on a leaflet dispenser using the same system as a carousel slide projector (Figure 5-5). This was presented graphically as a starting point for them to take forward. In other cases, we provided actual concept models that learners could handle and explore before getting in to the detail of developing it.

Structuring responses
Early trials produced an incredibly mixed and interesting set of responses from learners. But we soon realised that the resulting work was not easy to assess. The source of this problem was that, although there was evidence of hard and continuous work on the part of the learners, the **evidence** was very one-sided. There was plenty of evidence of the **outcomes** of the thinking (sketches and notes), but very little evidence of the quality of the thinking itself, which could only be diagnosed by inference from the sketches.

To give a specific example, suppose a learner was developing a cooker timer for the elderly and produced a series of developing design ideas towards a solution that might be made to work. How do we know whether that learner has thought about its durability, or its portability, or its ease of assembly? They might or might not have. Sometimes it might be deduced from the ideas implicit in the sketches, but usually we can only know if specific reference is made to these things on the sketches. Are learners to be judged on the amount of their thinking that they happen to jot down in their sketches?

We considered that this was fragile evidence, and set about structuring the activity in ways that encouraged learners to make their thinking explicit without placing cumbersome burdens on them.

Substructuring the activity

Part of the strategy involved subdividing the activity and building in questions that would provide the evidence we needed. Tentative moves in this direction showed us not only that the answers enabled far more successful assessment to take place, but also that in thinking through and producing the answers, the learners had been provided with a valuable 'pause for thought' which was positive in helping them move forward.

Our 'prompt' questions that initiated the pauses for thought were explicitly targeted at the evidence we were seeking. If we wanted evidence of their investigation needs, or of their ability to plan, we built in a question that required them to reflect on this. The tasks became divided up into a series of subtasks, some focused on active designing, some on reflection, but all aimed to reveal to us the learners' thinking, their intentions, and their ability to realise these through the development of the outcome.

This strategy of using subtasks to structure the activity proved to be a much more important device than we initially imagined, for as we point out later, it provided an important means of differentiating the tests. Many short subtasks gives a tight structure which is highly supportive but within which it is difficult to operate really creatively. Fewer, longer subtasks provide a more open and less supportive structure – but one that is more conducive to autonomous creative responses.

Learner response booklets

We were aware of the intimidating nature of blank sheets of white paper when learners are trying to get started on a task, and we sought to develop an unfolding booklet that progressively led learners through the subtasks (Figure 5-6).

The booklets were effectively folded sheets of A2 which were designed to unfold so that each unfolding revealed a new – related – subtask but without hiding all the work that learners had just been doing. We sought to get away from the idea of turning pages in a book as each turn of a page obliterates all previous thinking.

The approach taken in the development of these booklets turned out to be of great significance for this and further research projects – and this is discussed in more detail later in the chapter and in further projects.

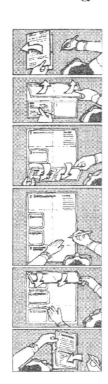

The task is on the front of the booklet

More task information and first thoughts are on the bottom inside fold

The top section opens up for idea development while first thoughts and the task are still visible

The bottom section folds down for further working

Reflections on the development are put on the folded-down top flap – still leaving the ideas being considered visible

Final information is recorded on the back of the booklet

Figure 5-6. The unfolding booklet

4.3.5   The Administrator Script

It was also clear from our trials that we could not just give the task and the booklet to learners and then collect the work 90 min later. We needed the teacher/administrator to choreograph the activity in a systematic way. This ensured both a standard form of test administration (for fairness across schools) and also ensured that learners spent equivalent amounts of time on the various elements of the activity.

We therefore developed an administrator script to talk learners through the subtasks of the designing. Both the booklets and the scripts were trialled to ensure that they provided not only the necessary guidance to learners, but also that the booklet had the subtasks sequenced appropriately and with the right amount of space for each section. The two acted together to support and enable the learners, at the same time providing equivalent evidence without which accurate assessment was difficult. Teachers commented positively on this overall structure.

Very well thought out programme of work. Learners enjoyed it. Good format'. (Administrator comments database, school No. 6080)

4.3.6   Fair Assessment Requires Equivalent Opportunity

Individual learners inevitably bring to the test activities different knowledge, skill, understanding and experiences on which to draw. The point of the assessment is to diagnose these individual differences. As far as possible therefore – in the scientific paradigm in which this element of the survey was based – it was necessary to standardise as far as possible everything other than these individual differences.

- **Equivalent starting points**: using standardised video, booklets and administrator script
- **Equivalent environment**: in a neutral classroom setting of flat top work tables
- **Equivalent time**: using a common time plan for each test structure
- **Equivalent teacher support**: using the administrator's script
- **Equivalent learner interactions**: working individually or (at times) discussing in groups
- **Equivalent materials and resources**: using a resource kit of pencils, pens and basic instruments

Interestingly the most extensive debate was over the inclusion of erasers: if they were included valuable evidence was often rubbed out, if they were not included a resourceful learner always managed to 'acquire' one during the test. The final decision was to include one, but of such poor quality that even removed evidence could still be seen.

4.3.7   Developing the Modelling Tests

During the development period, we became increasingly aware of the gulf between the 90 min tests (the bulk of the sample) and the small number of Extended Project Work case records and the modelling tests were developed to bridge the gap between then. All learners who took a modelling test **also** took a 90 min test, so that direct comparison could be made between the capability demonstrated in each case.

The structure of the modelling tests was developed directly out of the 90 min tests and extended the available time to 150 min. For the first 45 min and for the final 20 min the activities were identical, and the differences lay in the active heart of the structure. Whilst the 90 min tests at this point allowed learners to develop their ideas with a further 25 min of pencil/paper design time, the modelling tests allowed 1½ hours of activity, including using 3D **modelling** and a structured **discussion**.

The **modelling time** provided access to a rapid modelling kit (card, plastic, fabrics, rods, tubes, straws, springs, rubber bands, balloons, gears, pulleys, string, plasticine, etc.). Learners did not **have** to model but could do if they so chose. The **discussion session** required learners to comment on each other's work. For logistical reasons the modelling tests were conducted in groups of six learners, and at a given moment (in the midst of the modelling time) they were required to bring all their work to a central table and – in turn – to explain three things:

- What I have done
- Why I have done it
- What I plan to do next

The rest of the group was then encouraged to comment on the work. Having spent 5 min on the first learner, the focus them moved to the second and so on until all learners had presented their work and had it reviewed by the group. We considered then – and still do – that such collaboration is a natural and very beneficial aspect of design & technology and an indicator of capability.

Training modelling test administrators
We trained 20 experienced design & technology teachers to undertake the modelling test administration. Each administrator was responsible for taking 12 learners each day through the modelling test – six in the morning and six in the afternoon. Our trialling suggested that this period of time would allow purposeful activity using the 'real' modelling materials, and resulted in a sample size of nearly 1,300 learners.

There were many complexities in the administration of this task – not least the problem of how to respond helpfully to learners when asked questions, **but without providing answer**s that advantaged them over others in the group. The learners were told on what terms the resources were available and they were encouraged to view the administrator as they would a 'shopkeeper', asking for anything they needed. The shopkeeper would see if this could be provided from the range available, and as long as they explained exactly what they wanted (or were trying to do) the shopkeeper would do their best to assist. If certain requests could not be met, learners had to modify their plans accordingly. The 'shopkeeper' was **not** there to provide ideas for learners, but as far as possible to provide the resources that were requested.

During the discussion session, the administrator could legitimately prompt or elicit further information when appropriate. To enable administrators to maintain a balance between supporting and directing, they were trained in the use of **neutral questioning** techniques. Rather than passing judgement on performance, they allowed learners to make their own judgements in relation to their work and ideas. Administrators used neutral probing questions that were designed to be value free, such as:

- Tell us what you have been working on.
- Are there any difficulties?
- What do you mean by 'better'?
- Do you all think that is a good next step?

Such questions were intended to stimulate responses that were valid for the group of learners as a whole. They encouraged responses that reflected the **learners'** opinions, choices and priorities, rather than those of the administrator.

The teachers trained as modelling test administrators all commented on the discussion session as being one of the most powerful – and unusual – aspects of the activity. At that time – the late 1980s – it was most uncommon for teachers to use group discussion as part of design & technology sessions, so the following comment was not at all unusual.

> This was a strategy that I had previously not put any emphasis on in my own teaching and I found it by far the most useful device for helping pupils extend their ideas. The pupils' response to each other's criticism was a major force in shaping the success or failure of the artefact in their own eyes. Pupils saw this as a very rewarding activity and would frequently change the direction of their own thinking as a result. I found the use of open-ended (non-directive) questions created the correct climate for this development. (Kimbell et al., 1991, p. 124)

4.4   Designing the Survey

Our brief required us to run the National survey with broadly a 2% sample of 15-year-olds. The tradition of Assessment of Performance Unit surveys has been of **randomly** selected samples of learners, achieved by drawing school numbers at random from the DES list, and learners by random dates of birth. A 2% random sample of the cohort (roughly 10,000 learners) was considered a big enough representative sample of the whole population to enable reliable conclusions to be drawn.

Because of the emergent condition of design & technology in schools at the time, it would have been rash to rely solely on this randomly selected sample for testing. We knew from the Trent Survey (Assessment of Performance Unit, 1983) that a number of subjects in the curriculum were responsible for making major contributions to the development of capability, but we also knew they were thin on the ground as a proportion of the whole school population. In advance of the pilot (1987) survey, we explored this problem to see how far we could trust a random sample to throw up sufficient learners from examination courses of interest. We developed a school questionnaire that we sent to 600 schools in England, Wales and Northern Ireland and that enabled us to identify the uptake of particular courses and the composition of the learner groups within them. We used the results from that questionnaire to enrich the random sample with 'target' samples drawn from courses of interest, particularly in Art & Design, Craft Design & Technology and Home Economics.

4.4.1   How Many Tests Should a Learner be Asked to do?

The principle that had traditionally informed Assessment of Performance Unit surveys was one of **light sampling** learners, i.e. if there are 100 tests in total, 100 learners can do one test each and the national position is arrived at by aggregating the individual results. The aim of light sampling is to minimise as far as possible the load on any one learner or school whilst at the same time making it possible to compile a representative national picture of performance.

There are, however, problems with this procedure. Suppose a learner takes test 4A and proves to be brilliant at evaluating painting aprons for young children. What does this tell us about his/her capability? Does it tell us that they have a wonderful understanding of the needs surrounding the use of painting aprons (perhaps they have worked in a playgroup or a reception class) or does it tell us they are good at evaluating products? Or is it both? To sort out this problem we set a **parallel task**, e.g. 4C where the effectiveness of three different types of garden plant-ties has to be evaluated. If the learner proves equally adept at this task, then that is evidence of transferable evaluative capability. If not, it may well be that the original test simply happened upon a particular strength, which should not be seen as representative of more generalisable evaluative capability.

In short, two tests give far more than twice the data. Because of the comparability of the data, they make it possible to **interpret** performance in ways that are simply not possible with single tests.

In terms of the 90 min tests, the survey design was based on 240 randomly selected learners (20 schools × 12 learners in each school) for every test in the three major contexts. Because all learners were doing two tests (A–C, A–E or C–E), this gave us 480 responses per test, which the APU Statistics Advisory Group accepted as appropriate sample sizes. This number was enhanced by 'target' samples in a selected number of tests. With the modelling tests, we allocated 1,596 learners across the three pairs of contexts, i.e. 36 schools × 12 learners to each pair. This enabled us also to get some target learners into the modelling tests such that three target groups each had nine schools in a test (i.e. 27 target schools) the remaining nine being randomly selected.

The final survey design for the main (1988) survey is shown below and amounted to tests of 9,005 learners, all of whom undertook two activities, giving us 18,010 pieces of work for assessment Figure 5-7). This was in addition to the approximately 1,000 learners who had taken part in the pilot survey a year earlier (1987).

| | contexts | | | | | | |
| | 'people' | | 'environment' | | 'industry' | | |
	children & play	problems for the elderly	growing places	Post Office	quality with quantity	packaging business	
starting points	480		480		480		1440
early ideas	912	192	912	192	912	192	3312
developing solutions	2832 + 920	192	912 + 1020	192	2832 + 920	192	10,012
evaluating products	480		480		480		1440
modelling tests	532		532		532		1596

test sample size   = 17,800
EPW case records   =   210
total sample size   = 18,010

Figure 5-7. 1988 survey structure

4.5   Marking the Resulting Work

The markers for the main survey represented the largest single group (112) and posed the biggest recruitment and training problem. Although many of our (by now very) experienced fieldworkers and administrators were ready to take on another *APU Design & Technology* challenge they fell far short of the number required.

Phase one marking focused on making **holistic** judgements on a 6-point scale (0–5) and then – subsequently – breaking these down into major category judgements on a 4-point scale (1–4). These categories were broadly of three kinds:

- **Procedures** – e.g. ability to identify key issues; ability to develop the product for the user/manufacturer
- **Communication** – e.g. clarity, skill, complexity
- **Concepts used** – e.g. materials, energy systems, aesthetics

We developed assessment guides using a range of carefully selected **exemplar** scripts and used Optical Mark Read assessment forms to speed the process of data management. Phase 2 marking was more diagnostic – seeking to **illuminate** qualities of the responses that helped to **account for** the level of performance. This required clear exemplars. If phase 1 marking provided us with measures of learners' 'capability', phase 2 marking helped us to understand and illustrate what that level of performance was composed of.

Of all the judgements asked of markers, the overall or **holistic** was statistically the most reliable (Spearman rank-order correlation between markers and research team – median of 0.74.) and therefore, we conclude, the easiest. Given the judgemental nature of the assessment, and the fact that this holistic judgement reflected an overview of everything in the learners' booklet, this result was both surprising and reassuring – validating our belief in the importance of holism.

5. SIGNIFICANT FINDINGS

Our approach to analysis and reporting – in line with the **illuminative** principles of the research design – was to seek first to **describe** and second to **explain** the kinds of performance that we uncovered.

5.1 The Balance of Capability

We used the *APU Design & Technology* activity model to create a short-hand way of describing capability. When working on a task, learners operate in both active and reflective mode. They **generate** ideas – **express** them through talk, drawings, models and prototypes – and review and **reflect** upon them. This process is iterative and – in the case of fluent experienced designers – virtually simultaneous. In the case of learners' designing at age 15, we found many kinds of response that can be broadly categorised in three forms; **balanced** performance (Figure 5-8), performance with a **reflective** bias (Figure 5-9), and performance with an **active** bias (Figure 5-10).

Performance with a **reflective bias** is characterised by a concern (typically expressed in words) with the **issues** that are central to the task. 'It's got to do this – and that – and be able to do the other'. Having raised all the issues, the script then fails to deal with them in any significant way. There are no **proposals** for action leading to a prototype solution.

Performance with an **active bias** is characterised by a concern (typically expressed in drawings/models) with **prototype solutions** for the task. In extreme cases, these solutions are **developed** with a complete disregard for the **issues** that need to inform the solution (e.g. durability and usability). They are therefore somewhat 'thoughtless' solutions.

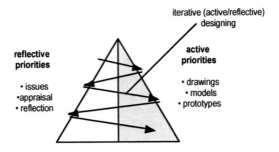

Figure 5-8. Balanced response

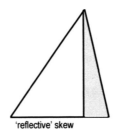

Figure 5-9. Reflective skew

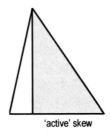

Figure 5-10. Active skew

5.2   Test Context and Structure Effects

As we explained, the different tests have broadly different structural emphases. In summary, 'starting points' and 'evaluating products' had a more reflective structure (prioritising awareness of issues), and 'developing solutions' and 'modelling' had a more active structure (prioritising the search for solutions. The 'early ideas' test was the most balanced of the five test forms.

There is a remarkably close association between this analysis and the performance of girls and boys. Generally, girls did far better on the more reflective tests than boys, and boys did somewhat better than girls in the more active tests. In other words, girls appeared to be better at identifying tasks, investigating and appraising ideas, whilst boys seemed to be better at generating and developing ideas. However, it is also possible to analyse the test structures in terms of their procedural tightness and looseness. Broadly, is the test comprised of many short subtasks (tight structure) or fewer longer ones (loose structure)? This was not something that we were consciously manipulating at the time, but rather something that we became increasingly aware of as we observed learners doing the tests.

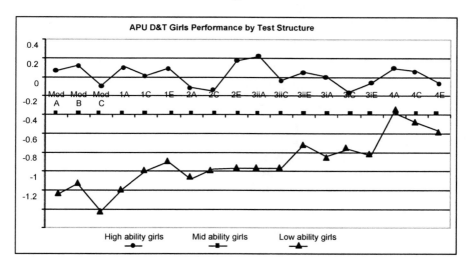

Figure 5-11. Test structure influence on girls' performance

In collecting demographic data about the learners who took part in the activities, in addition to their gender, we also asked each school to provide information on the public examination grades that were predicted for each learner in mathematics and English. We used these as a surrogate measure for general ability and all learners were categorised into one of the three 'ability' bands – high, medium and low. While not perfect, it allowed us to get some handle on the relationship between perceived general ability and the level of design & technology capability they demonstrated through the test activities. In terms of the structure of the tests this turned out to be important, as is demonstrated in Figure 5-11.

This chart has been structured to show the differences in performance between the mid- and high-ability learners and the mid- and low-ability learners – and hence the mid-ability learners appear (somewhat unusually) as if an axis. The tests at the opposite ends of this chart are complete opposites in test structure; the 'modelling' tests (MOD A, C and E) being the most active procedurally and the most loosely structured, while the 'evaluating products' tests (4A, C and E) are the most reflective and the most tightly structured. The combined effect on low ability girls is enormous. There are clear messages here about the sort of strategies that need to be adopted to help girls (and especially low-ability girls) to perform well in design & technology tasks. The messages are not about the **content** of the tasks but about the ways in which tasks are **structured** to support their performance.

In the case of boys, there is a different set of messages. Low-ability boys do relatively well in 'modelling', and low-ability girls in 'evaluating products'. There is generally less effect on the high ability groups, though again the tendency is for boys to outperform girls in 'modelling' and girls (dramatically) to outperform boys in 'evaluating products'. We discuss these and related issues in more detail in Chapter 13.

5.3   Effects in Combination

Wherever the effects that we have described above overlap and operate to the advantage of the same group, then we must expect that group significantly to outperform other groups. Only occasionally, of course, do the effects all operate in the same direction. More often, if one effect operates in favour of one group this is balanced by a different effect favouring other groups, and a good example of this was test 3iA. Here, the fact that it is in 'Context A' (designing a moving toy for babies and toddlers) appears generally to favour girls, but it is also one of the more 'active' and procedurally 'open' test structures, that generally appear to favour boys. The total effect is to reduce the gender bias in the results, and there is no significant difference in holistic performance between girls and boys.

It was as we were compiling these analyses of performance that we became increasingly aware of the subtle ways in which learners' performance can be supported or depressed. Summarising these effects, we pointed out that teachers should be very aware that

- The **context** of the task will affect how it is received and understood – and particularly so in the case of lower-ability pupils.
- The details of the **specific task** – and particularly its 'open-ness' or 'closed-ness', and the conceptual demands that it makes, will affect the ease with which pupils can deal with the task.
- The **procedural structure** that you build into the activity, particularly the active/reflective balance and the 'tightness' or 'looseness' of the structure, will seriously affect pupils' ability to get to grips with the task.

5.4   The Power of Discussion

The **discussion** session emerged as the one that was rated as 'very helpful' by the highest percentage of learners and – given the comments of the 'modelling' test assessors (see above) – we did not find this in the least surprising. Judging from the reactions of these assessors during the training session it was clear that in the late 1980s, discussion was not a widely used technique in design & technology teaching. Moreover the feedback from the same assessors **after** the 'modelling' tests had been run, suggested that all of them (without exception) found it to be the major area in which they felt they would significantly change their own teaching. They were astonished at what they described as the generally beneficial effects of the discussion sessions.

5.5   The Value of Curriculum Experience

We designed the *APU Design & Technology* survey so that we might be able to say something about the effects on learner performance of having curriculum experience of, for example, Craft Design & Technology or Home Economics. But we should not underestimate the difficulty of making these comparisons. Even though we enriched the survey sample with groups that explicitly had this experience, the data was confounded by all the other effects that we have described above; context effects, gender effects, task effects, test structure effects. If a learner was **not** doing Craft Design & Technology, he or she would be doing something else instead, and that **something else** would not have been the same for them all.

Nonetheless, we were able to identify some effects of curriculum experience. And the most obvious effect was what might be termed a 'smoothing' effect. Experience of studying design & technology in the curriculum had the effect of **reducing the impact** of the gender effect, the context effect, the task effect and so on. Whilst these effects were still discernible, there was a greater tendency for learners with design &

technology experience to have developed a more robust capability that they were able to demonstrate regardless of context, gender and so on.

6.   CONCLUDING COMMENTS

6.1   APU: Understanding Design & Technology

APU Design & Technology was the first major research and development project for design & technology. Previous projects – for example, those for the Schools Council: Project Technology (Schools Council, 1970) and Design and Craft Education Project (Schools Council, 1975) – had been explicitly concerned with curriculum development. But the DES established *APU Design & Technology* to find out about what learners could do in design & technology and about how their curriculum influenced this. Accordingly, we were committed to describing what (at that time) was meant by performance in design & technology. Equally, we felt able to go beyond those descriptions of the time. In our report we analysed the pre-existing models to describe performance and outlined both our doubts about them and our arguments for our *APU Design & Technology* model of performance.

Unlike any previous project, however, we had the opportunity to go well beyond these abstracted descriptions of capability. We had nearly 20,000 pieces of work by learners on 24 tests, conducted in 700 schools across the country. Using this huge resource, we were able to analyse and describe capability. This analysis enabled us to describe two facets of capability; **active and reflective** and we warned about the dangers of their separation. We made the case for testing **thought in action** rather than thought separate from action. Having described these two sides of capability, we then sought to analyse the influences upon them in learners' performance. We created a set of diagnostic tools that enabled us not only to talk about capability, but moreover to speculate on the **development** of capability.

Beyond the accumulated wit and wisdom of practicing teachers, there was – prior to *APU Design & Technology* – no research data to inform the development of tasks, or to advise teachers on the consequences of this approach or that strategy. What makes a task easy or difficult? Is this the same for all learners or does it vary from learner to learner? For the first time, *APU* data allowed us to create a framework of guidance to support the teaching and learning of design & technology. We discuss the issues arising from this in Chapters 10 and 11.

6.2 APU and the Unpickled Portfolio

The approach to performance assessment that we developed during *APU Design & Technology* has had a profound impact on our work since that time. Partly because of the reactions of teachers, but principally because of the responses from learners, it was apparent that we had evolved an approach that was not only very different from the prevailing project-based methodology of teaching but was also very effective in **promoting** performance. Our choreographed (90 min) activities were designed to promote **evidence** of learners' performance but wherever we tried them we discovered that they also had the effect of promoting the performance itself.

In a recent development of the approach for *Assessing Design Innovation* (see Chapter 6), a learner commented on the approach in relation to this tendency to encourage and enhance performance.

AB324 – I realised that I could do more than I thought I could.

Throughout *APU Design & Technology* we received innumerable comments of this kind and they encouraged us to see the 90 min tests as more than just an APU assessment tool. We realised that they were better seen as an **approach** rather than a product. Not so much a test … more a way of working. Having **supported** learners' performance through the activity, they inevitably make it more **apparent** and therefore more available for assessment.

Having come to this realisation, we were subsequently able to modify the approach for other projects where we were seeking either to support or assess learners' performance in one way or another, for example:

- 1995 *Decisions by Design* – to help school managers understand designerly ways of thinking and acting (see Chapter 8)
- 1998 *Wholes and Parts* – to compare different design styles of young learners (see Chapter 7)
- 1999 *North West Province Technology Education Project* – to evaluate the impact of a new technology education curriculum (see Chapter 9)

By the time of the Design & Technology Millennium Conference in London we had created a whole series of variants on the approach with different time scales, different activity focus, even with different purposes, but all based on the idea of choreographed, structured activity. We wrote about the approach for that conference – describing the approach as **the unpickled portfolio**. (Stables & Kimbell, 2000). The title may need some clarification.

'Normal' design portfolios tend to exist and grow over an extended period of time and involve the learner becoming 'pickled' in the juices of the task. Our approach is far too quick-fire to allow such pickling. The portfolio that results is fresh and 'unpickled'.

In the following chapters, the reader will find several references to these unpickled portfolios, and it is worth reporting that wherever we have used them they have always – without a single exception – been well very received by learners. They provide something of an antidote to the conventional routines or 'rituals' (McCormick et al., 1994) of design project orthodoxy.

6.3   APU and the National Curriculum

APU Design & Technology came at an awkward moment in time with regard to influencing development of the National Curriculum framework. The first framework for the overall structure of the curriculum emerged through the Task Group on Assessment and Testing (DES/WO, 1988a) that defined the framework for assessment in terms of Key Stages, Programmes of Study and Attainment Targets. From this starting point, subject working groups were required to define the content and organisation of the Programmes of Study and to draft Attainment Targets (Figure 5-12). The Design & Technology Working Group produced its Interim Report on these matters in 1988. (DES/WO, 1988b) We were able to offer advice to the Working Group but based only on our descriptive model of capability (published in 1987) and on the test development for the pilot survey. During 1989, the Working Group was writing its final report that would become the Statutory Order for design & technology in the National Curriculum, but we were in the midst of data analysis and had not developed the findings that – 2 years later – would form the heart of our own final report. So our influence on the National Curriculum was more at the broad-brush overview level. We did influence the overall description of design & technology, and our framework of tests proved to be a remarkably good fit to the original form of the 1990 Attainment Targets.

APU tests	NC Attainment Targets	
starting points	Attainment Target 1	'identifying needs and opportunities'
early ideas	Attainment Target 2	'developing a design proposal'
developing solutions	Attainment Target 3	'planning and making'
evaluating products	Attainment Target 4	'evaluating outcomes'

Figure 5-12. APU Design & Technology tests and National Curriculum Attainment Targets

But in 1989, we did not have the detailed data to inform the specification of Attainment Target levels, and in any event our data was restricted to 15-year-old learners. Our repeated attempts to persuade ministers to allow us to run a parallel survey (particularly at age 11) fell on deaf ears.

However, one of the main research and development spin-offs of the National Curriculum was in relation to the development of Standard

Assessment Tasks for 5–7-and 11–14-year-olds. The *APU Design & Technology* research team was uniquely placed to undertake these developments, and we were instrumental in both projects – as is outlined in Chapter 6. Before embarking on that story however, it is worth identifying a very significant issue about assessment practice that we were increasingly convinced of, and about which we did manage to persuade the Working Group. It concerned the importance for assessment of the relationship between holistic capability and the attributes that make it up.

6.4   APU Assessment and Holism

The traditions of teaching in design & technology all centre on 'the project', which might run for several weeks and in which learners typically take a task from initial clarification to evaluation of an end product. Broadly speaking, the pedagogy might be described as holistic. We felt that – in principle – this approach should be replicated in the approach to assessment.

As a start, we believed that teachers could make overview judgements about a whole piece of work by a learner, and that **thereafter** the teacher could drill down into, or tease apart this overview judgement into a series of smaller judgements of qualities that make up the bigger 'holistic' capability. It is one thing, however, to establish a position of principle, and quite another to show that it can lead to reliable assessments. Nonetheless this was the approach that we developed with the team of nearly 120 *APU Design & Technology* markers.

As we outlined in Section 4.5, we were able to establish that, given suitable training, our marker team held a sufficiently secure **construct of capability** to make holistic assessment a valuable and reliable tool for the assessment of design & technology activities. This might not sound to be a particularly remarkable achievement, but it has to be understood against the traditions of assessment that pertained in design & technology at that time. These traditions demanded that the process of design & technology be divided up into parts; that these parts be separately assessed; and that the final mark awarded to the project was simply an addition of all the part-marks.

Our view of the assessment was that whole projects have first to be judged **as a whole**, and that only thereafter is it helpful to tease apart this holistic judgement into a series of smaller (atomistic) judgements.

This was an area in which we were able to influence the National Curriculum Design and Technology Working Group. We were pleased when their Interim Report expressed the view that:

> These considerations point to the conclusion that, because Design and
> Technology activity is so integrative, the approach to the assessment of

learners' performance in this area should ideally be holistic. (DES/WO, 1988b, para 1.30)

It is a matter of record that the subsequent (1991/2) distortion of this policy by the Schools Examination and Assessment Council towards the ludicrously atomised assessment regime for Standard Assessment Tasks, resulted in 1992 in a complete boycott of the assessments by schools and the sacking of the Secretary of State for Education. These and related issues are discussed in detail in Chapter 6.

6.5   APU: The Human Factor

Finally, in reflecting on *APU Design & Technology*, it is important to remember the human element. The project was sufficiently well funded to bring together a core research team of five specialists in design & technology – and to keep them together for 5 years. This, in itself, was a fantastic resource. But beyond that team was a series of wider circles of individuals:

- An expert steering group (15) formed by the DES
- A group of 'modelling' test administrators (20) trained by the research team
- A group of markers (120) trained by the research team
- A group of schools (700) that ran the tests

The effects of *APU Design & Technology* can in part be measured through its impact on policy. But we believe that the greatest contribution that the project made to the advancement of design & technology was in the effects it had on these people. Many are still active in the education service – as teachers, heads, advisers and examiners – in the UK and overseas. And 20 years on, they are still informing us of the benefit they derived from the project.

Our subsequent research projects in TERU have benefited hugely not just from what we learned as researchers in that project, but equally from the massive stock of good will and expertise that was developed amongst the teachers and other participants who were involved (in one way or another) with *APU Design & Technology*.

Chapter 6

FURTHER PERFORMANCE ASSESSMENT

Why you might find these projects interesting

This chapter extends the story of our research endeavours in assessment, the first two projects dating from the early 1990s and the introduction of the National Curriculum. The importance of this first pair of accounts lies in the challenge of developing assessment instruments commissioned by a very assertive government agency, the School Examinations and Assessment Council. The politics of assessment is right at the surface of these two accounts and they illustrate our attempts to remain true to the spirit of the curriculum and supportive of teachers whilst managing the politics.

The particular significance of the third project, for the Royal Society of Arts and the Engineering Council UK, lay in the fact that we were not assessing design capability, but were rather commissioned to examine **generic** *capabilities such as 'citizenship' and 'managing information'. We demonstrate how our APU style (unpickled portfolio) performance tasks were used for this purpose.*

The final two projects followed after a decade of national curriculum implementation, when the Qualifications and Curriculum Authority (SEACs successor body) finally recognised some of the distortions that had been created by its hard-line approach to assessment. In Assessing Design Innovation, we were commissioned to develop a new approach to assessment embracing the rediscovered qualities of 'teamwork' and 'creativity'. The final project, e-scape, grew out of that innovation project and explores the world of e-assessment through e-portfolios. Whilst the project depends upon some innovative technologies, the key messages concern the impact of the system on learning, teaching and assessment.

***

1.   INTRODUCTION

The first two projects dealt with in this chapter are from the early 1990s when
the introduction of the National Curriculum (DES/WO, 1989) forced some
fundamental changes in assessment policy at a national level. They involved
establishing the initial assessment resources for the new curriculum that the
UK government announced whilst we were in the midst of *APU Design &*
Technology. The Curriculum included a new assessment regime which for the
first time legislated for what was to be taught in schools – the Programmes of
Study, and what was to be assessed – the Attainment Targets. Within this
structure there was a requirement to develop Standard Assessment Tasks for
7- and 14-year-olds. TERU joined forces with King's College London, the
Institute of Education London and Hodder and Stoughton publishers to form
the Consortium for Assessment and Testing in Schools (CATS). When the
contracts for developing the Standard Assessment Tasks for technology were
let, the Consortium was successful in winning development contracts for both.
The projects, *CATS KS3 Technology* dealing with 14-year-olds (1989–1991)
and *CATS KS1 Technology* dealing with 7-year-olds (1990–1992), were
conducted by TERU.

     Having concluded these projects, it was a decade later that we turned once
again to the challenges of performance assessment when it became apparent to
the Department for Education and Skills and other public bodies that the
Curriculum was in need of refreshing. The third project discussed here is one
in which we worked with the RSA Opening Minds project team. This team
proposed a radical, competence-based curriculum, as an alternative to the
subject-based National Curriculum. The new Opening Minds curriculum was
trialled in a range of secondary schools across England and had a strong focus
on formative and portfolio assessment. TERU was commissioned to research
alternative approaches that complemented these. This project, *Researching*
Assessment Approaches, created opportunities to explore assessment in other
curricular settings and also to consider the assessment of teamwork.

     In parallel with this, we were involved in a project that arose through the
growing awareness (in the government Department for Education and Skills
and elsewhere) that assessment processes were suppressing creative performance in design & technology. A mismatch was perceived between the
visionary 'Importance of Design and Technology' mission statement (DfES/-
QCA, 1999) and the reality in classrooms, where teaching and learning was
increasingly being driven by the demands of assessment – particularly for
GCSE examinations. As a result, the Department for Education and Skills
commissioned TERU to undertake research into the development and assessment of creativity and innovation. The *Assessing Design Innovation* project
(2002–2004) was born.

In the course of developments for this project, in an attempt to overcome the age-old problem of ephemeral evidence of 3D modelling, we explored the power, both in assessment and development terms, of the immediacy of digital photography for capturing evidence. The success of this step encouraged us to explore the power of other digital tools and a further project was funded by the Department for Education and Skills – to research the potential for e-portfolios in this area. The *e-scape* project is resulted and is underway as we write.

This chapter charts the distance travelled in our understandings of assessing design & technology from the *APU* project to the present.

2.   CATS KS3 TECHNOLOGY (1989–1991)

2.1   Context

The new National Curriculum came into force in 1990, and it was widely acknowledged that the original conception was both a massive innovation and a somewhat odd step for the Thatcher (Conservative) administration. Thatcher will forever be associated with a ruthless policy of decentralisation; breaking up great government run monopolies (British Airways, British Telecom, etc.) and selling them off to the private sector. But in her education policy she was a massive centraliser, and just as she was ousted from power, the country received (for the first time ever in its history) a nationalised curriculum. But the sting in the tail of Thatcher's vision of the National Curriculum very soon became evident in the priority attached to assessment. The first committee to sit (1987) when deciding on the shape of the new curriculum was the Task Group on Assessment and Testing. This group created the framework for the curriculum. Programmes of Study would identify what was to be taught at each age range or 'Key Stage': Key Stage 1 age 5–7, Key Stage 2 age 7–11, Key Stage 3 age 11–14 and Key Stage 4 age 14–16. Performance was to be measured on a 10-point scale with Attainment Targets detailed into criterion-based Statements of Attainment. The achievement of Statements of Attainment was used to derive a level (1–10) for each learner in each Attainment Target and these levels were used to derive an overall level for the Subject. Subsequently, subject groups were created to put flesh on the bones of this framework. The Technology group (responsible for two curriculum areas: design & technology and ICT – Information & Communications Technology) identified four Attainment Targets for design & technology based on the process of designing:

- Identifying needs and opportunities
- Developing a design
- Planning and making
- Evaluating

The Task Group had recommended that learners should be assessed primarily through a judgement by their class teacher – 'teacher assessment' – and that this might be checked, selectively, by a range of Standard Assessment Tasks that could be administered from the centre. But this proposal was incrementally overturned as the externally set tasks became increasingly seen as the dominant assessment mode.

The administration of the National Curriculum and its associated assessment regime was run by a new body; the School Examinations and Assessment Council. Thatcher put one of her close associates in charge of this body and it rapidly emerged as the policing arm of the curriculum. Teacher Assessment became of little significance and as the New Order took shape, Standard Assessment Tasks were seen as the tool to be wielded. Every learner in the country was to be tested on every Attainment Target in every subject at the end of every Key Stage. The scale of this undertaking is, in retrospect, absolutely mind-boggling. Gipps (1992) initially described the whole development as an extraordinary innovation, introducing criteria-based authentic assessment on a national scale. She viewed this as the logical extension of coursework assessment, the Assessment of Performance Unit approach and another national initiative – Records of Achievement. But the original intention for Teacher Assessment to lead was overturned as the Standard Assessment Tasks became the dominant assessment mode and the potential Gipps identified was never realised. (Gipps, 1992; Brown, 1992; Kimbell, 1997)

CATS KS3 Technology was initiated as *APU Design & Technology* was nearing completion and we were in a strong position to utilise our expertise in performance-based assessment. The National Curriculum development environment was intense, dictated by an increasingly aggressive School Examinations and Assessment Council. Hindsight has highlighted the over-engineering of this early national assessment system and the modifications that made it less specific and more manageable by the mid-1990s. But it was against this extreme background that the TERU developments took place.

2.2   Brief and Outline Methodology

The overarching brief for the team was to develop a range of Standard Assessment Tasks that would enable end of Key Stage (i.e. 14-year-olds) summative assessment of performance. The project moved from early research explorations, leading to trials in 1990 and a full pilot in 1991.

Our starting point was that the Tasks should be designed as surrogate (but real) design projects within which learners have to demonstrate that they can identify a task (Attainment Target 1), develop a design (Attainment Target 2), plan and make it (Attainment Target 3) and evaluate its performance (Attainment Target 4). We were doing this not only just from personal conviction, but also by taking seriously the Design and Technology Working Group who had recommended (as identified in Chapter 3) that

> because design and technological activity is so integrative, the approach to the assessment of pupil's performance in this area should ideally be holistic. (DES/WO, 1988b, p. 12)

The difference between this 'whole project' approach and the approach we had adopted for *APU Design & Technology* is important. This approach to tasks made them closer to the kinds of tests that the School Examinations and Assessment Council would have preferred, but the problem with it relates to the different purposes of *APU* and National Curriculum assessment. Each *APU Design & Technology* test was designed to tease out a restricted range of abilities. The national data that we derived from the survey was an amalgamation of 24 different tests. Taken together it told us a great deal about what **the nation's** 15-year-old learners could do – but it told us relatively little about what **any individual learner** could do. Because of the need for National Curriculum Standard Assessment Tasks to evidence 'complete levels' (i.e. all Statements of Attainment at a level) it was simply not an option to use *APU Design & Technology* style tests. They could not produce this broad data at the level of individual performance. This issue of the **purpose** for assessments is a crucial matter for assessment researchers and one that we discuss in more detail at the beginning of Chapter 12.

We were therefore left with the decision to go for 'whole project' Standard Assessment Tasks, and innumerable problems arose as to how we were to operationalise them. The problems included how to define the tasks in the first place, and how to standardise the conditions under which learners did their work.

Trials utilised a range of approaches, involving using different Attainment Targets as starting points and working in different contexts. All Tasks required 10–12 hours of activity. The trials involved 55 schools in 18 LEAs. Following the trials, a need was identified to supplement these extended activities with short focused Tasks (more like *APU* tests) that could target specified Statements of Attainment and selectively validate the broad brush stroke assessment of the extended Tasks.

The 1991 pilot involved 6,219 learners in 101 schools in 29 LEAs, divided into three groups (hot, warm and cold), depending on the school's familiarity and involvement with the earlier developments.

To evaluate the pilot the following data was collected:

- Performance data from both the Standard Assessment Tasks and the Teacher Assessment
- Learner evaluations on whether the Standard Assessment Tasks allowed them to demonstrate their capability
- Teacher evaluations, considering manageability and their qualitative experience of being involved
- Information on the nature and management of project work
- Questionnaire data on the readiness of the school; manageability and impact of running the Standard Assessment Tasks; support from the LEA; and training needs

2.3   Development Challenges and Significant Findings

2.3.1   Holism and 'Reviews' for Ephemeral Evidence

A major challenge for the team was to develop assessment tasks that allowed for the demonstration of full capability and assessment of all four Attainment Targets. This was undertaken through the combination of the extended and focused Tasks. In addition, the extended Tasks included a set of 'reviews'. The reviews were undertaken at three points: once the brief was established, in the middle of the project and at the end. Each review was designed to provide an *APU Design & Technology* style 'pause for thought' by requiring reflection on each of the four Attainment Targets at each review. The reviews operated by posing a series of questions for the learner – about the task itself, about their design ideas, about their planning and making, and about their evaluative thoughts on it. Their responses provided snapshot images of their evolving perception of their work. Teachers saw reviews as effective in supporting learners and in promoting evidence for assessment. They also gave an indication of overall progress being made; those not seen as making 'suitable' progress at review points proved less likely to maintain the level they were working at. But interestingly, more boys than girls fell into the 'not making suitable progress' category and this was probably related to the dominant response mode adopted by learners in the reviews, i.e. writing.

2.3.2   The Impact of Structure on Performance

In common with pictures built from earlier research, girls generally outperformed boys – most in Attainment Target 1 with its strong emphasis on evidencing reflective skills and least in Attainment Target 3 – the more active 'making' attainment target. This was further affected by the structure of the task – when the starting point was Attainment Target 1 or Attainment Target 4 (also predominantly reflective), the girls performance was highest, when it was Attainment Target 3 the boys performed well. There was more balanced performance overall when the entry point was Attainment Target 2.

At a more general level, performance was depressed when the Task challenge was set too low or too high and if the school reduced the amount of time available. When looking at the detail of individual Statements of Attainment, the nature of attributes within a Statement affected performance. The higher the number of attributes, the combining of reflective and active aspects and the focus on attributes where existing practice did not match expectations of the new Order (e.g. discussing work, estimating resources, reflecting on working procedures reflecting on implications), all diminished attainment.

2.3.3 A New Curriculum as Well as New Assessments

Although teachers of this age range (11–14) were experienced within their own 'contributing' disciplines (e.g. Home Economics or Craft, Design and Technology) the newly formulated design & technology involved a paradigm shift away from teachers' traditional subject-based experience. Before they could take on the challenge of the new assessment regime, they needed support in shifting the learning and teaching practices in their classrooms. As one teacher commented, if design & technology was fully established, then 'running the Standard Assessment Tasks would be like falling of a log'. Consequently, the research team linked assessment in-service training into local training and support mechanisms.

To develop the confidence and understanding to make valid and reliable assessment judgements, 'agreement meetings' became very important. At these meetings samples of work were moderated by groups of teachers, LEA advisors and also by a panel of experts. Interestingly, while marks changed quite considerably at the agreement meetings, teachers were more consistent with their moderation than with the marking of the expert panel. The research team suspected that teachers were prepared to work with 'provisional' truths and standards, allowing them to evolve towards the order, whilst the experts were expecting absolute application of the law.

2.3.4 Holism and 'Level Guides'

The challenge for teachers in making assessments of learner's performance became greater and greater as the School Examinations and Assessment Council pursued its policy of requiring assessment data for every Statement of Attainment. The design & technology Statutory Order contained something approaching 150 such Statements, each one contributing a little bit of performance at an individual level on the 10-point scale. How were teachers to undertake such an assessment?

We were deeply opposed to the idea of ticking boxes and adding up results, and therefore devised a different approach. We developed a series of 'level guides' that were essentially A3-sized fold-out sheets that summarised all the critical information about a level. When folded out, the left column summarised the Programme of Study for the level and the right column contained the Statements of Attainment and Attainment Targets. But the critical thing about these level guides was in the central column.

> The central column was written by us as a capability guide; summarising the things to look for and the critical components of capability at that level. By folding forward the left hand side you turn up the SoA for the level below, and by folding forward the right hand side you turn up the SoA for the level above. If you are going to pitch a level – you need the key information at that level. But having made the pitch, you then need to cross-check up and down to be sure that you have got it right. (Kimbell, 1997, pp. 77–78)

Teacher evaluations and moderation trials suggested that the guides were effective in enabling teachers to assess learners' integrated performance. But they didn't promote the assessment of the 150 disintegrated Statements of Attainment. Accordingly, it was seen by the School Examinations and Assessment Council as contrary to their desired model of assessment. We saw performance assessment as starting with the big picture of whole performance (using the level guides) and thereafter teasing out the detail. The School Examinations and Assessment Council saw the assessment process as a matter of looking for the existence (or not) of the 150 Statements of Attainment. We never reconciled this difference.

If the School Examinations and Assessment Council's agenda for tightly focused assessment was evident in the pilot Standard Assessment Tasks of 1991, it became a bald imperative by the time that the specification for the 1992 round of Tasks was released. Essentially, the need was for Standard Assessment Tasks that

1. Were shorter
2. Were sharper – i.e. tightly focused to 'performance criteria' (the Statements of Attainment)
3. Would provide a set of Statement of Attainment scores – not an overall score for technological capability.

These demands simply did not fit to our model of assessment, and we were removed from the development process.

2.4 Concluding Comments

It is a matter of record that the approach the School Examinations and Assessment Council was insisting on, of using Standard Assessment Tasks to derive assessment data on every single Statement of Attainment, was very rapidly seen to be utterly unachievable. Not just in design & technology but across the whole spectrum of subjects the process of National Curriculum assessment was so burdensome – and the whole system so bureaucratic – that schools eventually boycotted the entire 1992 exercise, blankly refusing to administer the tests. The shock waves that this created through the DES, and its creature the School Examinations and Assessment Council, were such that the Secretary of State was forced to resign and a new regime was rapidly implemented.

Ironically, one of the principal shifts in policy that resulted from the debacle was to establish the idea of holistic professional judgement as the leading assessment approach, subsequently supported by 'illustrative' detail in the Statements of Attainment.

Whilst in many ways a challenging and frustrating experience, this project provided further validation of the *APU Design & Technology* model of designing activity and of our view of how task and assessment structures impact on performance. Moreover, the close involvement with teachers, and the need to support them in making assessments also laid foundations for work that was to follow. In particular, two areas of work proved important in the longer term; the capability-based level guides and the mechanisms we developed for operationalising the 'reviews'. Both were warmly received by teachers and both took forward our own understanding of the assessment process.

3. CATS KS1 TECHNOLOGY (1990–1992)

3.1 Context

The *CATS KS1 Technology* story is somewhat different. The Specification for these Standard Assessment Tasks was issued a year after that for Key Stage 3 and reflected a growing sense of the stranglehold that over-assessment was having on early years classrooms. As a result a decision was taken that, for Key Stage 1 Foundation subjects (of which Technology was the first to be assessed), Standard Assessment Tasks would be non-mandatory. This created a more liberal environment for developments, effectively creating a mandate for the team to see the teachers as the key client group, as Tasks not perceived to be directly beneficial to teachers would simply not be used – a scenario that the School Examinations and Assessment Council wanted to avoid.

The newly defined subject of Technology was one in which most early years teachers had limited experience. This gave the Standard Assessment Tasks a dual role – to be assessment instruments **and** to contribute to teachers' professional development. Thus, our task was to produce assessment resources that supported teaching, learning and assessment.

3.2   Brief and Outline Methodology

As these were the first 'non-mandatory' Tasks to be developed, the School Examinations and Assessment Council provided guidance on their overarching purpose and criteria, stating that they were to be used for both formative and summative assessment, at the teacher's discretion and in conjunction with normal classroom work. This position was endorsed by the Secretary of State for Education (DES Circular 14/91).

Within this context, the Specification required the Tasks to

- Provide reliable and valid assessments
- Be interesting and motivating
- Be manageable for assessment, recording, administration and resources
- Be effective with all 5–7-year-olds, promoting capability development
- Provide coverage of the Programmes of Study and support for the rest of the curriculum

The combination of these requirements created a compulsion to produce assessment materials that were empowering for teachers, that gave guidance rather than prescription and that enhanced confidence in teaching and assessing this 'new' subject. Development was carried out in conjunction with consultants and classroom teachers, trialling the Standard Assessment Tasks from reception to Year 3 (across Key Stage 1 and its borders), including children with Special Educational Needs. There was also parallel development in the Welsh language.

Trialling was undertaken on a rolling programme, initially involving eight LEAs and 40 teachers, and then a further three Authorities and 100 teachers. A range of tasks was developed that spanned the requirements of the Programmes of Study (Figure 6-1). Materials were evaluated under two headings: support for running activities and support for assessment.

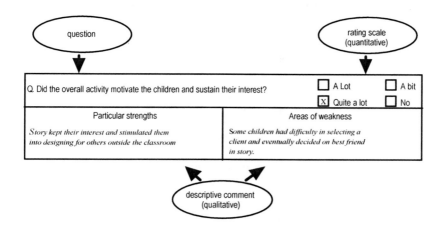

Figure 6-1. Example question from teacher feedback questionnaire

The evaluation strategies included: ongoing evaluation in the classroom; post-trialling evaluation through group feedback sessions and written questionnaires; scrutiny of work produced; and consultation over specific issues with experts. This provided a mix of qualitative and quantitative data – in the case of the questionnaire explicit data of both types.

The final suite of activities included in-service training support materials and a subsequent trial explored the development and use of the materials with 8–11-year-olds.

3.3 Development Challenges and Significant Findings

3.3.1 Creating Valid Activities

The Specification required valid tasks and reliable assessments and, based on our previous experience, this pointed directly at the need to create authentic design & technology projects that complemented good early years practice. Our approach was to create topic-based Standard Assessment Tasks into which teachers could embed other curriculum areas as they chose. We placed a strong emphasis on first hand experience and on discussion before and after experiences. Exploration and problem solving are key features of both early years learning and design & technology and we exploited this fortunate synchronicity.

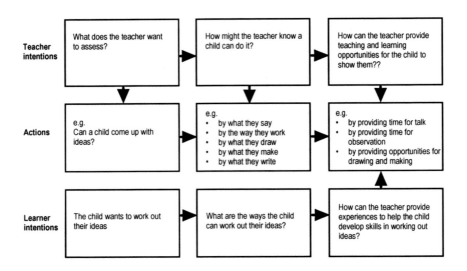

Figure 6-2. Linking learning, teaching and assessment: the relationship between the intentions
in the activity and its assessment

To underpin our approach we developed a model that showed how
learning, teaching and assessment should link in valid assessment activities,
stressing the importance of matching the teacher's assessment intentions
with the learner's intentions for progressing their designing (Figure 6-2). We
shared this model with teachers as a means of developing their own
understanding

We also explored ways of creating activities that gave sufficient structure
to provide consistency and manageability and at the same time remained true
to the iterative model of action and reflection developed through *APU
Design & Technology*. We took the view that it was inappropriate in early
year's classrooms to present ready-made worksheets or booklets as we had
done in *APU Design & Technology*. We considered it important that the
activities were mediated by the teachers who had a close knowledge of
these young learners. Consequently, we developed teacher guidance, based on
the principles developed through *APU Design & Technology*, and broke the
activity down into three phases ('exploring', 'creating' and 'measuring
success'), each of which was presented as a double page spread with 'what
to do' guidance on the left and 'what to look for' on the right. Each
subactivity was linked to an Attainment Target and 'what to look for'
included exemplification of Statements of Attainment (Figure 6-3).

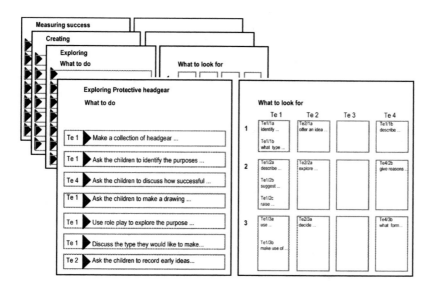

Figure 6-3. Structure of the activities

At the heart of our approach was an emphasis on creating validity both in terms of design & technology **and** young children and teachers' feedback showed the approach to be a resounding success (Stables et al., 1991).

3.3.2   Supporting Reliable Assessment ... and Teacher Development

However, while the children were quickly motivated, early work with teachers soon highlighted the difficulties teachers had in making assessments. A reality of the *APU Design & Technology* iterative model is that it refuses to deny the complexity of designing – that you cannot separate out neat 'stages' in the process undertaken. While taking a stand on this was important for validity, at the same time it created a hurdle for the teachers in achieving reliability. There were two challenges to be tackled.

The first related to assessing supposedly individual Statements of Attainment. With the huge number of individual Statements to assess (all **criteria** referenced rather than **norm** referenced) it was like trying to find a needle in a haystack. So we drew on our previous experience of holistic assessment, treating the collective Statements at any level as a 'basket of descriptors', encouraging teachers to assess to the 'spirit' rather than the 'letter' of the statement (Stables, 1992c). Once teachers worked in this way, they could see the Statements in the context of the level (i.e. 'normed' to the level) – either confirming their overall assessment, or diagnosing a strength or weakness where there was a mismatch.

The second challenge was to help teachers see the Attainment Targets as representing dimensions of capability rather than a linear process, starting with 'identifying needs and opportunities' and ending with 'evaluating'. The activity structure, illustrated above, included all four Attainment Targets in each phase and to help teachers 'see' these dimensions within the integrated whole, we colour-coded the guidance materials, each Target having its own colour.

> In effect we were saying to the teachers that the Activities could run in an interactive way, but that if they put on their 'pink glasses' they could see how to assess (AT1) or their 'green glasses' to assess (AT4). In doing this we were attempting to assist both validity through the way the task was structured and reliability through the way assessment opportunities were highlighted. (Stables, 1992b, p. 7)

The team took the view that if the materials enabled teachers to understand the nature of capability and what valid activities were like, then valid and reliable assessments would follow. This became an overarching driver in all developments. Further support was provided through exemplification. First, we exemplified Statements of Attainment in the 'What to look for' pages of the guidance materials, effectively giving teachers a cumulative level descriptor that qualified and contextualised each Statement. Then we provided whole project exemplification through an anthology 'Children's work assessed' which illustrated whole projects highlighting both the assessment evidence and judgements. Strong graphic approaches to presenting materials to aid understanding, such as the colour coding and exemplification were strategies that proved successful in this project and that we have built on since.

3.3.3   The Challenge of 'Client' Pressure

The non-mandatory nature of the Standard Assessment Tasks allowed us to focus heavily on the needs of the teachers. But at the end of the day our main client was the DES, mediated through the auspices of the School Examinations and Assessment Council. The Key Stage 1 team had fewer battles to fight than the Key Stage 3 team, but the pressure to compromise in the face of 'client pressure' was still present. Evaluations showed certain aspects of manageability to be problematic, particularly the issue of time (both time available and timing within the school year). As a result we were subjected to pressure to provide different routes through the tasks that could minimise the time required. There is no denying that design & technology tasks, involving all dimensions of capability, take time if they are to be effective learning experiences. But bowing to pressure we provided three alternatives: identifying specific Attainment Targets only for assessment; taking a 'minimum evidence' route through the Task – following a highlighted core; or following all activities, providing full assessment. Our preferred option was the latter. Against our advice, teacher guidance stated that the minimum evidence route would allow each Attainment Target to be assessed in 'about 30 min' – an outlandish claim. A 'manageability rationale' also resulted in cuts to guidance materials, notably cross-referencing with the Programmes of Study (the **content** of the curriculum) – a move that hindsight indicated was flawed, as one of the biggest problems with the implementation of the initial iteration of the Curriculum was the false split between what was to be taught and what to be assessed.

3.4   Concluding Comments

This project highlighted the power of developing assessment materials that start with the development needs of the learner, the training needs of the teacher, and of taking validity as the key driver. For the team, it was our first venture into work with young learners and the corresponding support needed for their teachers, many of whom lacked confidence and expertise. The creative strategies we developed to address these challenges provided a foundation for projects that followed.

Several of our projects in the years immediately following involved some **unpickled portfolio** approaches but not because the research purpose was explicitly to develop performance assessment tools. Rather, we developed the tools so we could gather data to better understand some other issue (e.g. the effectiveness of an experimental curriculum – see Chapter 9).

So almost a decade elapsed before we returned, in 2002, specifically to the challenge of performance assessment. Then – seemingly on top of each other – we were immersed in two very contrasted projects that were explicitly concerned with performance assessment.

The first was commissioned by the Royal Society of Arts and required us to develop performance assessment tools in the context of a broad, capability-based curriculum, but not explicitly concerning design & technology. This project enabled us to explore the unpickled portfolio methodology in a wider frame of reference.

**4.   RSA OPENING MINDS: RESEARCHING
         ASSESSMENT APPROACHES (2002–2003)**

4.1   Context

In 1999, the RSA had published a radical new curriculum framework,
'Opening Minds: Education for the 21st Century' (Bayliss, 1999), which
proposed new ways of providing coherent and integrated curricula based on
competences (such as systematic thinking; managing risk and uncertainty;
accessing, evaluating and differentiating information) rather than regular
school subjects. Based on this framework they had initiated a pilot project
that was being undertaken by a number of 'volunteer' schools, working with
Year 7 learners (11–12-year-olds). Work had already been undertaken to
develop assessment guidance using a portfolio approach. Some teachers
were finding this guidance helpful, others were finding it burdensome.
TERU was engaged to research an approach to assessing the competences
that would address this problem by providing complementary systems –
Researching Assessment Approaches. The research was joint-funded by the
RSA and the Engineering Council UK, who were particularly interest in the
innovative curriculum model.

4.2   Brief and Outline Methodology

The research aimed to establish the feasibility of using the 'unpickled
portfolio' concept to enable valid and reliable assessment across the 'Opening
Minds' competence framework. We were asked to explore using this approach
in practice-based and humanities settings and to explore the impact of the
'Opening Minds' curriculum.
     We surveyed four cohorts of Year 7 learners:

- Those who had experienced an integrated 'Opening Minds' curriculum
- Learners in the same school who had not experienced this curriculum
- Learners who had experienced a citizenship-focused 'Opening Minds'
  curriculum
- Learners in a school not involved in the initiative

Schools were asked to provide two groups of 18 learners that had a balanced
spread of abilities and equally split in terms of gender. All learners did two
activities so that we could explore the transferability of their competence.
Each cohort was split in half, one half undertaking one activity first, the
others undertaking the other first to cancel out the 'learning effect'.

The approaches to deriving data were:

- Assessment activities to derive performance data
- An 'about you' questionnaire that probed each learner's perception of their own level of competence
- An 'about the activity' questionnaire that gauged learners' reactions including how well they had been able to demonstrate competence

Each approach addressed the same set of competences, providing a matrix of related data. The competences chosen to be focused had to lend themselves to the focused 'unpickled portfolio' approach. This immediately discounted those warranting a more gestational approach, such as 'managing their own learning through life'. The final list comprised competences for:

- Learning (systematic thinking)
- Citizenship (ethics, values, personal behaviour and contribution to the society)
- Relating to people (teamworking and communication)
- Managing situations (managing risk and uncertainty)
- Managing information (accessing, evaluating, analysing, synthesising and applying: reflecting and applying critical judgement)

Two activities with parallel structures were developed. First, 'have your say', was linked to citizenship and focused on the setting up of a youth council. Second, 'special spaces' engaged the learners in redesigning an area of the school for a specific purpose.

4.3 Development Challenges and Significant Findings

4.3.1 Assessing Teamworking

A new challenge of this project was to assess individuals on their competence in teamworking. Drawing on experience gained elsewhere (Kimbell & Stables, 1999), we created a hybrid task in which learners worked in teams of three, had their own subtask and completed sufficient work on their own to be assessed individually. We also asked learners to identify which team jobs they would and would not like to take on – and why, and what their major contribution to the team had been. We created a teamworking observation sheet, recording how individuals operated and how the team operated as a whole. This tool proved valuable for research (and was also used in *Assessing Design Innovation*) but was too cumbersome for general day-to-day classroom use.

4.3.2   Comparing Impact

Gauging the impact of the 'Opening Minds' initiative through comparing performance turned out to be problematic. We had attempted to produce comparable cohorts by asking the schools to provide mixed ability and mixed gender groups. Despite this, variability between groups resulted in us only confidently being able to make comparisons between groups coming from the same school, focusing on a broad mid-ability band only, as the profiles of the upper and lower ability bands were somewhat polarised. Some useful insights were produced, the general picture indicating that the 'Opening Minds' curriculum particularly supported boys, who outperformed the 'control' group in all competences in both tasks. It also enabled girls to have higher performance in the 'have your say' activity – the task that learners generally found more challenging.

4.3.3   Structuring Tasks for Multiple Chances to Evidence Competence

As stated above, an early task for the team was to decide which competences lent themselves to assessment through a short, focused activity. Having made our decisions, created the task and assessment structure and run the activities, interesting differences between competences emerged. Some were rated highly for the perceived potential they held for valid assessment, such as **team operating** and **communicating**. The learners were particularly clear on this. Some were rated less highly, most notably **accessing information**. To confirm reliability, we compared the assessment profiles of each task – which were remarkably similar, and also the need to moderate marks. With the latter we found the percentage of marks needing moderation was very small except for one problematic statement – **accessing information**. Reviewing the activity it became clear that there was only a single opportunity provided to evidence competence in this area – whereas with other competences there were multiple opportunities throughout the task. This provided a valuable lesson on task structuring, validity and reliability – the more opportunities for providing evidence, the more valid the learners find the activity and the more reliably it can be assessed.

4.4   Concluding Comments

This project provided invaluable experience of exploring our approach to performance assessment beyond a design & technology context, demonstrating that the approach transcends subject boundaries when the assessment of procedural competence is the target. However, it also highlighted the importance of careful selection of areas to be assessed, and the way these are structured into the assessment task. *Researching Assessment Approaches* also allowed us to develop further approaches to assessing learners working in teams – valuable experience that we drew on in the subsequent project *Assessing Design Innovation.*

5. ASSESSING DESIGN INNOVATION (2002–2004)

After 10 years of implementing the National Curriculum, fears were being expressed about the excessively constricting nature both of the curriculum and its associated assessment regime. This deadly combination was finally being recognised (even in government circles) as damaging to learners' creativity. Creativity, remember, was central to the UK Prime Minister Tony Blair's agenda for Cool Britannia in the new millennium.

The time was ripe to attempt to reinvigorate both the curriculum and the assessment of performance. Had we been operating in the high-stakes world of English, mathematics or science we would probably not have got away with it, but being in design & technology we were able to engineer a commission to assess learners' innovation, and the new project *Assessing Design Innovation* was launched.

It was only the success of that project that has subsequently allowed us to expand our frame of reference to the humanities and sciences with project e-scape. The rest of this chapter is concerned with these two projects.

5.1   Context

One of the critical differences between the 2000 version of the National Curriculum and the preceding versions (1990 and 1995) was that the new version contained a vision statement that articulated the **importance** of design & technology in the curriculum. The Department for Education and Skills Strategy Group (charged with supporting design & technology through the early years of the new decade) were delighted by the visionary statement, especially as it reinforced the importance of creativity, innovation and teamwork, but they were concerned that it was somewhat mismatched with the rest of the document. Specifically, it was not clear where these key features existed in the Programmes of Study, and even less clear how they fitted with the Attainment Target (Prest, 2002).

There were also related problems evident with GCSE assessments, partly through the syllabus specifications themselves (which equally lacked reference to innovation, creativity and teamwork), and partly through the impact of school 'league-tables' which were heavily dependent on examination results. The resulting tendency in schools was for teachers to use ever-more rigid formulae on learners' project portfolios to 'guarantee' pass rates, and this tendency produced less and less creative work. The Strategy Group was concerned that innovative learners were being penalised by comparison with well-organised, rule-following learners. They recommended that research be conducted into effective design & technology practice and assessment. In particular, the focus was to be on creativity and innovation, the ephemeral nature of design decisions, the use of new technologies in creative activity and the relationship between process and product. TERU was asked to undertake the research.

5.2   Brief and Outline Methodology

The major aims for the project included:

- Exploring the mismatch between the **importance of design & technology** statement, examination grade descriptors and modes of assessment
- Developing strategies that would encourage a range of approaches to curriculum delivery and assessment processes from Year 6 to Year 11
- Seeking ways to en-skill teachers in fostering and assessing creativity and innovation, using new technologies in creative activity and understanding the relationship between process and product
- Seeking ways to increase teacher confidence in developing innovative and challenging projects, and effective teamwork.

The project developed through three interlinked phases: phase 1 exploring performance descriptors of design innovation; phase 2 examining classroom practices that encouraged it; and phase 3 developing assessment activities that promoted evidence of innovative performance (Figure 6-4).

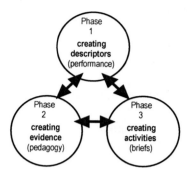

Figure 6-4. The interlinked phases

Throughout each phase the team worked closely with a small group of LEA advisors, teachers, General Certificate of Secondary Education Awarding Bodies and Chief Examiners (also practicing teachers) and the design & technology officers at the Qualifications and Curriculum Authority.

5.2.1   Phase 1 – Analysing Existing Work

Phase 1 centred on analysing existing work from the schools and the Awarding Bodies to identify categories, groupings and ultimately **descriptors** of design innovation. In total, 96 pieces of work were analysed. Teachers involved provided four samples of project work that they considered to be 'good', comprising two examples of innovative work and two non-innovative. For each example submitted the teacher rated the work on a continuum from 'highly innovative' to 'not innovative', explained their rating and underlined words that described the project from a list provided. The most commonly used words for 'innovative' and 'non-innovative' are shown in Figure 6-5.

innovative work	*non innovative work*
different	controlled
exciting	focused
novel	orderly
unusual	predictable
risky	honest
bending the rules	reliable
brave	thorough
determined	thoughtful
marketable	
professional	
'wow'	
confident	
powerful	
unique	

Figure 6-5. Rankings of 'innovative' and 'non-innovative' descriptors

With this starting point we derived an initial draft assessment framework. This framework was shared with the teachers who, along with their advisors, then scrutinised a range of work, modifying and validating the initial draft framework and developing a shared vocabulary describing design innovation.

5.2.2   Phase 2 – Exploring Pedagogic Strategies

It is one thing to have a vocabulary for innovative **outcomes**, but we recognised that learners' design innovation will be significantly affected by the **repertoire of pedagogic strategies** that teachers use. Accordingly, phase 2 centred on examining teachers practices in promoting teamwork and innovation in learners' designing and to observe the effects of these strategies on learners' performance. To do this we asked teachers to run a two-day project in their school, based on an outline structure we provided, and focused on a task and way of working that the teacher felt would promote creative work. We explicitly asked the teachers to ignore the need for assessment, to liberate them from the constraints it can cause. In all the schools that ran these activities we had two researchers present, one observing the teacher and one the learners, paying particular attention to the work of four individuals, chosen to represent a span of abilities and creativity. Data were collected via a set of observation sheets developed from those initially used in the *Understanding Technological Approaches* project (see Chapter 7) and supplemented by group observation based on the methodology developed for *Research Assessment Approaches* (see above). We were interested to see what teacher actions prompted and supported design innovation and the way learners reacted to these tactics. In addition, photos were taken of the developing project work, learners completed an evaluation (indicating what had and had not helped) and teachers were interviewed to explore the techniques they had used.

5.2.3   Phase 3 – Developing Performance Assessment

The challenge of phase 3 was to create some assessment activities that built on what we learned from phases 1 and 2 and provided valid and reliable assessments of learners' design innovation. Once again we returned to our *APU Design & Technology* experience and, with the understandings gained in phases 1 and 2, revisited the 'unpickled portfolio' (Stables & Kimbell, 2000).

'LIGHT FANTASTIC' TASK

A light-bulb company wants to minimise packaging waste and extend the product range they offer. They want a new range of light-bulb packaging that people won't throw away.

Your task is to come up with exciting ideas for light-bulb packaging that people won't throw away because it transforms into interesting lighting features & structures.

By the end of the activity you must have produced

• a working light-bulb package containing everything for the lighting feature;

• an assembled lighting feature

• a persuasive argument for your product to attract purchasers.

Outline structure

1. read task to the group and establish what is involved

2. explore a series of 'idea-objects' on an 'inspiration table' and in a handling collection designed to promote ideas for transformation

3. put down first ideas in a designated box in the booklet

4. swop work within team - for further development by team mates

5. work returned to 'owner' to consider which ideas to pursue

6. teacher introduces the modelling/resource kit

7. learners develop their ideas through drawing – and/or through 3D modelling.

8. learners reflect on the *user* of the end product and the *context* of use, before continuing with development

9. at set intervals, learners pause and throw a 'questions' dice, e.g. "how would your ideas change if you had to make 100?". Answers recorded in their booklet

10. approximately every hour photos of modelling taken to develop *visual story line* of evolution of design ideas

11. end of 1st morning, learners reflect on own and team members work

12. 2nd morning starts with celebration of work from day 1 using 'post-it' notes to highlight 'best' idea, 'wackiest idea' biggest problem' and 'next steps'.

13. prototype development continues

14. hourly photos and pauses for reflective thought continue

15. final team reflections on each others' ideas and progress

16. learners 'fast-forward' their idea - what it will look like when finished

Figure 6-6. Outline structure for the 'light fantastic' task

Certain features were adapted from previous versions – most notably the subtasks promoting iteration between thought and action, the evaluative 'red penning', the unfolding booklet and the administrator's script. Phase 2 had highlighted the effectiveness of 3D modelling for growing ideas and this led us to include modelling resources – and to expand the timescale for the activity so as to allow them to be used effectively. We also included a 'handling collection' to resource thinking and ideas, based on our experience in the curriculum initiatives reported in Chapter 9. However, a number of quite new features were included, most notably the use of supportive teamwork, the introduction of a 'photo-storyline' of the developing product, the use of 'prompt' questions identified randomly through throwing a dice and the requirement to 'fast-forward' ideas to show final design intentions. The first activity developed, 'light fantastic', was a 6 hour activity that took place over two consecutive mornings and involved designing light bulb packaging that (when the bulb was taken out for use) transformed into a lighting feature. The outline structure is shown in Figure 6-6.

While the majority of the development work was undertaken as 3D modelling, the whole activity was recorded in yet a further iteration of the unfolding (unpickled portfolio) booklet – an unfolded example of which is provided in Figure 6-7.

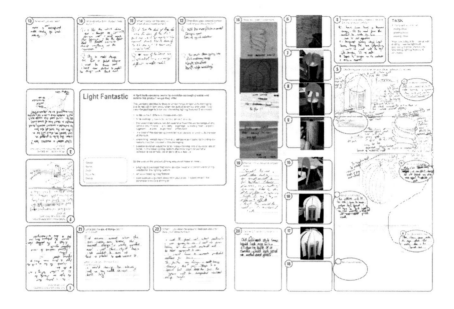

Figure 6-7. The unfolded workbook of one learner's developments for 'light fantastic'

The 'light fantastic' activity was trialled in a range of schools and age groups (from Year 6 to Year 12) and formed the basis of a template for further activities. We were working in collaboration with the General Certificate of Secondary Education Awarding Bodies, each of which offered two of their Senior Moderators who were all experienced and able teachers of design & technology. They each developed a variant of the light fantastic task with a focus on different specialist areas of design & technology (textiles, systems and control, graphics, etc.), so that in total we had eight new assessment tasks covering the full range of design & technology.

These tasks became the basis for a national pilot, with learners undertaking one of these eight tasks and (wherever possible) also the light fantastic task (for standardising/benchmarking purposes). The tests were undertaken in 12 schools, with 390 learners, 100 of whom completed two activities.

5.3   Development Challenges and Significant Findings

5.3.1   Counter-Intuitive Nature of Structure and Creative Freedom

From the teacher-led activities in phase 2, certain things became immediately obvious. The first was the empowering effect of having a block of time to work on the project. However, across 2 days the learners' productivity varied and this appeared to relate partly to their energy levels (the mornings generally being the most productive) and partly to the teaching strategies that variously challenged, motivated and rescued them. Observing the activities we were conscious of our *APU Design & Technology* experience where the pace of work was heavily influenced by the way we structured the activity to iterate between action and reflection. So once more we created a tight structure for the activities, anxious to see the impact on creativity. Despite the tight structure, the learners felt they were being provided with freedom to be creative, to develop their ideas in the way that **they** wanted to. This issue is picked up again in Chapter 11.

5.3.2   Recognising and Enabling the Power of Modelling

The second aspect that emerged from the teacher-led activities was the major (and untypical) use of 3D modelling, including at an early stage in developing ideas. Released from the requirements of assessment, the teachers appeared comfortable legitimising this way of working and many learners gravitated quickly to the opportunity, using modelling as a powerful thinking tool. Consequently, we felt compelled to replicate the opportunity within the more formalised assessment activity, so provided a wide range of rapid modelling resources and 'permission' to use these from an early point. In the activity evaluation questionnaires, learners consistently told us that 3D modelling was a highly valued aspect of the activity.

5.3.3   The Impact of the Photo-Storyline

While modelling proved an effective way to develop design ideas, an abiding issue in the use of modelling in assessment activities is the extent to which evidence is often lost as the model is modified, 'canibalised' or discarded. During the 2-day activities we made extensive use of photographs to capture the trail of evidence and we were struck by how effectively the photos told the 'story' of the project (Bain, 2005) and the extent to which the photos facilitated assessment.

To replicate this type of evidence, we set up a system for taking, printing and returning photos of the developing models every hour, effectively creating a 'photo-storyline' of evidence. What we had not anticipated was the powerful effect the provision of these photos had on the learners who found the building of the photo-storyline immensely helpful in their ideation processes. In learner evaluations of the activity the photo-storyline has consistently received high ratings as a helpful strategy. Our appetite was whetted by the potential (both for learning and for assessment) of using digital capturing of evidence and has been significantly developed through the subsequent project, *e-scape* (see below).

5.3.4   Using Random Questions as Prompts for Lateral Thinking

In the original *APU Design & Technology* booklets 'thought bubbles' appeared throughout as prompts to reflective thinking. The aim was to make the learner think more widely, deeply or differently about their work and this aim has materialised in various forms over the years – for example, in the *CATS KS3 Technology project* 'Reviews'. In this latest version we randomised the thinking prompts, to further break the mould of a linear process, and required learners to answer questions that came up randomly through the throw a dice. Teachers universally thought the dice a really good innovation, but for the learners the questions seemed to be an unnecessary distraction, and the use of the dice consistently achieved low ratings in learner feedback.

5.3.5   Harnessing the Power of Collaborative Groups

Previous projects (*APU Design & Technology* – see Chapter 5; *Researching Assessment Approaches* – see earlier; and the *North West Province Technology Education Project* – see Chapter 9) had indicated the immense power that teamwork can have when developing design ideas, both when learners are working on a collective project and when a critically supportive team is providing a 'sounding board' to an individual. Our previous experience had shown the importance of giving individuals space to develop ideas on their own coupled with opportunities for feedback from peers in positive critical reviews. For this project we were keen to explore the potential for individual work that was undertaken throughout the activity in the context of a constructive, collaborative group and to use the group to support the generation of ideas as well as critical reflection. Consequently, once the task was introduced (supported by group explorations of the handling collection) we started the activity with a 5 min burst of individual idea generation. The working groups of three then swapped around their booklets so A was looking at B's work, B at C's work and C at A's work. Their task (in the next 5 min) was then to take forward their teammates ideas. This then went through a third cycle before A, B and C got back their own booklets. At that point, their, often hesitant, first ideas were reinforced by teammates additions, comments and suggestions. This approach proved immensely popular with learners. Other team collaborations were structured throughout the 6 hours of the activity – some generative and some more reflective comment from peers. We sought to create a working climate in which the collaborative teams felt able to discuss work during the individual development periods. Both learners and teachers found this to be an effective way of working and learners quickly fell into the 'critical friend' role, where support and advice was given, but at the end of the day, individuals' work was very much their own.

5.3.6   Developing a Creativity and Innovation Assessment Framework

In previous assessment projects, assessment frameworks had related to holistic design & technological capability. In this new project we were focusing explicitly on one dimension of capability – being creative and innovative. The vocabulary that emerged from the phase 1 analysis was significant. It also showed that innovative projects were principally driven by ideas whereas non-innovative projects were typically driven by the conventional and sequential steps of a linear design process. As a result we derived the initial assessment framework around **having** ideas, **growing** these ideas and **proving** the ideas would work, growing ideas emerging as the cornerstone of creative ability in design & technology.

The principles behind the approach to assessment remained similar to those in the *APU Design & Technology* project – that first an overall holistic judgement should be made that creates a frame of reference to which subsequent judgements of detail can contribute further illumination. The scale on which judgements were made was one of 'wow' to 'yawn', using the vernacular terminology derived from the initial analysis, that teachers felt comfortable with and that we found to be reliable (Figure 6-8).

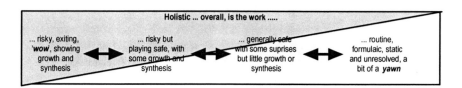

Figure 6-8. The wow-yawn continuum from the assessment framework

Interestingly, following a marking and moderation exercise, the holistic judgement and 'growing ideas through modelling' proved to be the most consistent, and 'having' and 'optimising' the least consistent. Teachers found it was straightforward identifying evidence and generally felt confident about making judgements.

5.3.7   Findings on Performance

Despite positive reactions to the assessment tasks, overall performance was low if considered on a normative distribution curve (see Figure 6-9).

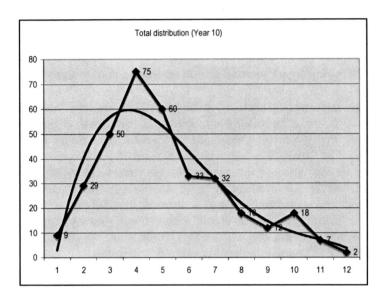

Figure 6-9. Overall performance

We believed this to be a reflection of the fact that design innovation has not received the attention that it deserves. But this overall data masked some interesting detail. While the numbers involved are too small to provide more than indicative findings, the following were noted:

- **Task effect** (i.e. the variability from task to task) was small, suggesting that the quality of **design innovation** is an identifiable quality in learners.
- Predictions of **learners' public examination performance** did not correlate with our findings on their design innovation. This was not a surprise since the whole point of the project was premised on the idea that GCSE examinations do not assess this quality.
- **General ability** did not directly correlate with innovative performance. This was not a surprise since our experience suggested that innovative learners are not necessarily the brightest by normal academic standards;

- Girls generally outperformed boys, but when the data were examined by individual activities, some of the traditional gender differences appeared to be being dismantled – boys outperforming girls in textiles and graphics projects.

5.4   Concluding Comments

This project confirmed once again the validity of the iterative action–reflection model and the importance of holistic assessment. The approach explicitly challenged the learners to step outside their normal way of working, into an environment of risk and innovation – and the learners rose to the challenge. The following comment from one teacher illustrates the sense of release that teachers typically felt when using the approach.

> The set task appealed to their imagination. The whole process is 'pacey' and nothing becomes overworked or laboured – the quick response time sharpened pupils' decisions and hence pushes achievements/attainment. Taking a chance/risky – as it is a prototype it matters but we can learn from the process. The end product is not just the key aspect of this task – it is how the task is undertaken. The exchange/evaluation of ideas in the initial part orientated pupils to be aware that other people's opinions could help and more importantly they function as a team. Pupils felt a range of emotions during the project – apprehension, edgy, risky, exciting, familiar but also a sense of achievement and pride. The photos spurred them to work at a pace and also gave a sense of achievement. (Kimbell et al., 2004, p. 35)

The power of modelling, of working in collaborative groups and of digital 'evidence' capture were particularly significant, and as a result of the project one of the Awarding Bodies has adopted the assessment approach into its GCSE assessments. Renamed 'the innovation challenge' the Qualifications and Curriculum Authority (responsible for overseeing UK school-based assessment) has monitored a 2-year national pilot of a new examination containing this approach and has now given the 'go ahead' for the new examination to be freely available. TERU continues to act as a consultant to the Awarding Body.

The challenge of capturing evidence in digital format arose initially through the photo-storyline for this project, and it set in train a series of explorations that enabled us to speculate on a whole new approach to digital e-portfolios for designing. This potential led directly to the final project in this section – the *e-scape* project.

6.   E-SCAPE PROJECT (2004–2009)

6.1   Context

At the same time that we were exploring digital data capture in the *Assessing Design Innovation* project, others were developing models of e-portfolios. This included the Qualifications and Curriculum Authority – who established their own e-assessment Unit – and the examination Awarding Bodies who were keen to explore e-assessment possibilities. Both we and they could see the benefits for learners in broadening the 'tool set' available for envisioning, manipulating and developing ideas, and the potential for assessment of having work held electronically for speed and ease of distribution and storage. But developing e-portfolios raised challenging issues at a technical level and in terms of learning, teaching and assessment in design & technology. Despite the challenges, the time for development was ripe.

6.2   Brief and Outline Methodology

Following from the previous project, we made a proposal to the Qualifications and Curriculum Authority and the Department for Education and Skills to take the model developed in *Assessing Design Innovation* and extend the digital aspects to create a dynamic e-portfolio. Current e-portfolio approaches, e.g. for GCSE assessment, typically involve learners working on paper-based systems that are subsequently scanned or otherwise digitised. *e-scape* involves a dramatic development from this position.

We were aware of the problems of mixing design & technology workshop environments with computers, and the typical set up that involves separate workshops and computer rooms or areas. Our belief was that the leading edge of this digital technology should involve peripheral, back-pocket technologies such as mini digital cameras, digital pens, digital personal digital assistants (PDAs or palm-held computers), rather than desktop or even laptop machines. This is third-generation technology (generation 1 = mainframes that dominated rooms: generation 2 = desktops that dominated desks) that can be used directly in workshop/studio environments alongside other designing resources.

e-scape is an acronym that broadly describes the ambition of the project; *e-solutions for creative assessment in portfolio environments*. A three-phase project was proposed, with phase 1 focusing on an exploratory 'proof of concept', phase 2 on building and piloting a prototype system and phase 3 on exploring **transferability** to other curriculum areas and **scalability** to a national system. At the point of writing this, we have successfully completed phase 1 (2005) and 2 (2005–2007) and are embarking on phase 3 (2007–2009).

6.2.1   Phase 1: 'Proof of Concept'

For phase 1 there were four distinct dimensions that needed clarification:

- Extent to which existing peripheral digital technologies could be adapted for our purposes in creating portfolios
- Extent to which the use of such a system for assessment purposes could equally support and enrich learning experiences
- Manageability – in the classroom and as a national assessment system
- Validity, reliability and comparability of the results of the assessment

To support learners' designing we took the light fantastic' task created in the *Assessing Design Innovation* project and explored digital enhancement of the approaches used. In every case the digital tools being explored are hand-held/back-pocket peripheral tools rather than free-standing machines that dominate space. Principally, using PDAs we explored

- Contextualising and task setting – creating a digital handling collection based on the successful features of the 'light fantastic' collection.
- Early ideas – exploring digital tools for generating and sharing ideas.
- Design-talk – exploring ways of capturing speech digitally that supported using discussion to enrich designing.
- Photo-storyline – moving the control of the PDA/camera to the learner.
- Design 'bot' – exploring the concept of 'chatterbot' technology to prompt development through questioning and providing task-related information via an 'intelligent digital assistant'. (To experience how 'bot' technology works, log in to http://www.elzware.com/).
- We were aware that all the above features needed to be integrated into a coherent interface that learners could understand intuitively and navigate simply.

Development was iterative between team exploration, sometimes with the technology suppliers, and trialling in school. We were frequently unsure what learners would do with the devices, and were continually astonished at their ability to assimilate the new technologies and make purposeful use of them.

In total, six trials took place, all using developed versions of the original 'light fantastic' task:

- Trial 1 with Year 12 exploring the impact of using digital pens, PDAs, infrared beaming to printers and between PDAs and 'design-talk' software
- Trial 2 with Year 10, replicating trial 1 with younger learners
- Trial 3 with Years 12 and 13 learners to try out the 'design bot'
- Trial 4 with Year 12 learners to collect video evidence or learners responses to the technology
- Trial 5 was with Year 6 primary learners who, through a separate initiative were all 'mature' users of PDAs
- Trial 6 with trial 1 learners, who carried out an extended trial having PDAs, for their own use in design & technology and other schoolwork – each learner producing a report on their use of the PDA

Alongside this the technical issues were being considered, particularly in relation to collecting and compiling files from different hard/software systems and data transfer to a web space that could facilitate assessment. Here, the challenge and methodology was different and not school-focused. We engaged with leading-edge systems developers – and to a lesser extent Awarding Bodies – to discuss the possibilities for developing systems that might be able to achieve what we increasingly saw as necessary.

We established relationships with two educational computing companies; one expert in programming for hand-held devices (especially PDAs) and one with experience of web site programming and management. Over the 9-month 'proof of concept' period, we articulated what the *e-scape* system might look like and how it might work.

See www.goldsmiths.ac.uk/teru/ for the full phase 1 research report.

6.2.2   Phase 2: The *e-scape* Prototype

The *e-scape* concept is that learners work on assessment tasks in normal design studios and workshops. In response to set tasks, learners will design and develop products using PDAs as digital sketchbooks, notebooks, cameras, and voice recorders. Their work is automatically and simultaneously sent through a wi-fi connection to a secure web space in which their virtual portfolio emerges. This virtual portfolio develops through the 6 hour activity and can be viewed alongside their real material modelling of prototypes.

Figure 6-10. e-scape digital tools

The wi-fi capability that is in-built in PDAs enables a class-set to be run from a laptop configured as a local area network and managed by the teacher/researcher administering the activity. The PDAs all have the *e-scape* software loaded into them in the form of 23 linked screens through which the activity progresses (Figure 6-10). These screens operate in a similar way to the boxes in the *Assessing Design Innovation* booklet. The administrator controls the activity through the laptop. As 'box 1' is activated on the administrator interface, the signal is sent (via wireless router) to all the PDAs and they all 'come live' with box 1. Learners can draw/make notes on the PDA, and at the end of the allotted time for box 1 a warning screen pops up prompting learners to 'tap-here' to save their work. This is then sent back through the router and stored in the laptop – as well as in the memory on each individual PDA.

By the end of the activity, learners will have created a mass of design data spread through the 23 linked screens. Their design development process will include drawings, notes, photos, and sound files. All these data are held (temporarily) on the PDAs, and on the laptop. We then link the laptop to an internet-connected computer so that all data is uploaded directly into a secure web space. Once completed, the work may be accessed remotely for assessment and moderation purposes.

As part of phase 2, we conducted a pilot of the system in 15 schools and now have approximately 300 e-portfolios live in the web space.

6.3 Development Challenges and Significant Findings

6.3.1 The Concept of 'Portfolio'

An early task was to make explicit the team's own definition of an e-portfolio in the context of design & technology. The term portfolio is used in a variety of ways and based on a classification articulated by IMS Global Learning (Cambridge et al., 2005), the essence of a design & technology portfolio can be seen as a mix of an **assessment** portfolio, a **learning** portfolio and a **working** portfolio. Considering how portfolios have been used historically in design & technology, they can also be seen variously as a **container** – where all the bits and pieces of a project are stored, as a **reported story** of the project, completed after the event, or as a **dialogue** – in which ideas are recorded and developed as they emerge. The first two approaches replicate the existing problems of design & technology portfolios, wherein the emphasis is on retrospective tidying and presenting of work. In our experience this mitigates against the more creative learners and also often against boys. Developments existing at the start of our project focused on variations within the above two approaches (Ridgway et al., 2005) but what we were seeking to do through *e-scape* was to create an e-portfolio based on the dialogue model. Through the use of the 'back-pocket' technologies, particularly PDAs and their facilities for recording drawings, writing, voice memos and photographs, we have incorporated the technology directly into the structure of the activity. It has been used for both ideation and reflection and for sharing of ideas between learners and the resulting design work directly transmitted to a webspace for assessment purposes. Thus we have created a 'real-time' portfolio, not an 'after the event' record. Indications are that the system will also have benefits for teaching – as the online work can immediately be displayed and discussed in the classroom.

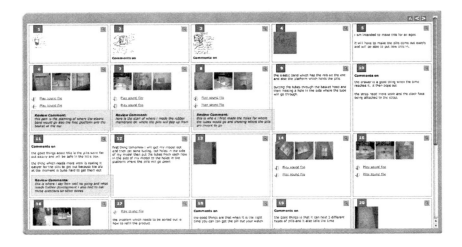

Figure 6-11. A snapshot of the web-based portfolio

The portfolio is structured through the 23 subtasks of the 6 hour activity, with response modes of various kinds (drawing, writing, photographing and speaking) and with both individual and team-based purposes. Like the paper portfolios that were the precursor to *e-scape*, these web screens provide a very real picture of the learners' evolving prototype and their thoughts about it along the way (Figure 6-11).

The snapshot of box 6 shown in Figure 6-12 illustrates the richness of these data. The three photographs show the drawing up to that moment and two photos of the model – from different angles. Clicking on the magnifying glass brings the images to full-screen size. The two sound files are the authentic recorded voice of the learner responding to two questions – what is working well? what needs further development? – and together these provide a real insight into their understanding of their work.

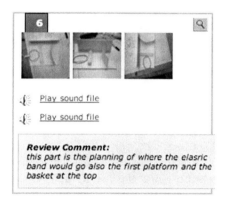

Figure 6-12. Snapshot of box 6

It is important to note that this 'photo and sound file' routine recurs throughout the activity – essentially once an hour for 6 hours. At least three significant things result from this. First, they get better – more articulate – in describing their work and the circumstances surrounding it. Second, the routine, taken together, leaves a real-time visual/audio evidence trail that is quite unique in the assessment of performance in design & technology. Third, learners' approach to the task is enriched as they are more motivated, braver (take more risks) and think more deeply about what they are doing.

Finally, the review comment (below the sound files) is a reflection by the learner made at the **very** end of the 6 hours of activity. Looking back over their whole work, we invite them to think about what they might have done differently if they had known then what they know now. Sometimes these metacognitive responses are descriptive – as in this case – and sometimes they are deeply analytic of their own performance.

We are not aware of any equivalent system of real-time, dynamic, e-portfolio assessment for any subject in any country. We believe this to be a world first. The 300 rich portfolios that inhabit the web site have now become the focus of our work in the project. The first challenge was to operationalise the assessment process.

6.3.2   Assessment Issues

We are very familiar with conventional marking procedures for portfolios. We develop a rubric that allocates groups of marks to categories of capability and we then scrutinise each portfolio to decide how many marks (in each category) it deserves. We then add them up and thereby arrive at a 'score'. This approach has recently been subject to serious criticism in England principally because of the reliability problems that are associated with teachers marking the portfolios of their own learners.

As with the previous project, *Assessing Design Innovation*, we have conducted *e-scape* in close association with the Awarding Bodies, and it was through this route that we met Alistair Pollitt – who was at one time the director of assessment research at the University of Cambridge Local Examinations Syndicate. He drew our attention to an alternative approach to assessment.

> The alternative approach to summative assessment that I would like to propose is based on the psychophysical research of Louis L. Thurstone, and specifically on his *Law of Comparative Judgement* (Thurstone, 1927). ... The essential point will be familiar to anyone grounded in the principles of Rasch models: when a judge compares two performances (using their own personal 'standard' or internalised criteria) **the judge's standard cancels out** ... a similar effect occurs in sport: when two contestants or teams meet, the 'better' team is likely to win, whatever the absolute standard of the competition and irrespective of the expectations of any judge who might be involved. (Pollitt, 2004, p. 6)

For a full account of the technicalities of the approach see Pollitt (2004). Based on this idea, he proposed a system in which judges compare two portfolios and decide merely which of the two is the better. The judges of course have to have some notion of what might be meant by 'better' and 'worse', so some shared values are important and these would helpfully be articulated as a set of criteria. The key point however is that criteria are not 'marked' in the conventionally way. Rather, a holistic judgement is made about which piece of work – overall – best represents an excellent piece of work. One of the beauties of this (Thurstone) model is that the idiosyncratic standards of the judges just do not matter. I may be a hard marker or a soft one – but I still have to decide which of the two pieces is the better. Judges' personal standards (the greatest source of error in current assessment procedures for GCSE examinations) therefore just cancel out.

The greater the true difference between the quality of the two portfolios that I am examining, the more likely it is that the better one will win each time they are compared. Thus a large set of comparisons does more than just generate a rank order; the relative frequency of success of one performance against another also indicates how far apart they are in quality.

The scale shown below is of the 249 pieces of work in the e-scape web site after three rounds of judging and the differences of quality of the portfolios are reflected in the 'value' axis. The portfolios have been sorted into order and are shown with their standard errors. Vertical lines on the 'rank' axis are drawn through five notional grade boundaries of equal size (see Figure 6-13). These boundaries were the focus of further judging to model the consequences on standard error. The approach might be described as objective relative measurement and since each portfolio was compared with a minimum of 17 others and by seven judges, the system generates very high reliability, in this case 0.93.

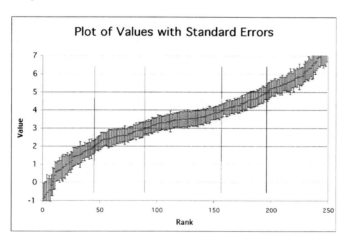

Figure 6-13. Plot of values with standard errors

Furthermore, if a few scripts that have already been agreed to represent grade boundaries – perhaps from a previous sitting of the examination – are included in the comparisons, the whole process of marking, grading and comparability of standards can be replaced by the collection and analysis of paired comparative judgements (Kimbell et al., 2007).

6.3.3   Pedagogic Issues

Our concern in relation to pedagogy was the extent to which the use an e-scape system can support and enrich the learning experience of design & technology. In this area, the findings from the trials have been quite unequivocal. The technologies were deftly assimilated into the learner's working, across all age groups trialled. The following specific examples indicate some of these aspects.

- Use of 'beaming' to share ideas and support teamwork
- 'Swarm' effect within the groups learning to use new technologies
- Using PDAs to build digital scrap books to support design development
- Learners taking control – deciding when to take photos or annotate work
- Using voice memos for on-task reflection
- Instant class display of work for discussing and critiquing

In every case in the national pilot, learners had no difficulty in adapting their design approaches to the use of PDAs as their 'leading' digital tool. They adapted their intuitive mobile telephone understandings and were fearless and very open to the potential of the hand-held digital technology. Teachers on the other hand were rather more wary of the process – but as the 6 hours of the activity unfolded they became accustomed to using the technology and lost their nervousness of it.

The pedagogic potential is huge for hand-held, mobile, sharing technologies on which learners can undertake their own design tasks, at anytime they choose (including breaks, after school, weekends, etc.) getting personalised feedback from their teammates, their teacher or any other external expert prepared to give the time. As learners and teachers in the pilot began to grasp the potential of the technology, they became increasingly aware of the limitations of their current practices.

6.3.4   Manageability and Validity Findings

From a validity stance, the activity was based directly on that developed through the *Assessing Design Innovation* project, where its validity as an authentic design & technology activity had been established. All comments on the new activity be they from the learners, teachers or other involved professionals, indicates that 'going digital' has not damaged this authenticity. Indeed, it might be argued that it has been enhanced – at least to the extent that 'real' designing (in industry) is now typically done digitally and in part so as to take advantage of the power of file sharing. Any of our e-scape learners could readily have contacted James Dyson or Jonathan Ive to comment on their work – **as it was underway** – and then incorporate their comments.

In terms of manageability, we were concerned to know if it was possible to make such assessments do-able in 'normal' design & technology workshops and studios. The pilot established beyond doubt that the system is quite manageable, but in the process it has thrown up a whole new world of possibilities that have yet to be tested.

See www.goldsmiths.ac.uk/teru/ for the full phase 2 research report.

6.4   Concluding Comments and the Launch of Phase 3

The impact of the phase 2 report has been substantial and rapid, and particularly so in policy circles. As we pointed out above, there has in recent years been such alarm about the reliability of coursework assessment that Department for Education and Skills have effectively banned its use from high-stakes examinations. Yet all teachers (and indeed those responsible for policy) realise the power of coursework portfolios in demonstrating the real learning that takes place in extended individual work. So there has been a considerable hiatus as everyone hunts around for alternative assessment approaches that offer the same degree of authenticity and validity, but at the same time offering much greater reliability. This is the Holy Grail of assessment, for the conventional wisdom suggests that these two (validity and reliability) are typically traded off against each other.

Multiple choice tests = low validity but high reliability
Portfolio assessment = high validity but low reliability

As the Head of the Office of State Assessment for New York State once told us, whilst attempting to justify all the multiple choice testing … 'we haven't lost a case yet'. The high reliability figures make him bullet proof when the State gets sued by unhappy parents. The fact that the tests have only the most tenuous connection to the measurement of anything useful is neither here nor there. As British policy moves incrementally closer to that of the USA, we find ourselves desperately trying to cling on to our tradition of process-rich assessment strategies whilst recognising their limitations. It was against this policy background that we concluded phase 2 of *e-scape* and presented our report to Ministers and their policy advisers.

They saw a system of what we might call 'school structured coursework' in which learners undertake real tasks over time in real learning settings (studios/workshops), but in a supervised and managed way that results in learner e-portfolios. Then they saw an assessment methodology that results in those e-portfolios being judged into a scale with very high reliability.

The upshot has been that phase 3 of *e-scape* is now underway with a double imperative. First is **transferability**. Is it possible to create *e-scape*-like portfolios in other areas of the curriculum like science or geography?

Second is **scalability**. Is it possible for the research-based approach that was demonstrated in phase 2 to be scaled up into a national system of assessment capable of being run by the national Awarding Bodies.

This research is now underway. We are creating development teams of specialists in geography and science and with them will conduct national trials in the summer of 2008. We will report our findings to Ministers in March 2009. If it can be demonstrated that the system is robust and transferable, we might expect to see it adopted into formal coursework assessment processes from September 2009. We shall see.

Chapter 7

CONTINUING FUNDAMENTAL RESEARCH

Why you might find these projects interesting

*Before 1985 design & technology was virtually a research-free zone and, using the **APU** project we had, by 1991, kicked open a few doors. But there had been serious limits to what we could do with APU, partly because it had been focused simply on learners at age 15, and partly because it was essentially one-time testing rather than longitudinal. Both of these limitations conspired to make it very difficult for us to say much about the **growth** or **evolution** of learners' capability over time.*

*We were determined to tackle this problem and secured funding for a 2-year project to explore (mainly through observation and interview) the nature of design & technology at every year-group in the national curriculum; from age 5 to 16 (Years 1 –11). We mapped for the first time the totality of the design & technology experience in compulsory schooling in England, and using properly grounded research data we could therefore begin to talk about **progression**. We highlighted some of the glaring discontinuities that only become visible from such a wide field of vision.*

The other project in this chapter illustrates our first cross-disciplinary project; with colleagues in Psychology. Their interest in object recognition (do we see bits and gradually assemble a whole view or vice versa) related to our interest in mechanisms of designing (do we design whole things and then detail the parts or vice versa). The parallels were obvious and compelling, so we explored the territory together ... with unexpected results.

***

1.   THE NEED FOR FURTHER RESEARCH

As we have identified earlier, one of the things about which writers in this field are agreed, is that there has always been a desperate lack of research to inform the evolution of design & technology as a teaching and learning activity in the curriculum. This was very much the case in the years leading up to the introduction of the National Curriculum. (DES, 1988b; Penfold, 1988)

Twenty five years earlier, design & technology did not exist in anything like the form that emerged in the 1990 Order. And twenty five years is an astonishingly short germination period for a new curriculum subject, especially given the timeless durability of the vast majority of them. As Williams observed:

> The fact about our present curriculum is that it was essentially created by the 19th century, following some 18th century models and retaining elements of the mediaeval curriculum near its centre. (Williams, 1965, p. 172)

Given this meteoric rise, it is perhaps not surprising that research had little opportunity to shape things. Indeed, design & technology in the school curriculum grew from **practice** rather than from theory; from teachers in the classroom trying out innovative and often idiosyncratic activities and programmes – rather than from an intellectual analysis of a field of knowledge. It has been hugely successful. Learners voted with their feet; courses expanded and proliferated; competitions and prizes led to high profile public exposure where politicians and others were delighted to shake a few hands for the camera. Even universities caught up with the fact that there was some quite exceptional young talent coming through this route to higher education.

As we discussed in Chapter 1, different arguments have been used to justify studying design & technology, from liberal/educational arguments, to vocational arguments to economic policy arguments. But as we explored design & technology through *APU Design & Technology*, these arguments did not seem to us to get to the heart of the matter. Design & technology is neither a liberal arts 'awareness-raising' study, nor a vocational training, nor a tool for macroeconomic planning. It might contribute to these things – but none is its driving purpose. We believe the core case is centred on the challenging and empowering notion that learners can identify aspects of the made world that demand attention, and can intervene creatively to improve it. This argument rests on the idea that design & technology presents learners with opportunities for exercising unique ways of thinking about the world and for intervening constructively to change it. It presents design & technology as a kind of concrete thinking process and an entitlement for all learners.

APU Design & Technology went a long way to creating understanding about capability, but that project was all with one age group (age 15), making it difficult to form arguments about the **growth** of capability in learners. This led us to see the need for further fundamental research, and to submit a proposal to the ESRC to scrutinise the evolution of technology projects in schools through the development of a series of learner case studies spanning the 5–16 design & technology curriculum. In June 1992, as the APU project was completed, the *Understanding Technological Approaches* project was launched.

APU Design & Technology had highlighted differences in the approaches of learners to designing – in that project most notably in terms of gender and ability. This new project gave us the opportunity to look in much more detail at individual learners, adding to our awareness that there are very different ways of approaching design & technology that are not necessarily better or worse – just different.

This interest coincided with other work being undertaken in design & technology (within and beyond TERU) in relation to cognitive style (Atkinson, 1995; Lawler, 1996) and we became aware of complementary interests in researchers in the Psychology department at Goldsmiths. Linking these two sets of interests was the springboard for a further project exploring fundamental issues of capability – the *Wholes and Parts Project* – that was undertaken during 1998–1999.

2.   UNDERSTANDING TECHNOLOGICAL APPROACHES (1992–1994)

2.1   Context

While *APU Design & Technology* had provided an immense set of data and insights into the nature of capability and its assessment with 15-year-olds, it had not provided detailed information into the way learners work through extended classroom projects, nor enabled understandings of different age groups. In England and Wales, design & technology National Curriculum had been launched with a curriculum providing, in theory, a continuous experience from age 5 to 16. The Design and Technology Working Group acknowledged the diversity of practice that existed before 1990, including the extreme patchiness in primary schools, and saw the

> attainment targets and programmes of study offering a clear and firm framework for existing practice ... without [which] ... it is difficult for schools to plan for progression (DES/WO, 1988b, p. 9)

But despite the brave aspirations, the lack of research on progression in design & technology inevitably meant that the way the new curriculum was both constructed and presented was based on assumption rather than evidence. Reflecting back on this era, Hope (2004b) comments on the confusion the National Curriculum caused for those involved with primary classrooms.

> Not surprisingly, many early conference papers and journal articles focused on what young children could not do, and whether or not what they could do was what the National Curriculum writers had in mind all along ... The lack of research into young children's design skills prior to the publication of the document made its instructions a cause for anger or despair among many teachers (Hope, 2004b, p. 16)

It was our desire for a more informed understanding of both the reality of classroom practice in design & technology in the early days of National Curriculum and the similarities and differences in approach across the ages of formal schooling that provided the impetus to acquire funding for this new research.

2.2   Brief and Outline Methodology

There were two broad sets of objectives underlying *Understanding Technological Approaches*. The first involved the construction of a series of detailed case studies following learners through technological projects. Within this, we sought to elucidate the influences on learners' initial ideas and to examine the development strategies they used. Our second set of objectives concerned the relationship between the data generated in this project and that which we had previously acquired through *APU Design & Technology*. The *APU* data was principally 'outcome' data based on the marking of learner responses to test activities. By contrast, this project provided 'real-time' process data that was complementary to that from *APU*.

To construct the case studies we identified 20 schools, broadly in the Greater London and surrounding area, through which we could gain access to design & technology project work in all four key stages. We collected data through observing learners in action, across the full length of projects derived from the teachers' regular way of working. In each project we observed four learners, where ever possible two girls and two boys. We also collected copies of their design portfolio work and took photographs of their modelling and making as it developed. The methodology was mainly observational with a data collection system based on trained observers watching literally every minute of the learner projects and recording what happened in 5 min time blocks. We created a common observation framework to enable us to compile comparative analysis across projects and thereby report on progression and continuity issues. While data in each case was highly detailed and rich, the total sample of 80 case studies across four key stages was of necessity small and did not claim to be representative. The findings were therefore illustrative, not generalisable.

2.3 Development Challenges and Significant Findings

2.3.1 Creating the Observation Framework

This project presented major challenges in terms of methodology, the most significant being the collection and management of the data. The extended project work case studies undertaken in *APU Design & Technology* were created by interviewing learners at three points during their project. While this provided an overview, it did not elucidate the level of detail we sought in *Understanding Technological Approaches*. Consequently, we decided to watch every minute of a learner's project, which presented two key challenges. The first was pragmatic – how many learners could we successfully observe at any given time – and through trial and error we established four as the critical number. The larger challenge was how could we standardise the focus and recording of the observation so that all potentially relevant data would be collected consistently and reliably across the team. We evolved an observation routine that could be used over and over again (every few minutes) so that each of the observational 'snapshots' could be welded into a continuous and unfolding story. After trialling observation intervals ranging from 1 to 15 min, we settled on 5 min as an appropriate interval (Figure 7-1). In each interval we collected both narrative and precoded data – the coding providing us with a sharp analytic tool, the narrative providing the context for what was coded. The categories were developed through an iterative process of observation and analysis. The areas targeted in each 5 min were:

- Level of learner engagement and **pace** of work – stationary, poddling or motoring
- Teacher intervention – directive or supportive
- Design issues being dealt with – task, communication or making)
- Learner's design intentions – the 'why' of their actions
- Manifestations – the 'what' of the learner's actions

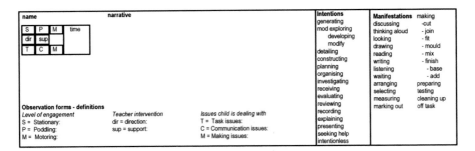

Figure 7-1. A 5 min block showing the structure of the observation framework

To develop consistency in the use of the framework within the research team, we undertook independent observations of the same learners at the same time and comparing our interpretations to derive and agree definitions and procedures. These were then turned into a guidance sheet to accompany the framework. Our major concern at this stage was to ensure shared understandings within the team and in doing so we found ourselves using vernacular language to encapsulate these understandings. This approach was epitomised in the way we monitored engagement/pace. We believed from the start this would be important and assumed it would be difficult to observe. However, we quickly found we could do it very reliably using 'car driving jargon' – making a judgement about whether (in any 5 min block) the learner was 'stationary', 'poddling' or 'motoring'. Not only did these terms suit the team well, they also allowed the UK audiences to understand the data quickly – although with other audiences the concept of 'poddling' has sometimes been challenging to convey. But for the team, this use of the vernacular (an approach we have often taken in our work to share meanings, see Stables & Kimbell (2006)) was extremely effective.

2.3.2   Managing and Interpreting the Data

The classroom reality of design & technology projects is inevitably different across the age groups in a range of ways. The biggest problem this caused for comparability was the different lengths of projects – the shortest was a Year 1 project that in total lasted 4.5 hours, the longest a Year 11 project that lasted 48 hours. From our observations, what was clear was that, however long a project was, there was a sense of flow through various phases, from introductory and 'getting going' to 'bringing it all together' and completing. So, after entering the data into spreadsheets, we compacted it into five equal phases. This allowed us to compare, for example, teacher intervention in the first 20% of each project, or the level of learner engagement across all phases of a project. This latter example, shown in Figure 7-2 plots the summary data on the percentage of time spent 'motoring' in each phase by learners in each Key Stage. Managing and presenting the data in this way makes differences in engagement 'flow' clear. Thus, aggregated data allowed us to portray and compare learners' approaches.

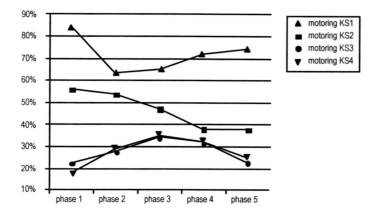

Figure 7-2. 'Motoring' across all four Key Stages

2.3.3 Evidence of Iterative Processes

Analysis of the learners' design intentions showed no evidence that designing is a step-by-step linear process in which learners pursue certain activities (e.g. modelling, making and evaluating) in a set order. Whilst the balance between such activities varied across the length of a project, all activities were present in all phases. This reinforced the iterative model we derived through *APU Design & Technology* and held true for all Key Stages. However, the ways learners' intentions were achieved did vary. For example, in primary classrooms, work tended to be collaborative, with an emphasis on discussion. With 11–14-year-olds work was much more individual and learners spent a great deal of time listening to the teacher. As we found in *APU Design & Technology*, there were gendered differences in approach, girls being more comfortable with reflective activities and boys with those that are more active. Boys appeared more able to handle reflective aspects through practical activity, which was most notable at Key Stage 4 (15–16-year-olds).

2.3.4 Key Stage 'Cultures'

From both the aggregated and narrative data we found that distinct differences in approaches emerged across the four Key Stages, such as:

- Length of projects
- Pattern of engagement
- Contexts of projects
- Tasks learners were set
- Level and nature of teacher intervention

Taken as a whole, the *Understanding Technological Approaches* data suggested that design & technology tasks – and hence the projects that flowed from them – were seen as very different things in the four Key Stages. When the observation data was combined with the more discursive and interpretive data, different Key Stage 'cultures' began to emerge:

- **Cultural** technology characterised Key Stage 1 (5–7-year-olds) 'technology is part of life and always has been'. Projects tended to be derived from cross disciplinary topics, such as 'explorers', involving tasks such as designing a shelter, having been shipwrecked and washed up on a deserted island.
- **Problem-solving** technology characterised Key Stage 2 (8–11-year-olds) 'can you make it work'. Projects were still linked to topic work, but the focus was typically on products that provided technological problems to be solved – using a pulley system to make a merry-go-round work, or elastic bands to power a toy car to be as fast as possible.
- **Disciplinary** technology characterised Key Stage 3 (12–14-year-olds) 'you need to know about this (knowledge/skills)'. Projects were contrived specifically to teach particular skills or knowledge, such as brooches to teach metal fabrication and enameling, or alarms to teach simple circuits. The product outcome was the motivational sugar on the pill.
- **Simulated** technology emerged at the interface of Key Stage 3 and 4 (15-year-olds) 'this is how real designers work'. Projects were largely individual – identified by the learners themselves and therefore having some reality – within which they were expected to be rigorous in the application of an abstracted designerly process and the development of a portfolio that reflected it.

Given the aspirations of the National Curriculum Design and Technology Working party, these differences might seem surprising. But variety in approach, and focusing work appropriately for an age group are important in planning learning experiences. The bigger question is whether these approaches provided for continuity and progression in learning. Our view was that this was not always the case – and the most extreme evidence of discontinuity was between Key Stage 2 and Key Stage 3 – particularly between Year 6 and Year 7, the primary/secondary divide.

2.3.5   Transition and Discontinuity

In exploring differences between Year 6 and Year 7, it became apparent that almost everything about the corresponding experiences was in contrast:

- Year 6 projects took place in classrooms; Year 7 in specialist workshops.
- Year 6 tasks were open ended and negotiable; Year 7 were specific and controlled by the teacher.
- In Year 6 materials were not specified; in Year 7 they were largely fixed.
- In Year 6 designing was carried out largely through 3D modelling; in Year 7 it was done on paper, in advance of making.
- Year 6 teachers acted as progress-chasers; Year 7 teachers as instructors/-facilitators.

The overarching contrast related to learner autonomy.

> The primary children were expected to operate in an autonomous way within a context of uncertainty. There was no guarantee that they would hold in advance any of the technical knowledge or skills needed to create a successful outcome. ... By contrast the secondary children were operating within a context where many of the skills and techniques were new to them but where the teacher systematically introduced them ... any previous skills they had ... were effectively being put 'on ice'. Looking at these different demands raises some interesting questions. Did the children have the skills required to cope with the demands being placed on them? (Stables, 1995, p. 161)

We concluded that they did not.

2.4   Concluding Comments

This project provided fundamental insights into design & technology that built on and complemented those derived from *APU Design & Technology*. The combination has provided the foundation to much of our future work. In particular, by looking in such detail at individual learners, the research enabled us to unpick further issues of difference in both approaches and capability, and this focus was picked up directly in the project reported next.

3.   WHOLES AND PARTS (1998–1999)

3.1   Context

In the mid-1990s our interest in different approaches particularly to designing focused on that of **designing styles**, and on how this might – or might not – relate to the wider issue of learning styles. Atkinson (1995) was simultaneously exploring how learning styles might bear on performance in design & technology – particularly in the context of gendered performance. We were drawn to a somewhat different challenge concerning the tantalising relationship between the **whole** task, and the **parts** of it that one is almost bound to focus on at different times in the activity. Do learners conceptualise a 'whole' solution – and then work out how all the bits fit into it, or do they systematically work out the bits and gradually assemble a whole solution?

At the same time that we were toying with this idea, Jules Davidoff, a psychology professor at Goldsmiths, was exploring views of object recognition, particularly is the object recognised because the viewer 'sees' the whole object, or does the viewer rather see components and build a picture of the whole. This research was focused on face recognition. Is it the nose or the eyebrows or the hairline that we 'see', and thereby we assemble a view of the whole face? Or do we rather take a snapshot of whole faces and only afterwards begin to disassemble them? These distinctions had been found useful to account for data drawn from both normal and brain-damaged populations (Davidoff & Donnelly, 1990; Donnelly & Davidoff, 1998).

Our intent was to meld these two sets of ideas into a new project. Does the way a learner 'sees' the world predispose them to design it in the same way? If they tend to see in parts and gradually assemble wholes, do they do the same when designing? If they are 'holist' designers, starting with big pictures of a solution and thereafter moving to flesh out the detail, does this reflect the way they perceive the world through their image recognition?

3.2   Brief and Outline Methodology

The objectives of this project were to examine the connections between perceptual 'input' (the manner in which we 'see' the world) and designing 'output' (the manner in which we create new products for the world). A preliminary literature review suggested that there were some points of contact. Both areas for example used terms that refer to a preference in individuals for global or specific ways of operating: **seeing** the whole or its component parts; **designing** the whole or its component parts. We designed a study to see if the same processes were involved and that addressed the question 'Does the way that you perceive the world affect the way you operate on it as a designer?'. Are perceptual 'wholists' also design 'wholists'; are perceptual 'partists' also design 'partists'?

We used a combination of psychology and designing tests. A battery of perceptual tests was selected and customised taking into account the reading age and attention span of the subjects (Davidoff and Warrington, 1999). For our purposes, the 'embedded figures' and 'block design' tests were used. (See Figures 7-3 and 7-4) Individual differences in performance on these tests are believed to be evidence of cognitive style; the way an individual processes information about their environment (Witkin et al., 1967; Baillargeon et al., 1998).

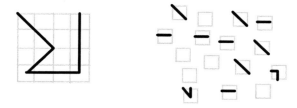

Figure 7-3. Block design test (can you make [i] from [ii]?)

Figure 7-4. Embedded figure test (can you see [ii] in [1]?)

The design tests used were based on the *APU Design & Technology* format. Two activities were devised, the first of which began with and prioritised a 'big pictures' approach to the task, while the second began with and prioritised a 'small steps' approach to the activity. Each lasted approximately 1½ hours and are outlined in Figure 7-5.

The focus of the study was a sample of 80 mixed gender, mixed ability Year 6 learners (age 11) who experienced design & technology through their curriculum, but (as *Understanding Technological Approaches* indicated) would not have been 'imprinted' with a particular methodological approach. Consequently, if designing styles could be identified in the cohort, it was more likely to be a reflection of their natural or intuitive approach to designing than a reflection of how they had been taught.

'Big pictures' activity	'Small Steps' activity

'Big pictures' activity

Task - Design of a water toy

Contextualisation -video on children and play.

Response boxes in order

1	Jot down first thoughts
2	Put down design ideas
3	Describe what you are setting out to achieve
4	List the things the design must do to be successful
5	Continue with designing
6	Comment on strengths and weaknesses of the work to date (red pen)
6	Put down what you would do next and why
7	Plan the stages to produce a finished item
8	Comments on the test

'Small Steps' activity

Task - Design of a Packed Lunch container

Contextualisation- Investigating and commenting on the contents of 2 packed lunches

Response boxes in order

1	Investigation activity of 2 different lunch boxes
2	Put down important points for the design of lunch boxes
3	Put down design ideas
4	Develop design ideas
5	Comment on strengths and weaknesses of the work to date (red pen)
6	Put down what you would do next and why
7	Comments on the test

Figure 7-5. Structure of design tests

3.3   Development Challenges and Significant Findings

3.3.1   Links to *APU* Findings

The software associated with the perception tests marked each test automatically. Assessing the design responses was far more complex and relied on expert interpretation of the nature of the designing being demonstrated. On a 4-point scale, three assessors independently rated each piece of work for wholism and for partism; e.g. a strong wholist would be a 4:1; and a strong partist a 1:4. However, we did not see the qualities (wholism and partism) existing at opposite ends of the **same** spectrum, but rather we saw them as separate qualities that can be assessed independent of each other. Our assessment therefore also made it possible for a learner to be a 4:4 (good at both) or a 1:1 (poor at both).

Replicating the *APU* data from 1991, this study provided clear evidence of the preference of girls for operating through small steps, and for boys through big pictures. Almost 47% of boys scored higher in the big-pictures activity and 45% of girls scored higher in the small-steps activity. In both cases, the majority of the rest scored equally on each test. Separating out the overall high scoring learners, 76% of the high-scoring boys did so through big pictures, whereas 66% of high scoring girls favoured a small-steps approach (Lawler, 1999). *APU* identified similar trends with 15-year-old learners – data from *Wholes and Parts* suggests that the trends are already established before learners leave primary school.

3.3.2 Relating Perceptual Style to Designing Style

However, the principal purpose of this study was to examine the relationships between perceptual style and designing style. We found a strong link between a combined group of the best wholists designers and the best analyst designers, and high scoring for the block design and embedded figure tests – interestingly, a similar finding to earlier work of Riding & Pearson (1981) on the performance of 13-year-old learners in art.

By relating the wholist and partist designing assessments for an individual, it is possible to see their performance as strong wholist, strong partist or balanced. Exploring the relationship between these groups with their performance in the perception tests showed that those with the strong wholist designing style perform better than the other two categories on the two perceptual tests, particularly the block design test. We concluded from these findings that there is indeed a relationship between the ways in which we *see* the world, and the ways in which we **operate on it** as designers.

3.4 Concluding Comments

The value of this project was twofold. First, it demonstrated the benefits of collaborating with another discipline to bring fresh insights. Second, it extended our previous understanding of gendered approaches to designing beyond the focus of 'action' and 'reflection'. Identifying and attributing qualities of 'big picture' or 'small steps' designing to a learners' approach helps us to understand and better support their designing. Critical in the findings of this project was that, when looking at the best designing, it could have been generated through either approach – once again showing that different design styles are not necessarily better or worse, and as such are a cause for celebration not concern.

Chapter 8

PUBLIC POLICY RESEARCH

Why you might find these projects interesting

The projects in this chapter fall into a 7-year period between 1995 and 2002, and in political terms these were turbulent times – the final days of 17 years of Conservative Party rule (Margaret Thatcher and John Major) and the opening period of 'New Labour' under Tony Blair.

The first two projects were commissioned by the Design Council (reinvigorated by the policy success of linking 'cool Britannia' to 'New Labour') and centred on the power of design thinking in non-design settings. In the first we explored management decision making: would it be more creative if it had more of the features of designerly decision making? In the second we explored the reciprocal question of what designers are good at other than designing. Both projects played into a public interest, and hence a public policy agenda.

The middle project was commissioned by the Department for Education & Skills. The success of design & technology had outrun our ability to recruit teachers and we were asked to undertake a research study to identify new sources of appropriately skilled teachers.

The final two projects were commissioned by the Engineering Council UK and both were linked to recruitment issues. The first explored what kinds of mathematics – and at what levels – is learned through design & technology. This was important in particular for admission to engineering degree programmes. The second provided a moment of reflection. While 'New Labour' was explicitly positioning the UK as a 'knowledge economy', what were the consequences of this for design & technology and for the engineering world?

***

1.   TERU AND THE CONTEXT OF PUBLIC POLICY

The environment in schools in the first half of the 1990s was extremely troubled. The National Curriculum had been introduced in 1990 and it involved far reaching transformations of practice for teachers. The whole curriculum was now circumscribed into 'core' and 'foundation' subjects – with design & technology sitting somewhere between these two groupings as part of what Ministers referred to as the 'extended core'. By the mid-1990s design & technology had become a fixed point on the educational landscape. Having escaped from the obscurity imposed by its fractured history, design & technology – as a single entity – began to assert itself into areas of public life.

Public policy research is typically funded by research councils, but there are other organisations with research-related remits for public policy, including of course government departments. We include in this chapter an account of a policy-related project for the Department of Education & Skills concerning the issue of teacher supply. Why is there a shortage of appropriately qualified recruits for teaching and why in particular is the shortage so acute in design & technology?

Beyond government departments there are organisations whose concerns are directly involved with design & technology, and whose activities sit at the public/professional interface, and the two most obvious are the Design Council and the Engineering Council UK. These bodies in addition to having some responsibility for managing, promoting, or regulating their professions, also have a brief to inform and educate the general public about their activities. To that extent they are involved in informing and influencing public policy and we describe in this chapter two projects that we have conducted for each of these bodies.

2.   DECISIONS BY DESIGN (1995–1997)

2.1   Context

In 1994, the Design Council launched an initiative entitled 'Total School Design'. This initiative invited practitioners, teachers and researchers to speculate on the many ways in which design might impact upon schools. The invitation for proposals therefore went well beyond the former territory of the Design Council concerning curriculum support for design teaching, and invited wider scale thinking. Within TERU we were pleased with this widening of the scope of design-related research and we proposed a project that explored decision making in schools. Specifically, we were interested in the decision making of school managers (head teachers and deputy head teachers). Amongst the questions that seemed to us to be interesting were:

- What is designerly decision making?
- Is management decision making a designerly kind of decision making?
- If not, would it be 'better' decision making if it was more designerly?

This project drew together the principal interests of the two project directors: Richard had long been intrigued by the generic value of design thinking, and by the idea that design decision making has some unique characteristics that might usefully be articulated within a wider (non-design) frame of reference. Pat Mahoney (Roehampton Institute) was working with school managers and specifically with the new government initiative on the training for head teachers. Specifically, we were interested in the extent to which decision-making processes reflect design behaviour; and in the consequences for decision making when those responsible for the decisions are made aware of the procedures of design thinking.

2.2   Outline Methodology

2.2.1   Brief

As a first step we developed the brief through a set of research aims:

- Examine and document – in case study schools – the decision-making procedures that operated in the Senior Management Teams in those schools
- Expose those Senior Management Teams to intensive design experiences – both direct and indirect – requiring them at the same time to reflect upon them
- Monitor the extent to which – and the ways in which – these experiences modified the decision-making procedures of Senior Management Teams

2.2.2   Auditing a Major Decision-Making Process

During the spring term 1995 a network of six case study schools was established, three primary and three secondary, each with differing organisational structures and systems in operation. One member of the senior management team – generally a deputy head teacher – of each school was appointed as **teacher fellow** to the project. During the summer term the teacher fellows were asked to stand outside their own school processes and draft a 'fly on the wall' description of what had happened 'from the cradle to the grave' of one decision. We asked them to record all the things that might have contributed to that specific decision-making process. The aim was to gain a comprehensive account of why and how the decision got made in the way that it did.

The reports were on very diverse topics including:

- School development planning
- Budget making
- Timing for a new school day
- Disciplinary procedures of a member of staff

The outcome of this first phase of work was a series of detailed case records that were both descriptive of the decision-making process and analytic in accounting for why the ultimate decision took the form that it did.

2.2.3   Observing Designers at Work

In the following autumn term we focused on design and designing – through seminars, literature reviews and the work of graduate design students, in order to provide the teacher fellows with some expertise in it and some familiarity with what it entails.

The main focus of the autumn term involved the teacher fellows observing designers at work and reflecting (in seminars) upon these experiences. Four sessions were dedicated to working in Goldsmiths with design students who were asked to work as they would normally in design activities. The teacher fellows were introduced to the students when the task was set and each was assigned to follow the development in a particular group.

Throughout the term the teacher fellows took on the roles of observers and participants in these design activities, and moreover they were required to reflect upon their experiences:

- Analysing the design techniques used
- Debating their strengths and limitations
- Reflecting on the transferability to other problems and settings
- Speculating upon their applicability to specific problems faced by the Senior Management Teams in their schools

Further, in order to consider the implications that these design experiences had for decision making within the school context, each teacher fellow was required to keep an ongoing log about any connections they made between what they had experienced in relation to design processes and their understanding and experiences of decision making in management processes.

At the start of spring term 1996, the teacher fellows returned to their original case records to review their former decision-making practices in the light of their new understandings about design and its relationship to decision making. A number of discussions were held around these reviews, which enabled us to identify some of the critical issues existing at the interface of design and management decision making.

2.3   Issues and Significant Findings

The teacher fellows identified the following design subactivities – we might call them designer strategies – to be of particular significance. They were significant in the sense that the designers' work appeared to depend heavily upon the benefits derived from these strategies and equally significant in that as management decision makers the teacher fellows were aware that these strategies were not typically evident in their own decision making.

2.3.1   Continual 'Unpacking' of the Task

The principal concern was that the task needed to be fully understood by all the participants in order to reach shared understandings. In design terms, the teacher fellows observed design students spending a considerable amount of time and effort understanding, developing and specifying the brief they were pursuing. Furthermore, they saw the students returning time after time to the original brief as a reference point throughout their designing activity. The teacher fellows were quite unused to this in their general management decision-making processes in schools.

2.3.2   Making Thinking Explicit

Designers' thinking processes emerge in more or less explicit terms in a design folio, which lays bare the designers thinking for all to see – and share. The process of making explicit renders an otherwise private process (thinking) into something that you can lay your hands on, inspect, criticise, encourage or disagree with. The teacher fellows expressed the view that exactly the same explicitness would enrich management decision making.

2.3.3   Clients and Values

It is well understood by designers that any design solution is a manifestation of a set of values. However, this came as something of a surprise to our teacher fellows. They were able to identify that differences of opinion amongst their Senior Management Teams were ultimately about conflicting values but it had not appeared important to them that these values should be made explicit at the outset of a decision making process. Once again it was by observing the design students that this was brought home to them. They saw the students debating their respective 'clients' who had their own wants and needs. Everyone involved in a decision, be they the head teacher, the Senior Management Team, the classroom teachers, the children, the parents, the governors, the government education department, the school contractors, the support staff, all have values that shape the ways in which they respond to the decisions that are made. To lay this out in the open at the outset is important if decisions are to be sustainable.

2.3.4   Innovation and Risk

The notion of 'risk taking' does not fit comfortably with the concept of making quality decisions, and many managers in the public sector would be uneasy with such a prospect. But 'safe' decisions rarely lead to any kind of innovation – since the concept of safety is tied to the idea of 'what we did last time'. The teacher fellows observed the design students mediating this risk partly through the involvement of 'others' (particularly of course the key clients) in arriving at important decisions, and partly through the complementary design practice of 'modelling futures'.

2.3.5   The Power of Group Work

Much successful design practice depends upon group activities of various kinds. The teacher fellows identified several significant features of design students' group work that could inform and improve their management of decisions in schools:

- Individual's perceptions of themselves – and others perceptions of them and of their roles
- Recognising the importance of the stakeholders/client groups
- Unpacking a task or problem in a group context to enhance a shared understanding of the task

2.3.6   Modelling Possible Futures

Decision making is essentially about the future. But how do we know that things will improve by taking a particular decision, since we are speculating about something that lies in the future. How can we be sure that our decision to change something will also improve things? Designers can never be certain, but they do typically engage in some processes that enable them to test their product idea against the future. They do it by 'modelling' the future and this modelling takes a number of forms:

- Verbal modelling – discussing it with clients and others
- Mathematical modelling – manipulating number to model possibilities
- Graphic modelling – sketching ideas in the context of the future

- Concrete modelling – building mock-ups of the real thing and trying it out
- Computer modelling – using computer programmes to simulate future scenarios

Not once – in all the case records – had our senior managers of schools modelled the consequences of their decisions. In this regard in particular, the observation of designers at work shocked the teacher fellows.

2.4   Moving into Phase 2

We had designed the above study to be followed by a supplementary one to explore the generalisability of this experience and specifically to see whether – or to what extent – it was possible to condense the experience of our teacher fellows into a 1-day training session.

A three-part training experience was developed and used with a new cohort of 12 senior managers in schools:

- A pre-course activity auditing a significant decision being made in school
- A 1-day training experience
- A post-course follow-up session 6 weeks later

By a long way, the most important element of this day – for us – was based on the development of some completely new *APU* style tasks. We explored with the new cohort some design decision-making situations through the vehicle of *APU* style 90 min tasks. Importantly however, we then created some new 90 min structured tasks that were based more on the kinds of things that schools managers were regularly called upon to undertake.

One of the design tasks was as follows:

- Design Task 1: Map 'To help you get here today, you were provided with information in the form of an existing design solution (the location map for visitors to Goldsmiths). Your task is to identify its strengths and weaknesses and to begin to generate ideas for different design solutions that work better.'

One of the management tasks was as follows:

- Management Task 1: Code of Conduct 'Your school has recently undergone an Office of Standards in Education (OFSTED) inspection and an issue has been identified in relation to the school's code of conduct. Your task is to identify its strengths and weaknesses and to begin to generate ideas for producing a more adequate code of conduct.'

The parallels between these two tasks were clear – and the structure through which we asked the teacher fellows to operate also underlined the designerly kinds of decision making that we sought to encourage.

A number of evaluative tools were used to capture the reaction of the teacher group to the messages of the day, amongst which was the question 'what made the biggest impact on you?' – to which the following replies were typical:

- Power of the process
- Importance of modelling the future
- Solutions are provisional – mark 1, 2, etc.
- Using a design model in a school context

2.5   Concluding Comments

This was the first project that we had undertaken that was specifically beyond the scope of the design & technology curriculum. It had its roots in design practice, but had implications that go well beyond designing and into the realm of 'management'. The team we put together reflected this wider concern, and we had expertise not just from the co-director Pat Mahoney (a professor of Educational Management), but also from consultants in the management world. The interest for us lay in bringing **design practice** to bear on this world of management decision making.

Methodologically, we were able to firm up this challenge by creating (in phase 2) what looked like a **management** task but that was procedurally conducted like a **design** task. It proved remarkably effective in exposing the differences between design and management traditions.

In the years that followed, two further projects presented opportunities for us to develop our understandings of 'designerly' activity through creating design-like challenges in which the tasks themselves were not centrally in the design field. In *Enriching Literacy through Design & Technology* we were evaluating curricular initiatives (see Chapter 9) and in *Researching Assessment Approaches* we were exploring assessing generic competences (see Chapter 6). For each, the *APU Design & Technology* test structure allowed us to create procedural challenges, the first allowing us to assess the use of literacy skills in primary age learners, the second to assess generic procedural competence (such as relating to people and managing situations) in young secondary school learners.

3.   DESIGN SKILLS FOR WORK (1997–1999)

3.1   Context and Brief

In the 1990s design courses in Britain were thriving. The expansion of 'new' universities (the previous polytechnic sector) led to a massive growth in university admissions, particularly in practically oriented degree programmes. Design courses, with their traditions of practice-based learning, benefited more than most. In 1997, the 'New Labour' Department of Trade and Industry undertook a study of these trends 'Innovative Britain at Expo '98' and the Design Council subsequently published an important reference guide (Design Council, 1999) that included statistics of students studying design at university in the UK. The figures painted an astonishing picture of the proliferation of design in higher education.

The Design Council was in two minds about this apparently amazing finding. Naturally, they were enthusiastic about the spread of the design culture through the university sector. But equally there was the sober reflection about what all these design students would do when they graduated and started looking for employment. How many new designers are needed each year?

The timing of our *Decisions by Design* report to the Design Council was therefore helpful, since we were able to illustrate – through concrete cases – the value of designerly thinking in everyday (i.e. non-design) settings. The issue focusing itself in the Design Council was around the question 'what are designers good at doing – other than designing'. Or to put it another way, what skills and understandings can designers bring to the world of work – if they are not going to practice as designers? Having studied design, does it make graduates more employable as journalists or social workers or police officers? In 1996, we were invited to undertake a new study 'Design Skills for Work' with a brief to investigate the extent to which the skills developed by design undergraduates have transferable currency to the world of work beyond design.

3.2   Outline Methodology

3.2.1   Phase 1 Methodology and Report

The project was again conceived in two phases. Phase 1 was a literature review culminating in a report (Kimbell et al., 1997a) concerning the theoretical and conceptual issues surrounding the challenge of 'generic' learning and the 'transferability' of skills, and locating these debates in the context of design education. Phase 2 was an empirical study of a selection of design degree courses that explored the practical realities of the debate presented in the phase 1 report.

One of the key themes of the phase 1 report was the **transitional state** of design and design education in the 1990s. This transitional state existed in a number of dimensions.

From modernist to postmodernist conceptions of design
Modernism in design – since the turn of the 20th century – has been associated with a rationalist view of the designer's role. The key transition from this modernist view of design arises through the belief that objects do not have fixed meanings that are the same for everyone, and that designing is better characterised as creating a dynamic relationship between the object and the user. What you see in the chair, filing cabinet or house, is different from what I see. The supposed universal values underpinning modernist design are replaced by individualised values (Margolin, 1989). This postmodern analysis of design sets it up as being a far more powerful social force than it has traditionally been viewed.

From vocational training towards mass higher education
Increasingly, the narrowness of a vocational conception of employment has been criticised, as reported by Temple and Morris (1995):

> The vast majority of students interviewed aspire to practice as designers in their chosen field, and that remains the rationale behind their choice of programme (nevertheless) Many educationalists consider that it is no longer valid or appropriate to train people specifically for one career function.... an expectation that any one student will remain in the sector in which she or he trained is no longer accurate. (Temple & Morris, 1995, p. 51)

From rationalist towards empiricist and 'situated' views of learning
We drew attention to the fact that these design debates are mirrored in wider debates about the nature of teaching, learning and education. On one hand, 'rationalist' ideology posits the certainty and superiority of value free, objective knowledge, and views the learner as a passive recipient of transmitted knowledge. Empiricists on the other hand view knowledge as tentative and hypothetical, are concerned with values and the individual, and view education as an active process of growth (see Berlyne, 1960).

In the final section of the report we examined the existing frameworks for transferable skills – as used typically by employment agencies. Such frameworks (e.g. Allen, 1993), proliferated in educational debate in the 1990s – not least through the 'key skills' initiative by the Qualifications and Curriculum Authority concerned with implementing the National Curriculum. In the light of an analysis of these frameworks, we postulated a framework through which we might locate the **design** dimension. We were drawn to a hierarchy of labels that moves from higher-order, generalised, intellectual **intentions** – through operational **strategies** – to functional skills. In the context of designing therefore, we might speculate on the examples described in Figure 8-1.

higher order (intentions)	operational (strategies)	functional (skills)
to plan / order	thinking *as* someone else	talking
to generate / create	modelling futures	writing
to investigate / find out	'playing' with reality	calculating
to evaluate / judge	unpacking tasks	drawing
to communicate / present	managing tasks over time	making

Figure 8-1. Intentions, strategies and skills

It is the intentions of the designer that – at particular moments in time – focus and drive forward designing (or indeed any other) activity. The central column of the spectrum outlines strategies that designers use to give effect to their intentions and readers will identify that the list there derives from the previous Design Council study (*Decisions by Design*). Thereafter in the right hand column are a group of functional skills that represent the necessary means by which we engage in the strategy. These are the 'observables' in a design activity.

3.2.2   Phase 2 Methodology

From *Decisions by Design*, we had identified a range of **operational strategies** that the teacher fellows had used to characterise designerly behaviour. Starting from this list, we enriched it from the design literature review arising from the phase 1 report so as to arrive at a view of the 'transferable' things that designers do as they pursue their work:

• Progressively unpacking wicked tasks
• Recursive, iterative thinking
• 'Playing' with reality
• Identifying, prioritising and optimising values (thinking as others)
• Modelling futures (balancing innovation and risk)
• Managing tasks over time
• Seeking knowledge (grappling with uncertainty – self-directed learning)
• Teamworking and collaboration

This became our framework for examining the extent to which design courses in higher education are able to develop robust and transferable design skills in students.

Ten undergraduate design courses were chosen to reflect the breadth of design disciplines. In each college the course tutor responsible for 2nd year students was interviewed. The 2nd year was chosen because this year would normally be not only the critical teaching year (the 1st year being introductory and the 3rd year being largely individualised), but also it is the year of teaching immediately adjacent to industrial/commercial placement. Three 2nd year students from each programme were also interviewed as a group. The students, selected by the tutor, were chosen to best reflect the philosophy and practice of the programme. The aim was to see the extent to which, and the ways in which, undergraduate design programmes recognised and reflected upon the nature of design skills as generic and transferable and whether or not this was structured into their teaching. Of course to see the extent to which these issues were evident in the capabilities and understanding of the students.

The interviews with tutors and students were semi-structured and allowed us to gather detailed, qualitative data concerning, for example:

- Principles that informed course design
- Procedures and strategies that were taught and/or embedded within them
- Design skills and qualities they had developed on the course
- Extent to which students were encouraged to see that they held these skills and that they understood they might have a wider transferable value
- What they thought were the particular qualities they needed to get a job when they graduated

Supplementary documentation from the course and the university was used to contextualise the data from these interviews.

3.3   Development Issues and Significant Findings

3.3.1   The Transitional Nature of Design in Higher Education

There was ample evidence of the transitional nature of design in mass higher education. With huge increases in student numbers, many courses were is a state of realignment from traditional (one to one) studio practice in the 'atelier' tradition, to mass, modular, unitised provision. We noted a trend away from the focus on talented individuals and towards the emergence of a culture of the design professional. Employment patterns were generally seen as being away from jobs for life and toward freelance portfolio careers.

3.3.2   Distinctive Design Skills with Transferable Currency

The interviews with tutors and students confirmed our view of the existence of a set of operational strategies that designers use and develop.

Unpacking tasks
The ability to unpack and tackle what the design literature calls 'wicked' tasks lies at the heart of these strategies (see Buchanan, 1995). It is a very real challenge therefore simply to get to grips with such a tasks.

Innovating risk takers

Innovation and creativity were central to many of the design programmes we saw, and there was an evident tension there. Do students go with a risky exciting idea (and invite failure) or do they identify the rules of the game, play safe and guarantee an outcome? There was no all embracing position in the courses that we saw, though the balance was towards encouraging risk-taking by students, and the attitudes of the tutors was a major determinant in how far students were prepared to go.

Identifying values

Identifying and accommodating the needs and the values of clients was a core part of the experience, and was typically explicitly acknowledged.

> It's absolutely about other people and not about themselves, we encourage positioning ... for people that do not necessarily look at the world from their point of view. (Kimbell & Miller, 1999, p. 10)

Modelling futures

The ability to model futures was universally seen as central to design capability. Modelling their concepts of the future enabled them to experience it, make informed judgements about it, and thereby manage the risk that is inherent in implementing the new and the innovative.

> [Modelling is] central – of paramount importance – unsurpassed medium allowing communication to others and self. Modelling allows students to gain a deeper understanding ... they are testing the future. (Ibid.)

Managing complexity and uncertainty

Wicked design tasks are typically multidimensional, messy and value-laden, and designers have to optimise solutions bearing in mind competing priorities. They have to take a project from inception to completion – often over an extended period of time; they have to manage their resources, and the appropriate supply of materials and equipment in ways that enable them to complete their task. At the end they typically have to bring together all the strands of thought and development into a single holistic solution. They need to be holistic integrative thinkers – whilst managing the messy and often contradictory strands of thought within a project.

Research in action

Two distinct forms of research in design practice were observed: research to stimulate creativity, and research to acquire information. The former was typically used as a starting point, but progressively, research was based on the need to acquire task-based 'need-to-know' information. The ability to recognise the need for information; the know-how to acquire it; and the capability to use it and all acquired simultaneously as part of their developing design capability.

Optimised decision making
Optimised decision making is one of the central features of life in a design project. We were confronted time after time with evidence of continuous reasoned decision making based on a whole variety of complexities: quantitative and qualitative; from the simple to the complex; from the technical to the emotional; from the local to the global; and from the individual and quixotic to the corporate and collective.

3.3.3   Personal and Interpersonal Skills

This grouping incorporated personal qualities (e.g. passion, commitment, tenacity, responsibility and confidence), teamworking skills and communication skills. The students were very articulate – using spoken, written, graphic and ICT language to convey their ideas fluently. But beyond this we observed a further communication quality – they were great 'presenters'.

3.3.4   The Pedagogy of Design Courses

In **every case** in our sample, the design programmes were conceived as serving vocational purposes and the students were clear that they were training to be designers working somewhere in the design industry. The role of former students (now graduated and employed) illustrates this issue neatly. The only former students that were invited to contribute to the programmes were those who had got design jobs. No teachers or restaurant managers, or police officers. Our evidence indicated that many design graduates developed and possessed an awesome variety of skills and attributes that they can deploy in pursuit of a variety of employment opportunities. But the students were quite astonishingly unaware of their own tremendous skills.

The pedagogy problem
Many of the qualities that we know are required of students, and which we saw demonstrated in students' work and through our interactions with them, are embedded in 'the design process'. But they are not articulated and our discussions with students revealed that these skills were seen merely as integral parts of the process of designing. For a significant number of the students interviewed, realisation that they held other generic, transferable, and highly marketable skills only began to dawn on them as we talked.

The need to be explicit
It is one of life's ironies that persons who have developed capability, say in designing, are not necessarily conscious of the skills they are using. They may have become embedded in their practice and, in terms of the designer's

priorities, may become almost entirely subsumed into a concern for the production of successful outcomes.

The evidence of our study is that the multitudinous skills of the designer are used tacitly, and this is of little benefit to students who need to be far more aware of the new skills they are developing. They need, consciously, **to stop and think about what they are doing** and how they are doing it in order to develop an understanding of the power of the skill and the ways in which they personally can operate it successfully.

Effective learning requires a meta-cognitive awareness of one's own processes; not just being able to do it – but being self-aware as one is doing it. That is why Schön (1983) talks of the 'reflective practitioner'.

We argued that design tutors need to make explicit through their planning and their pedagogy the skills and qualities they are seeking to develop. By articulating them, they will become part of the day-to-day discourse and will progressively empower the students.

3.4   Postscript to the Project

Our analysis of the fieldwork for this project was presented at a seminar at the Design Council in March 1999 as part of 'Design in Education Week'. The seminar involved representatives of the student groups and the tutors who we had interviewed, and the purpose of the day was to share our findings and to promote discussion of them.

One of the quite proper outcomes of the day was further suggestions of qualities that had not appeared in our analysis, but which – on reflection – the students and tutors felt might be important. One of these was put as follows:

> [T]he skill of synthesis ... not just being able to 'unpack', but also to 'put together' again (engineers for example tend to have good analytic skills but poor synthesis skills). (Kimbell & Miller, 1999, p. 21)

It is probably true that we understated this quality. The ability to create and hold a 'big picture' of where things are going, and to integrate different strands of development towards a composite solution is indeed an important strategic capability. The fact that we have not raised it through our framework is probably because we subsumed it somewhere between what we referred to as 'managing complexity' and 'optimising decision making'.

3.5   Concluding Comments

Of all the projects that we have conducted and reported, *APU Design & Technology* has been the most sought after by teachers and researchers. But a clear second place is held by this project 'design skills for work'. It originated in the Design Council project 'decision-by-design' and the interest that was created at the Design Council by that earlier work. This illustrates an interesting truth about our projects that all researchers should take to heart. When you get one project from a sponsor – it should ideally grow into another (and another).

This is not a matter of money grabbing, but is rather recognition of two things. First, that with initial projects one typically has to spend a lot of time and effort in acclimatising to the interests and (particularly) the **values** of that sponsor. Second, that opening up a new field of work with a new sponsor will typically result in many more questions than answers. Provided that the project has been conducted thoroughly and effectively, sponsors are typically more than happy to see some of those questions converted into subsequent projects. We have always taken the view that one of the best judgements on our work is made by looking at the extent of the second (and third) projects that we have been commissioned to undertake.

4.   THE ATTITUDES OF POTENTIAL TEACHERS OF DESIGN & TECHNOLOGY (1999–2000)

4.1   Context and Brief

We have described in Chapter 6 some of the turbulence that was so evident in schools in the early years of the National Curriculum. This turbulence was so profound, that it overspilled the schools context and became a very public debate and inevitably had a significant impact on teacher recruitment. The public image of life in schools had become somewhat tarnished. Whilst teacher recruitment became problematic for several areas of the curriculum, for design & technology teaching it was extremely serious. By September 1997 the issue was sufficiently urgent for it to be made the focus of an 'Invitation Conference' organised by the Design and Technology Association (DATA) and supported by the Teacher Training Agency (TTA). At that conference, the Chief Executive of the TTA put the problem bluntly:

> Without wishing to sound full of gloom and doom, for the academic year just starting … design and technology applications have been lowest of all, and our predictions were that around 46% of places on PGCE courses would be filled. So perhaps it is timely to concentrate on design & technology. (Millett, 1997, p. 5)

In March 1999, the Department for Education and Employment commissioned TERU to undertake a 12-month research project to investigate the attitudes of **potential** teachers of design & technology in schools. The study focused on final year undergraduates pursuing design and/or technology related degree courses, and sought to identify their attitudes towards embarking on a career in teaching.

4.2 Outline Methodology

4.2.1 The Sample

We defined the 'potential recruits' for teaching design & technology as those undergraduates from design courses (e.g. product design) and from technology courses (e.g. engineering). We set out to contrast these 'potential recruits' with students who had already made a commitment to train as teachers (e.g. on Post Graduate Certificate in Education and shortened BA in Education programmes). We were also aware of the influence of university tutors over the career choices of their graduates. We therefore sampled tutors' attitudes to teaching design & technology. In each of the institutions, we asked tutors to select a group of five or six students that represented the final year cohort of students in terms of gender balance, the spread of age and ability and any other variable that the tutor believed to be important in defining the group. The final composite sample therefore involved 130 students, on 23 courses, with 19 tutors in 18 institutions.

4.2.2 Data Collection and Management

Since we were seeking attitudinal data, we used interview techniques for the mass of our data, supplemented with a series of tick-box questionnaires that were designed to be completed in about 10 min at the start of the interviews. These 'hard' data were analysed and used to illuminate the interview data. The qualitative interview data started life as a tape recording. This was transcribed and the text transferred into QSR Nud*ist – a software package specifically designed to facilitate the analysis of qualitative responses.

There were two forms of quantitative data:

- The qualities that graduates looked for in a job set against how they perceive the teaching job in relation to those same qualities – aggregated to form a profile of the particular student groups.
- Student information at a more personal/individual level (e.g. age, gender and their employment ambitions).

4.3   Significant Findings

4.3.1   Graduates 'Ideal' Job

In the chart that follows, we present (on the left-hand side) the priorities identified by the groups for their ideal job. On the right of the chart are the priorities that they see applying to a job in teaching. We then connect the common items to create a visual representation of the attitude match. Some lines head downwards, indicating a deficit view (i.e. the student group believe that teaching offers them less than they would ideally like of the quality in question). Some lines head upwards – are 'credit' lines (i.e. they believe that teaching offers them more of it than they would ideally like).

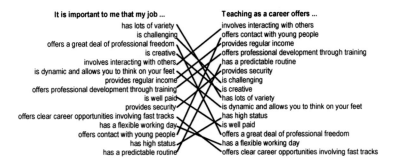

Figure 8-2. Students' perception of teaching as a career

Students on design courses see the job of teaching as having a lack of variety, challenge, professional freedom, creativity and dynamic; and they see it being too routine and involving too much contact with young people (Figure 8-2). The correlation is accordingly virtually zero. The most serious dislocation here concerns the professional freedom that design graduates seek. Students on technology courses had broadly similar profiles with the biggest misfits being:

- Lack of variety
- Lack of professional freedom
- Poor pay
- Lack of dynamic
- Lack of career fast tracks
- Lack of creativity

4.3.2 The Attitudes of Graduates and their Tutors

It was reassuring to find that where students had experience of design &
technology, the vast majority saw it as positive. There were commonplace
and recurrent references to the fact that their design & technology teachers
were 'good' teachers and influential in their schooling. We used the 'thumbs
up/thumbs down' example in Figure 8-3 to capture (in free-response mode)
students' recollections of design & technology.

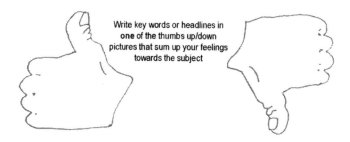

Figure 8-3. Thumbs up/thumbs down

The qualitative data from the student and tutor interviews revealed the
following broad issues

Summarising student attitudes
Very little careers guidance was provided in any of the courses. Typically,
there were very negative attitudes towards teaching, because it was seen as
stressful, uncreative and overburdened with paperwork. There was very little
knowledge of routes into teacher training and if students were conscripted
(i.e. forced) into teaching, only the design students would choose to teach
design & technology (engineering students more frequently mentioning
mathematics). To correct the situation, it was felt that teaching needed more
money, teachers more autonomy, and the profession needed to be far more
creative and be presented with a better public image.

Summarising tutor attitudes
The issues identified were broadly the same as those that arose from the
student interviews. Most tutors assumed that their students would be taking
up a career in industry. They knew very little about routes into teaching, and
the notion that their students should become teachers hardly ever entered
their heads. They believed that the teaching role was constrained by the
National Curriculum, uncreative and overburdened with paper work. Tutors
knew very little about design & technology, unless their own children were

studying it at school, and finally they regretted the low status of teaching and mentioned the damaging consequences of what they described as 'endless teacher-bashing'.

4.4   Recommendations to the Sponsors

The four most crucial recommendations to Department for Education and Employment from this project were as follows.

1. Focusing recruitment on the design group of students who had least resistance and (on balance) the most to offer to design & technology. We recommended the development of a 'designer in residence' programme and initiated one at Goldsmiths in association with the Design Council. This later evolved into the Design Council's 'Designers in Schools' initiative.
2. Focusing on design tutors, partly because they are a permanent feature of life in colleges (whereas students are transient), and partly because they have such a profound influence on the ambitions and expectations of their students. We recommended a series of conference/events be designed specifically for such tutors.
3. Informing students (and tutors) about design & technology teaching and about routes into it, we argued that the most transparent and available medium would be a web site, supported by (for group events) a state of the art video/DVD presentation of 'teaching design & technology'.
4. Countering the highly negative perception of teaching, policy bodies, in particular, the Teacher Training Agency, the Department for Education and Employment, and the Office for Standards in Education, need publicly to celebrate the creativity, diversity and risk taking in teaching design & technology in schools. It is interesting, and gratifying, that 5 years later, the Teacher Development Agency (who has subsumed the Teacher Training Agency) had such success with its teacher recruitment campaign emphasising the creative challenge of teaching.

4.5   Concluding Comments

There were many methodological challenges in this project that are worth a moment's reflection. The central problem was a national one; the source of potential 'subjects' from whom to gather data was huge; but the nature of the data being sought was personal and value-laden. We have no doubt that some researchers would have tackled this problem with large-scale questionnaires, but our approach was almost the reverse of that.

With attitudinal/value-based data we believe that it is essential to establish some **trust** with those from whom one hopes to elicit data.

Accordingly our approach is invariably to meet them face to face and in small groups.

In this case, despite being contracted by the monolithic Department for Education and Employment, we were essentially from the same design territory as the 'subjects' involved and it was easy to have preliminary discussions with the tutors and the students about their work, their institution and their ambitions for the future. These deliberately low-key discussions created a comfortable atmosphere in which the main data gathering could take place. We were not external busy bodies; we were co-workers/co-researchers sharing our thoughts. When we asked them to complete a questionnaire we handed it to them personally and invited them to tell us if any of it was not clear or not appropriate.

The downside of this strategy is that the **sample** we could cope with was far smaller than would have been possible with a blind questionnaire. Nonetheless we were able to create a carefully stratified sample – choosing institutions, courses and then students to represent the breadth of the national picture. The upside thereafter is that we can be confident that the stated views are real. We achieved a 100% return rate from the sample. We do not like '**missing**' data, since it is typically the most important data.

5. TECHNOLOGICAL MATHS (1996–1997)

5.1 Context and Brief

The Engineering Council (UK) regulates the engineering profession in the UK. Under its 1981 Royal Charter, the Engineering Council's role is 'to advance education in, and to promote the science and practice of, engineering (including relevant technology) for the public benefit and thereby to promote industry and commerce in Our United Kingdom and elsewhere'. Perhaps the greatest impact of the EC on educational matters has been through its long-running projects:

- The Women Into Science and Engineering (WISE)
- The Technology Enhancement Programme (TEP)
- Neighbourhood Engineers' scheme
- Young Engineer for Britain

The two Engineering Council funded projects discussed in the remainder of this chapter illustrate very neatly the public/professional interface at which the Council lives. The first looks inwards – to inform internal policy – and the second looks outwards to inform and seek to influence wider educational and public policy.

Technological Maths grew from one of these long-running projects; The Technology Enhancement Programme, which was established in 1993 to improve the quality of technology, science and mathematics teaching for 14–19-year-old students.

Engineering has always been seen as having very close interdependence with maths and physics, to the extent that they are invariably seen by university engineering departments as the core qualifications at A level for entry into an engineering degree course. But during the 1990s, the numbers of candidates coming forward with maths A level was rapidly dwindling, with serious consequences for engineering recruitment.

Technological maths was commissioned by The Technology Enhancement Programme in June 1996 and the brief was to examine the use of mathematics as a tool to support their activities in the school curriculum. The two interconnecting aims of the investigation were:

- Identifying the presentation of mathematics in selected Technology Enhancement Programme textbooks
- Investigating the use of mathematics in technology in three Technology Enhancement Programme schools

5.2   Outline Methodology

The review of existing research to inform the interface between maths and technology in the curriculum, was done particularly through three sets of sources:

1. The research project 'Maths by Design' (Design Council, 1996)
2. Work from the Centre for Innovation in Maths Teaching: University of Exeter (Burghes et al., 1994, 1996; Burghes and Blum 1995; Burghes, 1996)
3. The curriculum development project Science with Technology (Sage, 1996)

Thereafter – also as desk research – we examined the interaction of mathematics with design & technology in National Curriculum Programmes of Study and examination syllabuses. From this work we drew out the explicit and the implicit mathematical demands within design & technology.

The second focus for the project was addressed through empirical research in three case study schools. The framework for these investigations emerged from the result of the desk research and was shaped by research questions such as:

- How do Technology Enhancement Programme teachers understand the relationship between mathematics and technology?

- Are Technology Enhancement Programme teachers aware of any mismatch between the requirements in the mathematics and the design & technology National Curriculum Statutory Orders?
- What levels of collaboration exist between mathematics and design & technology teachers?

We conducted a series of visits to three case study schools from a short list provided by Technology Enhancement Programme. We used the above questions to produce a semi-structured interview format for use with technology teachers in those schools. We spoke to design & technology and mathematics teachers, to pupils undertaking Technology Enhancement Programme-related activities, and to school managers. We also examined Technology Enhancement Programme 14–16 textbooks.

5.3   Significant Findings

5.3.1   Findings from the Literature

The key issues and areas of difficulty emerging from the three texts were:

- **The mismatch of demand** – parallel ideas appearing in programmes of study – but at different ages and levels.
- **Making mathematics explicit** – mathematics lies implicitly in much of what is done in technology, and learners need to have it made explicit before they can grasp it.
- **Conceptual challenges** – specifically concerning the difficulty experienced by learners in translating knowledge acquired in one domain into practical action in another.
- **Cultural issues** – concerning different approaches to learning and teaching in subjects. Even in mathematics investigations, Burghes et al. (1996) judge that mathematics looks inwards (to purely mathematical phenomena) whilst technology looks outwards to the 'real' world.

5.3.2   Findings from the Fieldwork

Following the desk research, we launched the empirical case studies. With observations and interviews, we identified a set of issues and the most significant are outlined below:

- **Mismatch of curriculum** – we observed many examples of major concepts being taught at different times and using different conventions in mathematics and design & technology (e.g. Boolean algebra exists in some Advanced level mathematics though it has commonly now been dropped as 'too hard' – but is used regularly in 'truth tables' for GCSE design & technology). One head of mathematics was shocked.

- **Non-collaboration between teachers** – technology teachers were unaware of the sequence and age levels at which concepts were taught in mathematics. The consequence was that they ignored the mathematics department teaching and taught the concepts (again) to the pupils as part of technology (e.g. gear trains; Ohm's law).
- **Compartmentalising of learning** – there is plenty of evidence to support the view that as we compartmentalise the curriculum so pupils compartmentalise their learning.

'They take off their maths hat when they leave the maths room'. (Kimbell & Green, 1996, p. 14)

5.3.3   Findings from the Study of the Textbooks

The following were key issues concerning using the texts:

- **Presentation and accessibility of the materials** – the presentation is low key and bland and seemed deliberately to be aimed at a more academic and 'serious' technological audience. The materials were criticised by teachers as too 'wordy' and intimidating.
- **Technology Enhancement Programme 14–16 materials in General Certificate for Secondary Education courses** – there is considerable whole-group use made of TEP materials in Year 10 – which is an intensive 'teacher input' year – and considerably less in Year 11 – which is driven by individual major projects.
- **Technology Enhancement Programme 14–16 materials used for teaching younger age groups** – these materials are used for formal whole-group teaching in the early years of secondary schools, even though they are not designed for this age group.

Quite separate from the mathematics issues, there was universal acclaim for the imagination of Technology Enhancement Programme materials.

5.4   Concluding Comments

The central problem that lies at the heart of this project remains ubiquitous and intractable. In the observations we made of practice in schools there was no evidence that the use of Technology Enhancement Programme materials had enabled teachers and learners to move beyond the conventional problems arising from the compartmentalising of the curriculum. Typically, in Technology Enhancement Programme design & technology, pupils either work intuitively to solve problems that they only half perceive as being mathematical (i.e. the mathematics remains at the implicit level) or they work from the mathematics that is separately taught by technology teachers.

6.   DESIGN & TECHNOLOGY IN A KNOWLEDGE ECONOMY (2000–2001)

6.1   Context and Brief

In September 2000, the latest version the National Curriculum came into effect, including the most recent formulation for design & technology. At the time of publication, the Department for Education and Employment, in concert with the Design & Technology Association established a Strategy Group for design & technology, charged with the task of steering the subject through the following years.

In line with the innovation focus made explicit in the new design & technology Order, in November 2000 David Hargreaves, Chief Executive of the Qualifications and Curriculum Authority addressed a conference at London University Institute of Education titled 'Towards Education for Innovation' (Hargreaves, 2001). In his lecture he signalled both the importance of an innovative curriculum, and the overriding need for youngsters' developing innovation to be the focus of that curriculum. In this setting, Hargreaves was expressing the view that traditional schooling inside the security of rigid curricular boundaries was increasingly untenable. Much the same argument was coming from other writers of the time:

> [I]nnovation increasingly relies on the interface between different kinds of knowledge, for example, the combination of new information technologies with a new accounting system, or of design and technical skills in creating new websites. ... Value is realised when different bodies of knowledge are brought together. Interdisciplinary skills are more and more valuable to individuals and organisations. ... Interdisciplinary knowledge means far more than just specialisation in more than one subject. It requires the ability to understand the interface between different areas of knowledge and to apply insights from one to the other. (Seltzer & Bentley, 1999, p. 21–22)

Responding to this tide of thinking within educational circles, in November 2000, the Engineering Council presented TERU with the task of writing a report for them that would locate design & technology within this debate. We were asked that the report should be academically rooted, drawing from appropriate literature in the field, but reflecting directly on practice in schools. It should be linked with an Executive Summary – to be published separately – for audiences that demand the essence of the message with less of the supporting argument.

6.2   Methodology

In tackling this task we identified a group of teachers and researchers (8) with interests in this area, and invited them to a working seminar to arrive at a list of key issues with which the report would have to deal. From this debate, the structure of the report evolved into four sections:

- Part 1: The domain of design & technology
- Part 2: A distinctive pedagogy
- Part 3: A distinctive view of the learner
- Part 4: A distinctive view of the future

We completed the report and submitted it to the Engineering Council in February 2001 (Kimbell & Perry, 2001), including a Foreword from their Director General of the Engineering Council, Malcolm Shirley. The Foreword made clear the Engineering Council's support, both for design & technology generally and for the TERU report in particular.

The executive summary of the report has been further edited below.

6.3   The Report

6.3.1   The Domain of Design & Technology

The made world
The subject matter of design & technology is our made world; our clothes, our food, our means of travel, our shelters and our communication systems. But, more than that, design & technology is about creating change in the made world; about understanding the processes of change and becoming capable in the exercise of change making.

Design & technology in the curriculum
The curriculum manifestation of design & technology has evolved since the late 1960s. Schools Council projects, HMI and LEA initiatives, teacher education institutions and school examinations all contributed to its pro-gressive articulation, but the driving force behind its development has always been individual teachers exploring new approaches in their own workshops, studios and classrooms.

The 1990 Order for Technology was visionary; based on the best practice that could be found across the country. Good practice has now spread from a few centres of excellence to a far greater proportion of design & technology teachers.

This development has not been taking place in isolation from the rest of the world. In the UK, we originated the concept of design & technology and in England and Wales we were the first to establish it as an entitlement for all children from 5 to 16. In doing so, we have provided a model that much of the world has followed.

6.3.2 A Distinctive Pedagogy

Task-centred activity and learner autonomy
At the heart of design & technology lies a distinctive, project-based model of teaching and learning. It involves learners taking a task from inception to completion within constraints of time, cost and resources. The aim of design & technology is to develop students' 'capability'; that combination of qualities, abilities and experience that transcends understanding and enables creative development. The pupil is required to be an active participant. Not so much studying design & technology as being a design & technologist. The capable student sees the made world as inadequate, and can make it better.

Task-related knowledge and skills
In too much of the curriculum, propositional ('know-that') knowledge, has been elevated beyond its real value. Beyond a carefully defined core of knowledge, we emphasise the need for students to acquire and create new, task-related knowledge. The everyday experience of design & technology is of task-centred knowledge creation.

Performance assessment
In assessment terms, this throws the spotlight on students' ability to use their understandings and skills when they are tackling a real task. Capability in design & technology involves the active, purposeful deployment of understandings and skills – not just their passive demonstration.

6.3.3 A Distinctive View of the Learner

Individual learning styles and differentiated challenge
Learning is what happens when we realise that things are not quite as we previously thought. It is a constructive process – building on our existing framework of concepts and schema. Design & technology draws on a rich range of learning styles, so that the experience is customised to the requirements of individuals. The low truancy rates in design & technology provide one indicator of teachers' accomplishment in this process. Design & technology therefore offers a differentiated learning experience, in which we work from and promote learners' strengths, whilst encouraging them to grapple with their weaknesses.

Designers, decision makers, thinkers
The essence of the process exists in the interaction of cognitive modelling ('in the mind's eye') with the hard reality of the material world. It is iterative as ideas are bounced back and forth, formulated, tested against reality and then reformulated. It is best described as 'thought in action'.

Collaborative team players
Learners can regularly be seen subjecting their work to progress reviews; work in-process being critiqued by their teachers and their peers. Because of the openness of the visual, concrete language of design, students' work is public, viewable by others as it progresses.

Learning and valuing
We have described designing as a process of improving the made world. But improvement for whom? Tackling values in design & technology is not an abstract intellectual activity, for made-world products are the focus of attention. Teachers' experience of helping learners to make explicit the values underlying products, brings to life what can otherwise seem the remote, academic world of ethics and morality.

6.3.4   A Distinctive View of the Future

Modernising design & technology
Many initiatives are opening up imaginative opportunities, from high-tech 'smart' materials and programmable chips, to user-focused resources in an expanding repertoire of contexts. Designing and making is increasingly being explored through computer-aided designing and manufacturing techniques (CAD/CAM) and using electronic and communications technologies (ECT). The 'sustainability' and 'consumption' debates are real in design & technology and powerful in the lives of youngsters. Equally, design & technology is uniquely placed to contribute to the 'Young Foresight' initiative, exploring future trends, consumer behaviour and technological opportunities.

Modernising assessment
We are firmly of the belief that assessment must not be allowed to limit learning. Because of its long, project-based history, we have in design & technology, the most accomplished classroom practitioners of the subtle art of project-based assessment.

The challenge of a knowledge economy
Part of the discomfort that has been experienced by design & technology over the last 30 years arises from its awkward insistence on being neither a specialist art nor a specialist science. It is deliberately and actively interdisciplinary. It is a creative, restive, itinerant, non-discipline.

In the context of a knowledge economy, the interdisciplinary imperative of design & technology is increasingly recognised as strength rather than weakness. The 'skills challenge' of such an economy involves learning structured around projects; based on identifying and solving problems; in a range of contexts in which students (often in teams) transfer knowledge across different domains; using portfolio models of exploration, presentation and assessment. This is precisely the model of learning through which design & technology operates. We have been pursuing and refining these approaches for 30 years, and our teachers are in the vanguard of those preparing youngsters for employment in the knowledge economy.

6.4   Concluding Comments

Historically, the interest in this project is that it was essentially designed as a piece of propaganda. Not that we were trying to sell something falsely – but rather that in the circumstances of the time a clear manifesto was needed. Many interested parties in the design & technology world – including of course the Engineering Council UK – were alarmed at the direction that National Curriculum policy was moving in the late 1990s, and the fear was of marginalisation for the subject. We were asked to create a succinct statement around which the principal subject bodies and organisations could cluster and moreover one that would be meaningful to those beyond the subject (in the Department for Education and Skills and elsewhere) who would be making decisions about the future of the National Curriculum.

The report was very widely distributed and had a number of consequences both within the Engineering Council and beyond it. Perhaps the most significant external consequence was that the report was received by the newly established the Department for Education and Skills, Design & Technology Strategy Group that had been created as a joint venture between Ministers, the Design and Technology Association, the Office for Standards in Education and industry bodies (including the Engineering Council). At the first meeting of the Group (October 2001), our 'knowledge economy' report was debated and warmly received. Subsequently, the Group produced its report to Ministers 'Building on Success – the unique contribution of design & technology' (Barlex, 2003), the opening section of which drew heavily from our 'knowledge economy' report. This Department for Education and Skills report had a number of repercussions, one of which was to create the head of steam that resulted in **creativity** emerging as a key issue for research – and this eventually resulted in the TERU project '*Assessing Design Innovation*' (see Chapter 6).

Chapter 9

EVALUATING CURRICULAR INITIATIVES

Why you might find these projects interesting

The implementation of National Curriculum massively increased the need for new schemes of work that would meet the radically new curriculum requirements. Agencies undertaking such developments were keen to evaluate their efforts and in TERU we received many evaluation invitations.

The first venture was for the new Mandela administration in South Africa. A learner-centred pilot curriculum operating in schools distributed across miles of bush in the North West Province potentially transforming the life-chances of many young black learners. Who could refuse that?

Thereafter, we evaluated two projects for the London Design Museum, one based on the learning value of their tantalising 'mystery-box' of weird objects, and the other on their scheme for getting real designers to run development sessions for design & technology teachers.

Three other projects centred on the challenges of embedding new technologies in the curriculum. Two of these projects focused on the most sciency and typically the least imaginative of the areas of design & technology (systems and control). We explored the BBC's professional roboteers programme helping learners to design and build their own robots. A second project explored the power of LEGO for young learners working with programmable bricks on creativity projects of various kinds (including LEGO robots). The third 'new-technology' project – for the Design and Technology professional association – evaluated the impact of a new CAD initiative.

Finally, we discuss using our approach to assessment to evaluate a primary school initiative linking design & technology to functional literacy.

***

1.   INTRODUCTION

From the mid-1990s onwards, there was considerable development of technology education, both in the UK and globally. These developments saw the introduction of a whole host of curriculum initiatives aimed at supporting more formal requirements. To gain some measure of the effectiveness of their initiatives, the agencies responsible were seeking ways of assessing their impact and TERU was asked to evaluate nine such projects between 1998 and 2004. This chapter revisits these projects and their evaluations, providing history and insight into a group of projects that all aimed at breaking new ground. For TERU, evaluating the impact of each project also provided research opportunities to further understandings of design & technological capability and of assessment, learning and teaching.

During this era, national and provincial governments across all continents were legislating for the introduction or development of technology education and the first evaluation we were invited to undertake was in such a situation in South Africa. The project, the *North West Province Technology Education Project*, was part of the much larger 'Curriculum 2005' initiative, developing the whole school curriculum in the newly democratic South Africa. In the UK, a number of initiatives emerged as we approached the Millennium, many in response to the climate created by the changes to the English and Welsh National Curriculum, through the 'middle of the road' revisions of 1995 to the more visionary Curriculum 2000. The Design Museum was a key contributor in this era, active in providing both resources and in-service courses for teachers. In 1997, they launched an *Outreach Programme* based around two sets of handling collections and associated resources. First came the *Mystery Box* and then the *Architecture and Built Environment* collection. A further initiative, *Designers in Action*, set up a series of workshops, in which leading design companies ran workshops at the Museum to share their techniques and practices with teachers. TERU was asked to evaluate the impact of each of these initiatives.

Within TERU we had a long-standing concern over the suppression of creativity in the curriculum (Kimbell, 2000). This concern was shared by a range of groups including the National Endowment for Science, Technology and the Arts (NESTA) who, in 2001, established a pilot programme to explore the use of LEGO products both to enhance creativity and to develop interest in systems and control technologies. TERU was commissioned to assess the impact that the project had in schools across the UK – the *Energy & Environment Evaluation* project. Other initiatives to help learners engage with 'rapidly changing technologies' (DfEE/QCA, 1999, p. 15) brought two further evaluations to TERU. The first was the *CAD-in-schools* project, which launched a major programme to equip schools with the resources to introduce industry standard CAD programmes. The second, *Roboteers in Residence*, was a further NESTA-funded project, developed by BBC 'Factual and Learning' and which applied the model of artist in residence to professional roboteers.

A very different issue causing concern was the way in which a 'back to basics' drive for literacy and numeracy was driving other subjects (and hence breadth of experience) out of the curriculum. The National Literacy Strategy, introduced in England in 1998 was the first formal step taken that had a very real effect on timetables as it included a requirement that all primary age children followed a 'literacy hour' programme each school morning. A parallel initiative for numeracy placed similar demands on schools. The *Enriching Literacy through Design & Technology* project sought to take advantage of the potential for teaching literacy skills through design & technology and was introduced in a group of schools facing particular challenges. TERU was commissioned to evaluate the pilot year.

We will now look at each project to provide further detail and insights into what was learned.

2. NORTH WEST PROVINCE TECHNOLOGY EDUCATION PROJECT EVALUATION (1998–1999)

2.1 Context

The *North West Province Technology Education Project*, funded by the DFID, was a 3-year project, which came to completion in 1999. The initiative was a joint venture between DFID, the North West Province Education Department and PROTEC, a South Africa NGO who, since the early 1980s, had worked with disadvantaged students in townships and rural communities, developing technology projects outside the formal curriculum. The broader context of the introduction of 'Curriculum 2005' set an agenda for an entire paradigm shift from teacher, to learner-centred approaches. The funders wished to explore the impact of the initiative through performance based assessment of technological capability and we were commissioned to undertake this work. This put us back on old and comfortable territory, established through *APU Design & Technology*. We supplemented the performance data with the opinions and insights of those directly involved – the learners, their teachers and school principals.

2.2   Brief and Outline Methodology

The specific brief for TERU focused on the performance of learners and on implementation issues. Additionally, we were tasked with 'building capacity' in understanding performance assessment within the team running the project. The project had been piloted in 20 schools across the North West Province and, to conduct the evaluation, a sample of ten of the most mature schools (in terms of their involvement with the project) were chosen, along with ten 'control' schools equivalent in intake and environmental and economic setting but not involved in the project. The evaluation focused on mixed gender groups of 18 learners in years 11 and 12, providing a sample of 720 learners. A further six learners per school were involved in a group interview. We also interviewed the principals and technology teachers involved. To 'build capacity' we were supported by six fieldworkers, all experienced technology teachers within South Africa who understood the intervention project.

Broadly speaking the evaluation consisted of the following dimensions:

- Analysing the structure and materials used within the project
- Assessing the performance of groups of learners
- Collecting evaluative and attitudinal data from learners through questionnaires and group interviews
- Collecting interview data from teachers, principals and others involved
- Training fieldworkers to run activities and assess performance

We were interested in the learners' views on the assessment activity itself, on teamworking and on technology more generally. We created two questionnaires, both asking a range of questions linked to a four point 'Likert' response scale of 'strongly agree' to 'strongly disagree'. The evaluation questionnaire was in four sections:

- Definitions of technology
- Why the task experienced was technological
- Views on working in teams
- Free response questions about working with boys and girls

A separate questionnaire, that had its roots in the tradition of pupils attitudes towards technology (PATT) research, gauged the learners' attitudes to technology. PATT introduced an approach to exploring the ways young people conceptualise technology and their attitude towards it. Introduced in 1984 by Jan Raat and Marc de Vries, the methodology has been used extensively across the globe (see e.g. Raat et al., 1987). Our questionnaire addressed what learners believe technology to be and analysed attitudes to technology in the world around us (i.e. the value of technology, quality of life, prosperity and economy and environment) and learning technology (with reference to employment, gender and ability factors and enjoyment).

We wished to gather opinion from a range of groups and to have a basis on which to compare responses. Consequently, we developed a set of semi-structured interviews, customised appropriately for use with principals, teachers, group interviews with learners and other professionals involved with the project – the project field officer, the Provincial director of curriculum, the teacher trainers and director of PROTEC. Our overarching concerns were with the pedagogy underpinning the programme, teamwork, benefits for stakeholders, resource implications and dissemination.

2.3 Development Challenges and Significant Findings

2.3.1 Developing Assessment Tasks for Group Settings

The curriculum experience provided by the *North West Province Technology Education Project* was based on group work and problem solving. Content was structured under three broad headings: materials and processes, energy and power and communications (Figure 9-1). The assessment activity needed to reflect this experience, thus ruling out more conventional assessment devices such as multiple choice testing, which was standard in South Africa at the time.

Taking the *APU* task structure as a starting point, we evolved a short (75 min) technological activity, for mixed gender groups working in teams of six, designed to draw on the content areas of the curriculum, but not to be so dependent on prior knowledge to make the activity difficult for the control group. The task focused on safe transport of medicines to rural communities in hot climates with poor road conditions. Each team was divided for part of the activity into three pairs, each of which had a subtask, themed to a curriculum content area: pair A materials and processes; pair B energy and power; pair C communications (Figure 9-2). The pairs brought their ideas for addressing the subtasks back to the whole team who had to pull all ideas together and develop a coherent solution. As with previous projects, the task was standardised through structured test booklets and an administrator's script that provided instructions to guide each stage of the activity.

Medicines in Transit

Situation

Many medicines have to be transported to people living in remote parts of the country.

The medicines have to be carried in trucks on very bumpy roads.

The medicines need to be kept at specific temperatures to stop them being destroyed by heat or cold.

The medicines are very precious and need to be protected from thieves.

Team Booklet

School No. _____   Team No. _____
First name   Age   boy/girl

A { 1. _____
    2. _____
B { 3. _____
    4. _____
C { 5. _____
    6. _____

Date _____

Task

Your task as a whole group is to design a product that can be used to carry the medicines in. The product must:

 protect the medicines from heat and cold;

 keep the medicine containers secure so that they don't spill or get broken;

 send a warning if the temperature of the medicines gets too hot or cold;

 stop thieves trying to steal the medicine.

Figure 9-1. NWPTEP team task

Task for Pair A

The task for your subgroup is to tackle the problem of **insulation**. You will need to work on ideas for designing a product that will stop the medicines from getting too hot or cold and that will hold the medicines so that they won't spill or break.

Task for Pair B

The task for your subgroup is to tackle the problem of **securing the container** so that it doesn't move around in the truck and the medicines cannot be stolen. You will need to work on ideas for designing a product that holds the medicine container in place on the journey and that will stop a thief from stealing the medicines or the container.

Task for Pair C

The task for your subgroup is to tackle the problem of **creating an alarm** that will tell the user if the medicines are getting too hot or cold. You will need to work on ideas for designing a product that will have an inbuilt temperature gauge and alarm system.

Figure 9-2. NWPTEP pairs subtasks

Assessment focused on three dimensions: the procedural focus of the curriculum, the importance of group work and the content areas of the curriculum (Figure 9-3). Through these dimensions we created the parameters of capability we would probe through the activity and be able to assess from the evidence generated. Each dimension was further detailed to create a set of quality descriptors, provided at four levels for each assessment heading, the 4-point scale designed to avoid the trap of 'the middle ground'.

Dimensions	Sub Dimensions	Characteristics
Design / problem solving procedures	Identifying and specifying	• seeing clients needs • considering issues • seeing the whole task • thinking forward
	generating and developing	• range of ideas • development of ideas
	evaluating	• seeing strengths and weaknesses • dealing with strengths and weaknesses • compromising and optimising
Team working		• group decision making • addressing the whole task • amalgamation of ideas •supportive interaction
Application of knowledge	Materials and processes	• named material and construction processes • understanding of their properties • application to task
	Energy and power	• mechanical and electrical sources • understanding of their properties • application to task
	Communications	• systems communication systems • systems communicating with people • understanding the properties of communication systems • application to task

Figure 9-3. Dimensions of the assessment rubric

In line with previous experience the criteria were derived as characteristic rather than precise descriptors; they could be seen as indicative of a way of working, rather than as a tight definition to be matched. The rubric was illuminated by exemplars, in line with practices we had found successful in earlier projects. These tools proved extremely useful for training the fieldworkers.

2.3.2   Building Capacity in Performance Assessment

We trained the fieldworkers, all technology education professionals, to run the activities and assess the results. Training for activity administration took place through observation of a member of the research team running the activity with learners from a PROTEC Saturday school, followed by a workshop addressing issues essential for effective administration of a standardised task. Following a week running activities in schools we conducted further training, refocusing the fieldworkers as assessors. This involved a two-stage process, first identifying and colour-coding the **evidence** of capability in the scripts, then, through paired marking, agreeing the **levels** of performance the evidence demonstrated. The first-hand experience of having run the activity with learners proved fundamental to success – as evidenced by the fieldworkers' effectiveness as activity administrators, their reliability as assessors and their feedback on the value of the total experience.

2.3.3   Positive Impact of the Initiative: Particularly on Girls

We concluded that the initiative had been very positive in its impact. Evidence for this was seen in the performance of the learners, their attitudes to each other and to technology more generally, and in opinions voiced by all parties concerned. The assessment activity showed that, holistically, the project schools substantially outperformed the control schools, with significantly stronger performance in all dimensions assessed except **generating and developing** solutions (Figure 9-4).

Learners from all schools were generally positive about teamwork. However, analysis of responses to negative statements showed the most negative group to be girls in the control group. Responses to working with the opposite sex showed the *North West Province Technology Education Project* boys to be most positive about working with girls and the free response question (best things about working with girls/boys) showed boys and girls from the project schools consistently most positive about the opposite sex. This was illuminated by a rather stark comment from a boy in a control school who stated: 'To be realistic I don't know how to answer this one because I never worked with girls before.'

PERFORMANCE: Overall average scores	project	control	difference	t test probability
Holistic	2.53	2.18	0.35	0.03
PROCEDURES				
Identifying & specifying	2.63	2.32	0.32	0.03
generating & developing	2.43	2.33	0.10	0.50
evaluating	2.38	1.88	0.50	0.00
teamwork	2.65	2.27	0.38	0.02
USE OF KNOWLEDGE				
materials & processes	2.4	2.03	0.37	0.02
energy & power	2.18	1.6	0.58	0.00
communications	2.67	1.7	0.97	0.00

Figure 9-4. Overall average performance scores

This was further underscored by the attitude questionnaire, for example, by the divide between *North West Province Technology Education Project* girls and the boys in the **control** group over the statement 'girls think technology is difficult', to which the project school girls were most likely to disagree, and the control school boys most likely to agree.

Views of technology also produced starkly contrasted responses. In large measure learners in the project schools saw technology as a problem-solving process, while learners in the control schools saw it as products, typically computers (Figure 9-5).

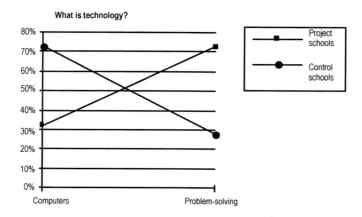

Figure 9-5. Percentage of learners seeing technology as 'problem solving' or 'computers'

The overarching picture that emerges is that the learners who have experienced the project have been empowered by the experience, particularly the girls.

2.3.4   Pedagogic Impact: Empowerment and Transferability

None of the teachers involved in *North West Province Technology Education Project* had previous training in technology. The subjects they had experience of teaching varied from science to geography to Afrikaans. Those involved in retraining these teachers adopted the project pedagogy as the training methodology and interviews showed that this decision was a good one. Although challenging, teachers found the pedagogic shift to be ultimately transformative and liberating, as the following comments show.

> In technology you are not spoon-fed – there is no authority there – you are there to help not to control. ... Professionally I am a changed person. For 13 years I have never had such a laugh – and such joy. I feel completely part of the African renaissance. ... I have acquired innovative teaching methods, which are transferable to other subjects. (*NWPTEP* Teacher Interview database, schools 5, 7)

The learners echoed this sense of liberation and empowerment.

> In other lessons the teacher says what is right – in technology I find out. ... In other lessons you are on your own – we prefer to work together and share ideas. (*NWPTEP* Learner Interviews, schools 4 & 5)

Teachers also introduced the new pedagogy into other subjects they taught as they saw its benefits and described seeing their learners become independent thinkers who could contribute to their communities. Although very positive, teachers did identify problems with the support materials, seeing them as too rigid and prescriptive. We saw this ability to critique the project as further indication of their professional growth.

2.4   Concluding Comments

The findings from the project enabled us to wholeheartedly commend the project to the funders, with recommendations that it should be pursued by developing a comprehensive technology curriculum from Year 7 learners upwards. For the research team it brought insights into assessing groups and ways of sharing assessment practices, and importantly huge insights into the issues and possibilities of introducing a technology curriculum in such challenging circumstances. We were full of admiration for those that had initiated and implemented the project, particularly the project officer, the teachers and the learners.

3.   DESIGN MUSEUM OUTREACH EVALUATION (1999–2002)

3.1   Context

In the latter half of the 1990s the London Design Museum provided a strong education programme to support design & technology. With their long-standing belief in the importance of visual literacy and learning through objects, they responded to the inclusion of 'investigating, disassembling and evaluating activities' in the 1995 programmes of study by securing funding for two outreach programmes, the first utilising their *Mystery Loan Box*, the second focusing on *Architecture and the Built Environment*.

> Design affects us all. We live, work and play in a designed environment, with designed objects all around us. Yet in our everyday surroundings, we tend to stop looking and discovering, often taking familiar objects for granted. In the same way, when children look at a product they do not automatically 'see' or learn from it. Like reading, writing and numeracy, visual literacy needs to be taught. (Shaw, 1996, p. 1)

The *Mystery Box Outreach* was a 3-year venture, starting in 1997, involving 19 LEAs covering a broad geographical area and involving schools working in urban and rural settings. In 1999, TERU was commissioned to evaluate the impact of the project. The *Architecture and the Built Environment Outreach* introduced in 2001, built on the original initiative and we evaluated the introductory phase, using similar methodology. However, since in research terms the *Mystery Box Outreach* evaluation was the major venture, it is reported here.

3.2   Brief and Outline Methodology

The *Outreach* was set up with the overarching aims of providing innovative training that helped teachers plan and teach successful design projects using quality 'loan box' resources. In particular, they sought to create resources that supported confidence and competence in teachers and learners by providing a structure for disseminating good practice. TERU undertook to evaluate the extent to which the *Outreach* provided a 'best practice' model and:

- Raised confidence and competence in teachers
- Raised standards achieved by pupils
- Improve the use of handling collections, including those of local and national museum services

The *Mystery Box Outreach* was developed as a 'mini museum on wheels' and contained a range of high quality, tantalising and mysterious objects that were guaranteed to provoke curiosity in young learners.

Each LEA involved was provided with a Box and also INSET for each school. We gathered data from teachers and LEA personnel through questionnaires that required them to report their experience in some detail, by observing in-service training sessions and making a small number of school visits. In total, 112 teachers provided feedback. Data were collected on teacher demographics, reactions to the in-service training, the use of the resource in school and the long-term impact of the approach. Quantitative and qualitative data were collected, including five case studies drawn from across primary, secondary and special education sectors. The case studies illustrated the use of the *Mystery Loan Box*, and its longer-term impact (Figure 9-6).

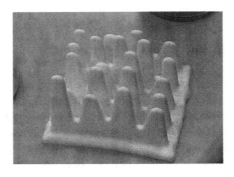

Figure 9-6. Examples from the Mystery Loan Box

3.3   Development Challenges and Significant Findings

3.3.1   The Importance of 'Hands-on' Experience

The *Outreach* was successful in a range of ways. There was noticeable impact on teachers' confidence and competence, particularly in primary and special schools. The in-service training sessions were particularly key in this. They were delivered with great enthusiasm and expertise and, as with the *North West Province Technology Education Project*, used a hands-on, discovery approach, replicating the model of practice being promoted for the classroom (Figure 9-7).

Figure 9-7. Hands-on experience for teachers

Questionnaire feedback and the case studies underscored how the 'detective' skills approach promoted by the project enabled development of observation, analysis and investigation skills. However, the teachers perceived the impact on children's **designing** to be far greater than on their **making** – possibly related to the teacher's own understanding of the collection's potential and something of a missed opportunity.

3.3.2   Support Provided for other Curriculum Areas

An unexpected finding was the way the collection supported other curriculum areas. The project was being undertaken at a time when primary teachers were under increasing pressure to teach subjects in a less integrated, less thematic way than had been the 'norm' and yet the evidence was that the handling collection promoted integration and enhanced learning in a range of curriculum areas, such as literacy, science, art and history. This finding played a significant role in creating a further initiative – *Enriching Literacy through Design & Technology* – reported later in this chapter.

3.3.3   Providing Access to High-Quality Handling Collections

Critical to the success of the *Mystery Box Outreach* were the artefacts included. The innovative nature of each item motivated less-confident teachers and engaged learners from reception classes to upper secondary. The approach enabled access to quality resources and the 'real-world' nature of the artefacts contributed to their success, encouraging children to think laterally and imaginatively. The collection provided a model for teachers to replicate, although the cost presented a barrier to some, highlighting the need to explore low or no cost collections with teachers.

3.4   Concluding Comments

The initiative provided genuine impetus for teachers to make more effective use of handling collections in their teaching. Using collections of carefully chosen items to provoke design thinking is a strategy we had used in a minor way in *APU Design & Technology*. This initiative refreshed the idea and we have made subsequent use in a range of projects such as *Enriching Literacy through Design & Technology* (later in this chapter) and also *Assessing Design Innovation* and *e-scape* (see Chapter 6).

4.   DESIGNERS IN ACTION EVALUATION (2001–2002)

4.1   Context

The *Designers in Action* initiative was a further Design Museum project, initiated in response to growing concerns over teachers' confidence and competence to enable creative responses in learners. This concern had been identified as a weakness by the Office for Standards in Education, who criticised this aspect of design & technology for being too linear, regimented and mechanistic and with

> many spend[ing] too much time on superfluous decoration of their design folders rather than on real design development. (Ofsted, 2002, para 2)

The Design Museum's approach was to engage practicing designers to run workshops with teachers, exploring the design company's approach to developing creative responses. A range of companies was involved, presenting different models of working, including Dyson, IDEO and Paul Smith. These hand-on workshops aimed to give teachers a real opportunity to get inside the 'mind' of the company and, in parallel, consider the curriculum and pedagogic issues the approaches presented. Once again TERU was commissioned to evaluate the initiative.

4.2 Brief and Outline Methodology

The *Designers in Action* workshops aimed to bridge the gap between education and the design industry, to stimulate teachers' own creativity giving them more confidence and strategies to adopt creative approaches in classrooms and to raise standards in design & technology teaching.

To evaluate the impact of the workshops we gathered data through pre- and post-workshop questionnaires, through observing the workshops and through interviewing a small number of designers, teachers and the Design Museum tutors. This enabled us to triangulate the data, and contrast views and insights from all parties.

The pre-workshop questionnaire enabled us to construct a demographic profile of participants in relation to gender, teaching experience, etc. and also their level of confidence in developing creative responses in learners. We also collected data on teachers' priorities for design & technology through their rating a list of design & technology aims (such as 'being practical', 'being innovators' and 'communicating ideas'). The same list was used after the workshop to gather data on what teachers considered to have been the strengths of the workshop.

4.3 Development Challenges and Significant Findings

4.3.1 Making Links Between Design Industry and Classrooms

Bringing designers and teachers into direct interaction involved an inevitable meeting of two distinctly different worlds. Important for success was ensuring that the activities stimulated and challenged the teachers in such a way that they could use the experience to enrich their own teaching. To manage this, the activities were originated by the designers, based on their own practices and mediated by the Design Museum staff. This had a dual lubricating effect; giving confidence to the designers that the tasks were appropriate to teachers and acting as intermediaries with the teachers, helping them tease out how to address classroom implementation issues and considering how to bring leading-edge design industry practice into the realm of schools and classrooms

4.3.2   The Importance of 'Hands-on' Learning

The designers all took a 'hands-on' approach to the workshops, directly engaging teachers in processes typical of the designers' studio practices. The teachers saw the success of the workshops lying in these hands-on experiences, giving them practical strategies and new modelling techniques. The impact of direct engagement echoed findings from other projects, not least the *North West Province Technology Education Project*, outlined earlier. From *Designers in Action*, one measure of the success was the increase in teachers' confidence that was manifest – 61% rating themselves as high or very high before the workshop, rising *dramatically* to 92% afterwards.

4.3.3   Using Designers' Approaches: Being Risky and Experimental

Designer brought with them their own designing 'flavour'. For example, one designer started by focusing attention on 'users' through picture profiles compiled from pictures taken (every hour of the day) by an unknown 'user'. The teachers were asked to build an image of the user from the illustrations in the photo profile. Who is the user? What do they value? How do they live their lives? What objects do they like? Whose life is this? The designer commented:

> Our special interest is in user-centred design. School projects seem removed from real clients. They are not grounded in reality. We taught them about human-centred design, with an empathetic project based on a disposable camera (IDEO designer). (Kimbell et al., 2002, p. 5)

The activity then moved to the challenge of 'can you design something for this user'?

> Then we taught them prototyping techniques – simple ones – from board to plastic – and more tricky ones like behaviour prototyping (IDEO designer). (Ibid. p. 5)

Overall, the designers' impression of design teaching in schools was that it is driven by different priorities, using different practices to those operating in industry. They drew out the following:

- It is not sufficiently 'real' (i.e. tasks are not based on real clients with real problems).
- It is not sufficiently questioning (i.e. briefs should be challenged and stretched, not just accepted).

- It is not sufficiently experimental (it remains on paper too long, then suddenly jumps to a final product).

The latter is a very important finding – designers used an iterative process of modelling, testing, refining and remodelling, seeing rapid-prototyping as being at the heart of their design development. The designers believed teachers saw experimentation as too risky a way of working because it is not given due credit in assessment systems at the GCSE and Advanced level examinations. They had the clear impression that teachers felt this approach was not 'allowed'. Encouraging the teachers to be risky and experimental in the workshops was key to their success.

> We try to inspire a more experimental hands-on approach – testing – curiosity – adventure – making things work – then making them work better. The teachers say they have to have beautifully made final pieces – even if they are not well designed. That seems daft (Dyson designer). (Ibid. p. 4)

The above quote highlights the distorted priority of 'playing safe' that the prevailing audit culture in schools has inflicted, and one that teachers are both aware of and constrained by, as can be seen by a comment from a teacher participant in the Dyson workshop.

> The 'look beautiful' syndrome in schools is crushing out real design – the stuff you find at Dyson. Assessment in schools is too rigid, making teachers direct students to safer outcomes. We need to give students knowledge about real world designs. (Ibid. p. 10)

4.4   Concluding Comments

The findings on growth in confidence and the value that teachers gave the workshops, showed the value teachers feel for working creatively and being innovative. But the research also evidenced the conflicting pressures teachers are under – of helping learners achieve high exam marks *and* helping them be creative. Teachers enthused about the value of practical engagement with a design ethic that is dramatically in contrast with the approaches that typify school-based (examination-oriented) designing. The priority given to spontaneity, quick thinking, quick modelling, instant trying-out and immediate modification as part of a process of iterative designing was warmly welcomed, and in many was echoed in later projects focused on creativity.

Although, in research terms, this evaluation was small scale, the significant emphasis on the contrasting practices of designing in industry and designing in classrooms was valuable in the impetus it gave for future work – not least *Assessing Design Innovation*.

5. ENERGY AND THE ENVIRONMENT EVALUATION (2001–2002)

5.1 Context

This project was a joint venture between the National Endowment for Science, Technology and the Arts (NESTA) and LEGO Education, combining NESTA's concern for creativity and innovation and LEGO's long-term commitment to hands-on learning. The two teamed up to develop materials to be used with 11–14-year-olds across the UK, based on a range of LEGO RoboLab and Mindstorm resources. These materials provided direct support to the 'system and control' element of design & technology. Ofsted reports had highlighted this area as having significant weaknesses and numbers taking the option at examination level were small. The LEGO resources were aimed at providing a stimulus to promote imagination and creativity and to inspire the learners sufficiently to encourage them to continue to engage with systems and control beyond the age of 14. TERU was commissioned to evaluate the impact the resources had in the classroom.

5.2 Brief and Outline Methodology

The LEGO materials comprised three linked resources: a kit of bricks and components, including 'programmable' bricks; supporting assembly guides; and a curriculum linking the above to KS3 design & technology.

NESTA's requirement from the evaluation was that we should assess the extent to which the materials and associated teaching and learning processes:

- Created interest and enthusiasm for teachers and learners in systems and control, and encouraged more students to take the option for the General Certificate for Secondary Education
- Encouraged creativity and innovation in the curriculum
- Encouraged cross-disciplinary work related to energy and the environment

We structured the research into three phases. Phase 1 utilised interviews, questionnaires and school visits to establish baselines of teachers' practice with systems and control and LEGO and their views on what fosters and inhibits creativity. Phase 2 looked at the reality in classrooms, through observing activities and interviewing teachers and learners. Phase 3 reflected on the project, drawing on teacher interviews, questionnaires and presentations on the projects undertaken, made at a plenary conference organised by LEGO for the end of the project.

Lesson observation drew on methodology developed through the *Understanding Technological Approaches* project (see Chapter 7) and took place on a sample basis – each school was visited to observe a project in its latter stages and in addition three schools were visited more frequently – early in the project, in the middle, and then again near the end.

At the conclusion of the project the teachers completed the same creativity questionnaire they had completed before the start, so that we could explore changes in viewpoints.

5.3 Development Challenges and Significant Findings

5.3.1 Adapting Tools and Methodology

Much of the methodology outlined above was based on approaches used in previous projects and adapting research tools proved relatively straight-forward. The exception was the observation of activities – which presented a challenge as the schools involved were geographically distanced from each other and from Goldsmiths. Funding allowed for only limited visiting. *Understanding Technological Approaches* (Chapter 7) provided a useful observation tool – the challenge was to adapt the model to the resources available and still gain insightful data. In the *UTA* project the aim had been to track the detailed approaches of **individual learners** through the life of a project – in this *LEGO* project we were using observation to gain insights into how the resource was used. Consequently, we adapted features of the *Understanding Technological Approaches* model to provide a 'dip-stick' we could use at different stages of a project to gain an overview of use and also to provide cameos that characterised certain aspects. This approach allowed us, for example, to identify characteristic ways in which teachers made use of LEGO guidance in the early stages of projects and then abandoned it once things were up and running. It also allowed us to identify that teacher 'direction' – which was a major pedagogic feature at Key Stage 3 in the *Understanding Technological Approaches* project, was contrastingly low in this project – teachers devoting on average 83% of their time in a 'supportive' role as the materials enabled more autonomous approaches by the learners.

5.3.2 Views on Creativity

About creativity, at the start there was a strong sense that teachers equated the term with **problem solving, risk taking, thinking laterally** and **using imagination**. From responses to the questionnaire completed **after** the project some shift in views about creativity was seen (Figure 9-8). Problem solving was still the strongest factor, but beyond this, 'risk taking', 'using imagination' and 'lateral thinking' were superseded by **spontaneity, chance and enthusiasm** – all things teachers witnessed in learners during the project.

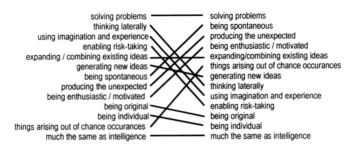

solving problems ———————— solving problems
thinking laterally   being spontaneous
using imagination and experience   producing the unexpected
enabling risk-taking   being enthusiastic / motivated
expanding / combining existing ideas   expanding/combining existing ideas
generating new ideas   things arising out of chance occurances
being spontaneous   generating new ideas
producing the unexpected   thinking laterally
being enthusiastic / motivated   using imagination and experience
being original   enabling risk-taking
being individual   being original
things arising out of chance occurances   being individual
much the same as intelligence ———————— much the same as intelligence

Figure 9-8. Comparing 'before' and 'after' responses to the creativity questionnaire

Teachers also identified 'promoters' of creativity that emerged, such as a 'play' element, 3D modelling potential and the speed at which ideas can be realised. Interestingly, the project appeared to be a catalyst to spur teachers to think **differently** and, possibly, less stereotypically about creativity.

5.3.3   Using the LEGO Resource

But while teachers identified ways in which LEGO kits supported creativity, it was also clear that this did not extend to the support materials. These were generally seen to act in the opposite way.

> In all probability the worksheets and the guides hinder creativity … they [the learners] tend to produce what they see. … The paperwork is certainly not a help. (Kimbell et al., 2002, p. 18)

Much of the learner support came in the form of step-by-step construction guides, which learners dutifully followed and which we came to term the 'LEGO Zone'. Creativity only came into play when the learners broke out of this Zone, at which point the guides were abandoned. What we witnessed was a clear conflict between the direction dictated by the resource and the refreshing actions of teachers wanting to run projects in their own free-wheeling way. The teacher support material took the form of an extensive curriculum folder (developed in the USA) that the teachers simply did not find helpful. The acid test was whether teachers would use the materials in the future – and here the typical response was yes, but on their own terms.

It will be integrated into all year groups (at KS3) but as shorter projects … what they did this year was too long and didn't sustain their interest. We will use bits and adapt it to our own needs. (Ibid. p. 28)

5.3.4 Enthusiasm for 'Systems and Control'

At the outset of the project teachers' views on **systems and control** exemplified the received wisdom from the Office for Standards in Education and others about the lack of enthusiasm amongst learners – it did not excite them and it did not encourage creativity. By the end of the project we were able to report that LEGO had the potential to turn this situation round. Its 'concrete' nature enabled learners to get to grips with systems and control concepts and rapidly model ideas. We also highlighted as strengths the quality of the 'kit' – the fact that all parts mesh together well, removing the frustration component that can kill enthusiasm in systems and control projects, and the way the foolproof construction guides freed the teacher to take a support role to the learner.

5.4 Concluding Comments

As with *Designers in Action*, this project added to our understandings of how teachers see creativity and how it can be enhanced or inhibited in a learning context. The project also highlighted the impact an underlying pedagogic approach can have on the potential value of a learning resource. LEGO kits have timeless and proven ability as imaginative, fun, motivating learning 'toys' – and these qualities held true in this project. But attempting to introduce a project pedagogy that was too tightly constraining, threatened the very strengths highlighted above. An interesting comparison is provided by the lock-step nature of the 'unpickled portfolio' approach to project assessment which seems to have the opposite effect – and this will be discussed further in Part Three.

6. CAD-IN-SCHOOLS EVALUATION (2000–2001)

6.1 Context

The introduction of CAD and CAM into schools in the late 1990s had been slow and steady but did not match the expectations of Curriculum 2000. Two problems held back developments: costs and training. DATA's launch of *CAD-in-schools* with ProDESKTOP software, heralded a new era for schools as the initiative made available to schools state-of-the-art software and a nationally established training programme. But, while CAD was seen as having huge potential in schools, no research had been conducted into the impact of this new 'tool' on the design capability of learners. At TERU we suspected that the impact would be sufficiently profound to deserve careful research. DATA and PTC (the software producers) agreed with this and we were commissioned to undertake a small-scale exploration into the matter.

6.2   Brief and Outline Methodology

The research was small scale and anticipated providing insights and questions rather than answers. We set out to explore how using CAD-affected capability, its potential for learning, and staff development issues. To undertake the study we conducted:

- Performance assessment, comparing learners' responses to a design task using either the CAD software or more traditional paper and pencil
- Teacher and learner interviews about the strengths, weaknesses and potential of using the software

The performance assessment was based on an original 'developing solutions' *APU Design & Technology* test, undertaken **either** as a 'normal' paper and pencil design activity **or** as a CAD activity using ProDESKTOP. Based on the design weaknesses of 'built-in' cooker timers, the activity invited learners to design a portable cooking timer for use by the elderly. In both 'paper and pencil' and 'CAD' modes the activity took 90 min. The task was the same, the procedures were the same and the assessment processes were the same. In the 'CAD' mode learners saved their work at intervals so that a record could be pasted into a paper booklet – in which the written (reflective) elements of the activity were undertaken. The activities were conducted with Year 9 and Year 10 learners (14- and 15-year-olds), who were identified as having had high quality design & technology experiences either **with** or **without** ProDESKTOP. The CAD-in-Schools initiative was new and consequently the sample meeting these criteria for CAD was small: in total four schools and 62 learners were involved. The learners undertaking the activity also completed a questionnaire inviting them to agree/disagree (across a 1–4 Likert scale) with statements about the activity and designing in ProDESKTOP and to identify the best and worst things about working in ProDESKTOP.

Parallel interviews were undertaken with groups of learners and individual teachers, including in additional schools recommended for their good practice. Questions included experience, pleasure and confidence in using ProDESKTOP; difficulties, benefits and advice to newcomers; and potential impact on the future of design & technology. Teachers were also asked about the ProDESKTOP training; and impact on developing capability.

6.3   Development Challenges and Significant Findings

6.3.1   Attempts at Creating a 'Virtual' Portfolio

The *APU Design & Technology* test structures and response booklets had been developed to maximise the impact on designing of adopting an iterative process of action and reflection. The ease, provided by a pencil, of moving between drawing and written notes facilitated this iteration. So with half of the learners working on computers, we explored ways of replicating this experience using the software. The lack of facility for adding notes within ProDESKTOP, coupled with complications for the learner of using two pieces of software in tandem (to say nothing of the tendency for the computer to crash) resulted in us finally creating a paper portfolio, similar to the *APU* test booklet, that was used for the reflective elements of the activity, into which we pasted printed images of the stages of product development from ProDESKTOP.

6.3.2   Differences in Performance

Although the samples were small, there were clear indications that performance in the paper and pencil format was better than in the CAD format – by a factor of approximately 15–20%. This was most marked in reflective areas such as identifying issues and evaluating and in communication, including communicating what was going on 'inside' the product. The ease with which paper and pencil allowed learners to iterate between thought and action, reflecting and annotating their designing as it progressed provided a flexibility not achieved by those working in CAD (Figures 9-9 and 9-10). As with any new 'language', fluency in CAD had not come quickly and learners showed evidence of being preoccupied by addressing issues of using the software, rather than those related to their design ideas. Two examples of work are shown here – both typical of the work produced in their respective modes.

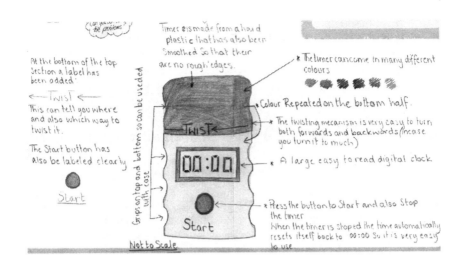

Figure 9-9. Example of work from the 'paper and pencil' mode

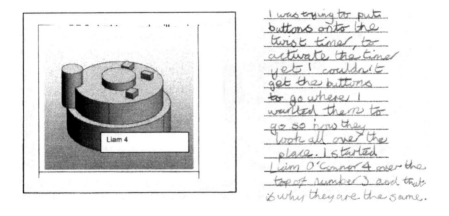

Figure 9-10. Example of work from the 'CAD' mode

6.3.3   Learners' Paradoxical Viewpoints

Through interviews and questionnaires, learners told us clearly that ProDESKTOP enabled accurate, professional presentation of work, helped them to visualise ideas and was 'easy to use'. At the same time, they told us it was stressful and confusing, would not let them do what they wanted and that the instructions were not good enough. But in the struggle between the frustration and seduction as a designing tool, the latter was the clear winner.

6.3.4 Training Teachers and the Conundrum of the Cascade

Training teachers to use the new software was developed as a 'cascade' system – a national training centre was initially created, and those involved in the first phase of training, once certificated, could set up regional and local training centres. This type of 'cascade' model is common, but often seen as a compromise between the ideal of receiving training directly from the first generation 'expert' and the pragmatism of taking large numbers of people through the training. But we encountered a curious twist – as there was evidence that the further the 'trainee' was down the cascade tree, the more satisfied they were with the training. A consistent criticism of the training at the first level of cascade was that it dealt with the potential of the software in technical design terms, but was not centred on classroom practice and did not address pedagogic issues. But as the training was cascaded, those experiencing the 'pedagogic-free' training mediating it through their own classroom experience before interacting with other teachers. However, despite such difficulties, teachers were overwhelmingly supportive of the initiative and what it offered to learners and to the subject as a whole.

6.4 Concluding Comments

It is important to remember that this project was undertaken when the use of CAD was still in its infancy in schools. It is probably fair to say we entered into it as 'healthy skeptics' – and some of our skepticism was confirmed, as the performance activity demonstrated. But we also could not deny the motivation and optimism created, amongst learners and teachers, and the undeniable view that **learners** articulated about the value of CAD for ideation. With hindsight, and the experience of the *e-scape* project fresh in our minds, this project provided the impetus for the later challenges presented by *e-scape*, not least the ongoing search for the holy grail of creating an effective 'dialogue' model of an e-design portfolio.

7. ROBOTEERS IN RESIDENCE EVALUATION (2002–2004)

7.1 Context

As with the LEGO project, this project had links to the systems and control component of the design & technology curriculum, but took an entirely different model – that of the 'artist in residence' – replacing 'artist' with 'roboteer'. The initiative, created by BBC 'Factual and Learning' and also funded by NESTA, was linked to the BBC's Techno Games series and proposed a series of residences involving five roboteers working with schools through Further Education College 'hubs' across the UK – two in England, and one each in Scotland, Northern Ireland and Wales. The project was provoked by a desire to explore deeper opportunities for learning about robots, both for fun and in real life. Original plans had all schools involved taking part in the BBC's Techno Games series. But the series was withdrawn half way through the residences, so as an alternative end point for the project, regional competitions were held and finalists were showcased at the Young Scientist and Technology Exhibition in Dublin.

7.2   Brief and Outline Methodology

The project aimed to show how deploying the skills, energy and ideas of expert roboteers could initiate a deep interest and involvement in robotics among learners in the 14–18 age group, and to provide high-quality, face to face learning opportunities. The evaluation addressed these aims.

The sample was chosen to include for each region a Further Education centre of excellence to act as a hub and four or five linked local secondary schools. The data collection methods were similar to those in earlier projects – questionnaires, interviews, observation and photographic and written recording. Data was collected from the roboteers, teachers and learners through three school visits, the first collecting background data, the second collecting data on work in progress and the third collecting outcome data.

7.3   Significant Findings

Overall there was no doubt that the specified aims of this project were met. The roboteers provided a high-quality experience enabling learners to grapple enthusiastically with highly complex technological challenges, creating a far deeper interest and involvement with robotics than hitherto. As a result some changed their career aspirations, one learner even going directly onto a mechatronics degree programme. Experienced teachers extended their knowledge, skill and confidence. Head teachers were enthusiastic about the impact in their schools. From the data it was clear that a number of factors contributed to this success.

7.3.1   The Enthusiasm, Skill and Teaching Style of the Roboteers

The pedagogic approaches of roboteers were excellent and seemed intuitive (none were trained teachers). For all, their approach centred on engaging the learners through curiosity and inquisitiveness, making good use of questioning and hands on exploration and introducing knowledge on a need-to-know basis. This provoked high levels of engagement from the learners who were particularly motivated by working with and controlling the robots and challenged by the opportunity of making one. Teamwork and peer support were encouraged and cooperation, communication and encouragement were frequently observed amongst the learners as they took responsibility for their own learning. The success of teamwork was identified by the learners as being one of the most impressive aspects of the project. A further contributor was the attitude of the roboteers and their expectations of the learners. What was interesting was the emphasis placed on personal and human characteristics, such as teamwork, enthusiasm and stickability, above subject-based knowledge and skill – and the empowering culture this attitude created.

7.3.2   Factors Hindering Success

The project was immensely successful but there were hindering factors, mostly related to practical and logistic problems. First was the use of Further Education colleges as hubs. The flaw in this model was that it assumed strong links between schools and Further Education providers that, by and large, were not present causing major coordination problems. Other logistic problems included the physical dislocation of key players that resulted, for example, in roboteers travelling long distances and problems in matching school and college timetables.

A second critical hindrance was the withdrawal of the Techno Games opportunity – which caused a major (albeit temporary) setback in motivation leaving the teachers and roboteers to manage the disappointment felt within the school communities.

7.4   Concluding Comments

As with *Designers in Action*, this project was an example of involving professionals to bring new approaches into classrooms – this time working with the learners as well as the teachers. Again, interacting with professionals improved teachers' confidence in a challenging area (this time systems and control). The resounding strength of the project was the roboteers themselves – giving a clear message about the potential of the 'professional in residence' model. In the words of one of the evaluators:

> The roboteers are super heroes. ... They are in a league all of their own. They come to the schools with a wealth of experience, accumulated from industry, tinkering with motorbikes and go karts, and from playing with

all sort of mechanical gadgetry. ... They just know this stuff and they are full of it. (Kimbell et al., 2004, p. 29)

8.   ENRICHING LITERACY THROUGH DESIGN & TECHNOLOGY EVALUATION (1999–2001)

8.1   Context

The development of the English National Literacy Strategy in 1998 coincided with evidence emerging from the Design Museum's *Mystery Box Outreach Programme* that engaging children in design & technology activities linked to handling collections had the added value of supporting the development of literacy, particularly in the areas of speaking and listening. The Education Officer leading this project moved to an independent consultancy (Bluefish) and developed a complete resource for teaching design & technology and literacy, through the use of handling collections, with direct links to the requirements of the literacy hour. Funding to engage with such projects was being made available through a Government initiative – that of the Education Action Zones (EAZ) – created to provide additional support for schools in areas of economic deprivation where standards in schools were well below average. One such EAZ (in North East England) saw the Bluefish initiative as having potential to raise standards in literacy in their primary schools and commissioned Bluefish to undertake an intervention project and TERU to evaluate its impact in the 1st year.

8.2   Brief and Outline Methodology

The **intervention project** worked with Year 2 and Year 6 teachers from six primary schools. Teachers attended a series of training sessions, were provided with classroom materials for design & technology and literacy-linked activities, including a 'handling collection' of products for children to interact with, evaluate and redesign, textual materials for use in the literacy hour and guidance for developing literacy skills within design & technology activities. They also received a small amount of classroom support.

   The **evaluation project** had two primary aims – exploring effects on the teachers' confidence, competence and practice in teaching literacy and design & technology and assessing the performance of the children in literacy and design & technology. The evaluation also explored:

- Extent to which design & technology and literacy could be effectively linked in the classroom
- Impact of the literacy hour on design & technology curriculum time
- Impact of using handling collections on teachers' practice
- Developing an assessment tool for literacy **and** design & technology
- Potential for using such an assessment tool with young children

Bluefish aimed to increase literacy levels by 'at least 10%'. We saw this as problematic, as it was not clear what baseline Bluefish was using. Our approach to exploring impact was to establish a comparative control group (from the same catchment with similar challenges) and then to identify differences in performance that might be attributed to the intervention.

To gauge the effects on teachers involved, two main strategies were employed: first, to conduct a 'state-of-readiness' questionnaire with all teachers and second, to conduct in-depth, semi-structured interviews with each teacher in the intervention schools. Teacher interviews focused on:

- Teacher's background and role within the school
- Teaching and learning literacy and design & technology
- Value of using 'handling collections'
- Quality of support provide during the year
- Value of the project to the teacher, the children and the school
- Implementation and development ideas and issues

Evidence of the children's performance was provided through an assessment activity once again derived from the *APU* 'unpickled portfolio' approach. In addition, for literacy, baseline data was collected from National Curriculum Standard Assessment Tasks. The assessment activity utilised a simple handling collection with complementary literacy and design & technology elements. The intervention group was assessed at the start and end of the school year, the control group only at the end of the year, resources not permitting an earlier test for these children. The Year 2 activities were based around clothes pegs and greetings cards, the Year 6 also around clothes pegs and lunch boxes. Each activity lasted approximately 75 min, involving predominantly individual work. Not all aspects of literacy or design & technology were assessed: the literacy assessment focusing on writing and the design & technology assessment on designing. The children's attitudes to the activities were gauged through an evaluation questionnaire. To enable indicative comparisons with the general population we compared current and previous years' SAT results from the schools with LEA and national levels.

8.3   Development Challenges and Significant Findings

8.3.1   Engaging Young Children in the Activities

This project was our first attempt at using the 'unpickled portfolio' assessment approach with very young children – previously, the youngest involved had been Year 6 learners in *Wholes and Parts*. We had the experience of *CATS KS1 Technology* to draw on and were aware of the value of engaging young children through handling collections and the potency of storytelling to help them understand and empathise with the concept of 'client'. Our approach is exemplified through the 'what a surprise' task, in which Year 2 learners (aged 6 and 7) were asked to design a surprise greeting card for someone they missed. The *APU* approach of an unfolding response booklet and administrator's script were retained (although the booklet size was reduced). The task was contextualised through the story of 'Amy' whose best friend had gone to stay with cousins. We also provided two handling collections – a set of 'surprise' birthday cards and a set of neutral concept models of paper 'pop-up' mechanisms.

The children found no trouble engaging with this task, as was demonstrated by the evaluation questionnaires completed. Asking young children to evaluate an activity was also new territory, but building on the ubiquitous 'smiley face' approach, we found them more than able to do so (Figure 9-11).

Figure 9-11. The smiley face scoring system

8.3.2   Developing Boys' Reflective Skills

The central positioning of 'handling collections' in the intervention project was key to success. Teachers pinpointed how exploring the collections sharpened analytical skills and the way product analysis, planning and sequencing work and evaluation were scaffolded across a range of projects as the year progressed. The assessment data indicated that this was a key contributor to the development of reflective skills, particularly in boys. From

APU Design & Technology onwards boys had generally demonstrated less well developed skills in this respect. In this project, comparisons between the performance of the intervention and control groups showed that, while the intervention group boys had higher levels of performance across all aspects, in the reflective elements the differences were most marked, with Year 6 boys scoring significantly higher on identifying user needs, evaluating their own procedures and product analysis.

8.3.3   The 'Added Value' *of* and *for* Design & Technology

It was evident that the project has made an important and valuable contribution to the children, their teachers and their schools. In respect of Bluefish's aim of a 10% increase in literacy skills, matters were less clear cut, although the intervention group did generally 'outscore' the control group, even though the control schools had higher SAT attainment. What was interesting was the aspects of literacy that were stronger in the intervention group – 'writing for the reader' and 'genre' – both elements one might expect to develop well when children are writing 'in context' – in this instance the rich context of the design scenario. The impact on boys was notably positive, for example, Year 2 boys outperformed both boys **and** girls in the control schools in 'genre'. There was also evidence from teacher interviews that working through the medium of design & technology had impacted positively on personal attributes such as patience and collaboration and on the development of transferable skills, most noticeably reflection.

The 'added value' **for** design & technology was the way design & technology was 'mainstreamed' in the curriculum of the Year 2 and Year 6 classes at a time when subjects beyond literacy and numeracy were having to fight hard for curriculum time, as was evidenced through the Office for Standards in Education inspections.

> The depth and breadth of design and technology activities have reduced this year. In a minority of schools design & technology has almost disappeared'. (Ofsted, 2001, p. 1)

The children's performance in design & technology showed categorically the value of engaging children in a broad, well-structured programme – the intervention group outperforming the control group in every aspect assessed.

8.4   Concluding Comments

This project was our first use of the 'unpickled portfolio' performance assessment with young children and provided the team with important insights into how to do this successfully. It also provided a new perspective on gender issues related to active and reflective dimensions of capability, particularly in terms of supporting boys to develop reflective skills. Despite being a small-scale study, it provided evidence to vindicate the inclusion of design & technology in the curriculum, not only for the important aim of developing design & technological capability, but also for the added value it brings more generally as a curriculum integrator and enhancer.

EMERGING ISSUES AND UNDERSTANDINGS

It is important for readers to understand some of the dynamics of the story contained in this book. We described in the introduction to Part Two the critical role that those projects played in developing our understanding about research. So it is perhaps not surprising that these project descriptions should precede Part Three – where we summarise what we now understand about learning, designing and so on. But more than that, we could not have written Part One when we launched our first major research venture in the mid-1980s. It was as we struggled with the hard reality of **doing** the research that we were increasingly driven to articulate the principles around which we were intuitively shaping it. The more we sought to articulate these principles (typically in drawings and diagrams), the better we were able to understand the research processes on which we were engaged. So whilst Part One serves as a useful introduction to our research ventures, in reality it (at least in this explicitly articulated form) has been a **product** of them.

So too has been this Part Three. If Part Two was a selected and heavily edited set of accounts of the 20 projects we have undertaken, Part Three explores some of the **issues** that have forced themselves to the surface in many of the projects. Some of the titles of the chapters look similar to those in Part One and again this should be no surprise since in many ways Parts Three and One were conceived in parallel. In retrospect, it has been possible for us to separate them out; to distinguish what were essentially our tacit starting-point beliefs from our subsequent, evidence-based understandings. The ideas in Part Three therefore draw heavily from the empirical evidence presented in Part Two and we have organised the evidence into five groupings:

- Activities and tasks
- Learning and teaching
- Assessment
- Learner difference
- Research methodology

Chapter 10

PROCESSES, ACTIVITIES AND TASKS

Why you might find this chapter interesting

*We open this chapter by analysing the activity of designing to explain our dissatisfaction with the models that we had inherited at the outset of our work. We present an alternative view of the process that emerges in part through our use of designing as a **pedagogic** vehicle rather than merely as a means of product development.*

*This pedagogic lens through which we view designing has a number of crucial consequences. It enables us to see 'making' and 'modelling' in a particular light; it asserts the value of the portfolio as a device to underpin the meta-cognitive growth of learners; it enables learners to see themselves as in charge of their own learning; and it enables them to situate themselves through the eyes of others – specifically their clients. We conclude the chapter by analysing the nature of **design tasks** using this explicitly pedagogic lens. How is the responsibility for task design to be shared between teachers and learners, and what are the consequences for the learning experience?*

***

1.   INADEQUATE MODELS OF PRACTICE

One of the recurring challenges of the last few decades – whilst we have been working on TERU projects – has been the need for clarity in what is involved in **doing** design & technology. We discussed in Chapter 5 some of the many attempts at describing the activity that proliferated through the

1970s and 1980s, all containing (broadly) the same features and all connected with sequential arrows representing (broadly) the same flow of the project. It was into this tradition that we were ourselves inducted, and it was these models of activity that we inherited when we launched *APU Design & Technology* in 1985.

Our difficulty with these process descriptions were many and profound, and arose even at the assumed starting point for activity; i.e. 'the problem'. The descriptions operated within what might be termed a 'problem solving' paradigm. But, for us, there are problems with the paradigm itself and three of the projects that we have described in Part Two illustrate our concern.

In Chapter 8, we described the two Design Council projects *Decision by Design* and *Design Skills for Work*. In the former, we had our own (Goldsmiths) graduate design students interacting with non-designers (school managers) and in the latter we interacted directly with design students and their tutors in many other design courses in higher education institutions. In Chapter 9, we described the Design Museum project *Designers in Action* in which leading-edge practising designers acted as tutors for design teachers in schools to help them to enliven their teaching of design.

Wherever we have observed the interaction of design practitioners with design & technology teachers in schools, we have noted the serious dislocation of their models of practice. In *Designers in Action*, the designers summarised their views in the following terms; design teaching in schools is not sufficiently **real**, nor sufficiently **questioning, nor sufficiently experimental**. The designers talked of 'wicked' tasks, 'risky' thinking, 'playing' with reality, 'imaging' possibilities and 'modelling' futures. By contrast the models of practice we inherited through the birth pangs of design & technology illustrate a pedestrian pursuit of 'solutions' to 'problems'. The cultures are worlds apart. As Buchanan (1995, p. 17) puts it, 'the problem for designers is to conceive and plan what does not yet exist' and this creative projection into the future is only very inadequately described as problem solving in the science-like school of inductive reasoning. Rather designers use exploratory and analytic heuristics.

This might be thought enough of a reason to throw out the notion of 'problem solving' as an appropriate paradigm for debating design. But there is a further reason, which is simply that not all design activity arises from problems. Sometimes opportunities arise that designers simply grasp and capitalise upon. The digital watch is an example. There was absolutely nothing wrong with analogue watches – they were (and still are) sought after and desired. But when a new technology presented itself it was just too good an opportunity to miss. Designers created all kinds of new watches, not because of a **problem**, but because an **opportunity** was available.

2.   DESIGNING AS A DYNAMIC PROCESS

Our concern with the early descriptions of designing might be summarised by noting that they were essentially behavioural and did not get anywhere near to capturing the important essence of the cognitive processes that are involved. As an example, one of the labels in the process was typically 'investigation', in which learners were expected to investigate the background issues or factors that inform the design task. So when designing a child's toy, learners would perhaps be expected to **investigate** young children's cognitive development (how toys help learning), compile anthropometric data (e.g. hand size), talk to parents about what they normally buy (consumer trends), etc. This **investigation** data was then presented on several sheets of the portfolio, and these sheets were then seen as a measure of learners' investigative capability.

When we began *APU Design & Technology*, the project-portfolio system was familiar to us as teachers. We had lived with it for years and knew how it worked. But we also knew that it had the effect of transforming a dynamic creative process (investiga**ting**) into a formulaic set of outcomes in a design folder (**an** investigation).

In our projects we have continually sought to deal with this problem by finding ways to focus attention on the **dynamic unfolding activity**, and playing down the prettied-up potential of final outcomes. The unpickled portfolio (see Chapter 5) has been our generic strategy and, the first project undertaken by TERU (*APU*) and our current project (*e-scape*) illustrate our continuing efforts to examine the dynamic intellectual processes of design and development rather than any post hoc post-rationalised story of the activity.

Whilst the iterative model that evolved from our *APU* work was unfamiliar (and therefore unsettling) to teachers at the time, it did match exactly with the view of invention characterised by Gorman and Carlson in their analysis of a considerably earlier innovation – the telephone. In this analysis, Gorman and Carlson had reconstructed the same dynamic cognitive processes, as used by Alexander Graham Bell and Thomas Edison when they invented the telephone.

> [T]he innovation process is much better characterised as a recursive activity in which inventors move back and forth between ideas and objects. Inventors may start with one mental model and modify it after experimentation with different mechanical representations, or they may start out with several mechanical representations and gradually shape a mental model. In both cases, the essence of invention seems to be the dynamic interplay of mental models with mechanical representations. (Gorman and Carlson, 1990, p. 159)

In the *e-scape* project we have tackled the very same problem that we see arising through the proliferation of e-portfolios. The concept of e-portfolio that is so often presented is one in which learners do their designing on paper and then present their prettied-up e-portfolio by selective scanning and other forms of digital 'touching up' – in PowerPoint or some other graphic or presentation software package. By contrast we have created an *e-scape* system that allows learners dynamically to build their web-based portfolio by direct iterations with hand-held digital tools. Just as with paper portfolios, our concern with the evolving iterative process results in portfolios that may not be so pretty, but the information that can be gleaned from them tells us far more about learners' designing processes.

3.   REDEFINING 'MAKING' AS *MODELLING*

Another dimension of the constraint that design teachers in schools feel obliged to cope with is the strange place that is characteristically accorded to modelling. Custom and practice dictates that models are allowed once the ideas have been sorted out and before we start making the real thing. We imagine that this idea of a process of designing originated (in someone's mind) because prototypes do typically precede production. But this misses the central point about the power of modelling as **idea development**. As Gorman and Carlson point out, the essence of invention seems to be 'the dynamic interplay of mental models with mechanical representations'.

For *APU Design & Technology* we sought to illustrate how ideas conceived in the mind's eye need to be expressed in concrete form before they can be examined to see how useful they are.

> It is our contention that this inter-relationship between modelling ideas in the mind, and modelling ideas in reality is the cornerstone of capability in design and technology. (Kimbell et al. 1991, p. 21)

This view of modelling has profound consequences for design & technology, effectively reconfiguring the concept of 'making' that lies at the heart of our collective history. Design & technology grew from essentially craft traditions. In craft activities, **making** is everything. The aim is to make; the activity is making; and the outcome is made. Not surprisingly therefore, **making** has played a big part in the debates about the formation of design & technology. In the 1995 version of the National Curriculum, design & technology was seen as having two attainment targets 'designing' and 'making', and in assessments for General Certificate for Secondary Education and Advanced levels, there are seen to be two assessment objectives; 'designing' and 'making'.

Our view of the activity – based on the values we articulated in Part One and emerging progressively through our experience of the projects – sits uncomfortably with these separations. Since we take the view that modelling is to be seen as the **progressive representation of ideas**, we cannot see how you could slide a cigarette paper between the ideas of designing and modelling. We are interested in all the forms of making that learners demonstrate in their activity, including what might be regarded at the finally emerging prototype.

In our projects we have always sought to embody this notion of making as part of the journey, and perhaps the best example was in *Assessing Design Innovation* (Chapter 6). There, we explicitly encouraged making (modelling) activities as a natural part of the designing process, and found ways to enable students to record their modelling through a photo-storyline. Subsequently, through *e-scape*, the recording was further enhanced through voice-memo annotation. These processes were hugely popular with the learners, widely applauded by teachers and invaluable as aids to the assessment process.

> Students *enjoyed* the challenge. Great atmosphere in the room. Students were totally engaged for the majority of the time. Loved the photographs! Teacher AMJ (Kimbell et al. 2004, p. 34)

> Using your own ideas; making models instead of drawing – they work better. Learner AB314. (Ibid. p. 37)

At the end of *Assessing Design Innovation* we could report to the sponsors:

> We strongly recommend that teachers be encouraged to see 'modelling' as one kind of 'making'; as prototyping; as provisional; as a means of learners thinking through their ideas. This kind of making needs to be understood as very different from the kinds of quality manufacturing that is appropriate once the ideas have all been fully resolved. (Ibid. p. 62)

Since our first articulation of the iterative *APU Design & Technology* process we have argued that all kinds of modelling go toward the evolution of a resolution:

- Visual modelling – through sketches
- Written modelling – through annotations
- Verbal modelling – through discussion
- Numerical modelling – through calculations
- Material modelling – developing 3D representations

Sometimes this modelling is future oriented, seeking to conceptualise the new. Sometimes it is just a way of 'talking' to yourself – or to a colleague. Sometimes it has a more reflective purpose, checking out how things might behave if they had these new components organised in this way. If we were looking for labels to distinguish these kinds of modelling, we might use 'concept-modelling' for the initial conceptualising drive and 'proving modelling' for the more reflective intent. Sometimes these purposes are wrapped up together in a single model. In any event they are part of the dynamic development process that Gorman and Carlson described and that we sought to embody.

This process has been described by others, including Archer and Roberts (1992)

> The conduct of design activity is made possible by the existence in man of a distinctive capacity of mind ... the capacity for cognitive modelling. ... (The designer) forms images 'in the minds eye' of things and systems as they are, or as they might be. ... Its strength is that light can be shed on intractable problems by transforming them into terms of all sorts of schemata ... such as drawings, diagrams, mock-ups, prototypes and of course, where appropriate, language and notation. ... These externalisations capture and make communicable the concepts modelled. (Archer and Roberts, 1992, p. 4)

4.   META-COGNITIVE DESIGNING

Seen in this form the designing activity is a uniquely public way of thinking, and the trace that is left behind in model form should be a powerful means for unpicking learners' thinking processes. For what we are doing when we design in this way is to lay out our thinking for all to see. If 'others' can see my thinking, then maybe I too (the designer/originator) can be helped **to see my own thinking**. I can accordingly become self-aware of my own thinking processes, and in the language of cognitive science this is meta-cognition.

> [A] design portfolio is a device that makes explicit the thought process of the designer. And in the process of making the thinking explicit it enables thinking to expand and develop. Portfolios lay bare the thinking of the designer. And this essential concreteness makes possible the development of the ability to stand outside oneself and look in upon one's own designing and reasoning. (Kimbell et al., 1998, p. 56)

Whilst at one level the portfolio might be seen as a **product development** tool as ideas in the minds of designers are externalised as discussions, drawings, models and objects, in **learning** terms it is also critically a **thinking** tool. Meta-cognitive awareness of one's thinking involves more than just being able to do it and requires being self-aware *as* one is doing it. Almost sitting outside oneself watching it happen. The criticality of meta-cognition for learning is widely acknowledged in the literature on learning (see, e.g. Donovan et al., 1999) and whilst it is quite possible to develop such meta-cognitive awareness in any discipline, it is particularly easy in designing activities. This is because the thinking does not just sit inside the learners head – but exists also in the external (portfolio/model) form.

It was in *Design Skills for Work* (see Chapter 8) that we uncovered an illustration of what happens when this meta-cognitive awareness is ignored and designing is projected as merely a set of behaviours. The surprise for us arose when we interviewed design students from a number of design courses as part of *the Design Skills for Work* project. Somewhat unnervingly, we found them **unable** to articulate the breadth of capabilities that they possessed. They said they could 'do design', but were unable to see how this capability might be cashed out into the full range of qualities that it contains. In discussion with their design tutors the reason became apparent. Tutors themselves were not using any language to articulate these qualities. All too frequently the students that we interviewed tended to see the skills and qualities we see as central to designing merely as part of an overall design capability. They had clearly not been encouraged to stand outside their practice – looking in on it from the outside – so as to develop robust self-awareness of what it involves.

> Design tutors need to make explicit through their planning and their pedagogy the skills and qualities they are seeking to develop. By articulating them, they will become part of the day-to-day discourse and will progressively empower the students. The strategies identified in our framework need to be *explicitly* identified and *explicitly* practised so that they become part of the metacognitive armoury of an effective designer. If they are not made explicit, if they remain as tacit practices embedded in thoughtless routines, then there is no reason to believe that the skills will become embedded as robust transferable skills. (Kimbell & Miller, 1999, p. 20)

Designing is far more than 'thoughtless routine', and the portfolio provides us with a wonderful vehicle for making explicit learners' creative thinking processes. In the process we have the potential to establish a robust and hugely valuable set of transferable capabilities. The pedagogic point that emerged so strongly from this project however, was that in order to establish them, they need to be made explicit.

5.   BECOMING SELF-DIRECTED

Being **aware** of the form of ones thinking is not quite the same as **taking responsibility** for it. One of the more obvious objects of schooling is to develop the ability of pupils to manage themselves; to bring them to the point where they not only understand what it means to take responsibility for their actions, but moreover they have expertise in so doing. Developing learners' personal autonomy would rightly be claimed by any teacher as a central goal for education.

In design & technology, we operate in a studio-workshop environment on projects that typically run over an extended period, and this is an environment and a structure that lends itself nicely to developing autonomous decision making by learners. We have long held the view that design & technology teachers are almost uniquely fortunate in operating within this rich setting.

> [T]he child will move in small steps from almost total dependence on the teacher to almost total independence. ... The function of the teacher ... is to to steer children towards the goal of independent thought and action along the tortuous path of guided or supported freedom. (Kimbell, 1982, p. 16)

'The project' has become the standard modus operandi in design & technology, and enshrines a subtle balance between the things the teacher wants to teach and the scope for learners to make decisions for themselves.

In terms of autonomous decision making, the technical content of projects is almost irrelevant, for the key issue is about managing the progressive pathway towards procedural autonomy. Projects would be expected gradually to place ever-greater responsibility on learners and accordingly teachers' frameworks for introducing projects might be expected to become ever looser. Early projects might be tightly constrained and might therefore allow little deviation from the parameters set by the teacher. But gradually these constraints would become negotiable and permeable to the point where older learners might be only very loosely controlled by the teacher and projects undertaken in the final years of schooling almost entirely at the discretion of the learner.

It was the *Understanding Technological Approaches* project (see Chapter 7) that enabled us to explore this continuum in detail. Through detailed case studies in 20 schools we articulated and exemplified the variety of forms that projects took through eleven years of schooling in design & technology. But we were genuinely shocked by the findings from the project. We had expected to find some form of a progressive transition from teacher-control towards learner-autonomy, but instead we found two such continua: one in primary years (1–6) and a separate one in secondary years (7–11). Critically, we found a massive discontinuity at the interface of the two (Years 6–7).

We point up this issue in Chapter 7. Year 6 projects take place in classrooms, Year 7 in workshops; Year 6 tasks are open and negotiable, Year 7 are specific and controlled by the teacher; Year 6 projects do not specify materials, in Year 7 they are largely fixed; Year 6 designing is conducted through modelling, in Year 7 it is almost exclusively on paper; Year 6 teachers operate as progress-chasers, in Year 7 as instructors.

This shocking catalogue demonstrates that far from progressively stretching the autonomous decision making of learners, our practices actually demanded far greater dependency in Year 7 than in Year 6. We would like to think that in the 10 years since we reported these findings, the situation has improved, since one of the strengths of a National Curriculum overview ought to be that it makes possible a sense of progressively evolving capability. Perhaps we should look again to see how things have changed in the interim.

6.   AUTONOMOUS STARTING POINTS

A further challenge in developing the autonomous decision making of learners was exposed when we were developing Standard Assessment Tasks for the National Curriculum (see Chapter 6). It is one thing to encourage learners to become autonomous designers taking ever-more responsibility through the life of a task. But what about the task itself? Is that something that learners should be choosing? Is it for them to decide what the topic might be – and who the client might be?

This issue has challenged teachers of design in schools for some years – and not least when the new (1990) National Curriculum declared that one of the key issues for assessment would be the extent to which learners could 'identify and state clearly needs and opportunities for design and technological activities' (DES/WO, 1989). In short, **learners** were to be in the driving seat. They were not to be seen as responding to tasks that had been given to them by their teachers. Rather they were to be deriving them for themselves. Ultimately, the issue might be seen as one of who is in control of this learning programme – the teacher or the learner?

But in the early Standard Assessment Task trials, as we shared with teachers the idea of progressively building learners' autonomy, the problem changed. Teachers became comfortable with the idea that learners could tune or refine or detail tasks from within wider contextual settings. It was all part of the subtle arts of being a teacher – helping and supporting whilst at the same time probing and pushing learners beyond their comfort zones.

Gradually, we draw back from making the decisions – encouraging learners to exercise their own decision making.

The problem then became our client – the School Examinations and Assessment Council – who had commissioned the Standard Assessment Tasks in the first place. They wanted tests that would provide a measure of learners' performance against prespecified Statements of Attainment. In an 'interesting' meeting at the School Examinations and Assessment Council we were asked what task we were setting and what Statements of Attainment it would measure. We had to explain that learners themselves would be making some of the key decisions about what the task would be like – and that the direction in which they took the project would to a significant degree control what Statement of Attainment would be evidenced. In short, the priority of autonomous decision making that was enshrined in Statement of Attainment in the design & technology Statutory Order gave learners significant areas of control, and this effectively undermined the concept of tightly targeted tests. This seemed to us to be a straightforward statement of the obvious. But the School Examinations and Assessment Council was not amused – and shot the messenger.

7.   'CLIENTS' AS A DEVELOPMENTAL FORCE

A number of our projects have highlighted the critical role of clients in the formation of design & technology activities. Design activity is driven by human desires – for comfort, power, money, convenience and identity. The boundaries of what is acceptable in the made world is equally defined by our desires, for any given design outcome only exists when there is an identifiable client-based need for it.

> It matters not whether this need/desire is for Sidewinder missiles (very few clients but very wealthy ones – hence sufficient development and production money) or for cups and saucers (very many clients – hence a big market creating sufficient development and production money). In either case the fact remains that *technology is client-driven.* (Kimbell, 1994, p. 242)

This issue has the potential to support the development of learners as autonomous decision makers. Wherever we have conducted 'unpickled-portfolio' projects with learners we have sought to instill the sense of a real client that lies behind the task. Perversely, this might be thought to have the effect of taking some of the decision making away from learners, since – surely – the design solution needs to be developed for **the client's** interests and priorities, rather than those of the learner.

What we have repeatedly found however is that by forcing the issue of the client we raise to the conscious level all the decisions that are being made. It is no longer good enough just to do it this way or that way simply because the learner likes it like that. Decisions need to be thought about in terms of what this third party might think. This process of conscious, deliberate decision making supports the growth in learners of their self-awareness of these processes.

What our research has shown is that even the youngest learners in our schools make rigorous, thoughtful design decisions when they have been immersed in a context and have a well-developed understanding of the 'clients' needs. The *Understanding Technological Approaches* project provided clear evidence of this. A classic example comes from a Year 2 class, working within a theme of explorers. The children went (through role play) on a sea-faring voyage, were chased by pirates and then shipwrecked. Cold, wet, tired and frightened, they designed and made shelters wherein every decision related to the needs of their situation – the shelters protected them from the weather, the pirates and wild animals they could hear howling in the distance (See Kimbell, et al., 1996, p. 49 for a fuller account).

8.   A HIERARCHY OF TASKS

Whilst it was in *APU Design & Technology* that we first outlined the idea of a hierarchy of tasks, it was *Understanding Technological Approaches* that enabled us to collect such rich data about practice across all the years of the National Curriculum. Accordingly, as we began to analyse the data derived from that project we started to theorise not only about the character of design & technology at the various years, but also to speculate on a hierarchy of task structures that might be applicable for all teachers.

It is self-evidently the case that tasks are not all the same. They have different content, some involving mechanical or electrical explorations and some focusing on the visual and aesthetic world. They involve different clients, from pets to grandparents. But it was not these content kinds of difference that we were struck by. The key difference lay in the procedural matters of scale or scope of the tasks. Sometimes the task is set in very inclusive, broad-ranging terms and sometimes it is tied down into specifics and details. As part of the *APU* project we had outlined a series of layers of tasks. We used the labels of **contextual**, **referenced** and **specific**.

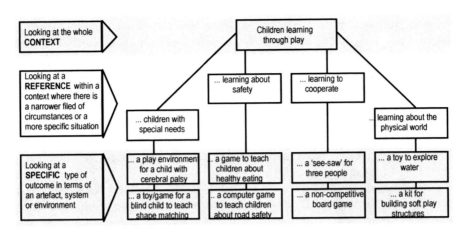

Figure 10-1. Context, reference and specific tasks. (From Kimbell et al., 1991, p. 107.)

Several issues arose from this initial analysis of tasks, some of which we were not aware of at the time but which subsequently emerged in the *Understanding Technological Approaches* project.

The first issue concerns the relationships between the layers. It is obvious that there is a contextual theme running through all the tasks in Figure 10-1; **children learning through play**. We have observed tasks set at this contextual level, encouraging learners to explore within the context to identify areas on which to focus their attention. Equally, we have observed tasks set at the opposite end of the spectrum, where a highly specific demand is made explicit in the task. These tasks typically provide more control for the teacher to introduce learners to particular areas of content. We have observed tasks set in between, in a midlayer of semi-specific-ness.

The second issue is about how these layers relate to each other in the conduct of the activity (Figure 10-2). For it is not that learners operate at a contextual level **or** a referenced level **or** a specific layer. They must always – in the end – get their tasks to the point at which they become specific. If the task is not specific it is not do-able. The issue is about **getting to** the specific. The learner has gradually to take responsibility for managing the process of pinning the task down to a point at which it has become specific.

generalised context

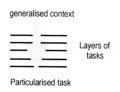 Layers of tasks

Particularised task

Figure 10-2. Layers of tasks

But equally it is possible to operate the other way. For if one was given a specific task, such as designing a water-based learning toy for 6-year-olds, it would be necessary as part of the activity to work out (or find out) what toys are for – what different kinds there are – and how they work to empower learning. In this case the activity requires the learner to flesh out the contextual background. Effectively, the 'task' is merely an entry point into a process of negotiation to arrive at a point where development can begin.

The teacher might wish learners to get involved in designing with textiles – and may set the task of designing **a traveller's body purse** to enable the user to carry around money or other valuables whilst on holiday. This specific task exists in its hierarchy in which the overriding context might be 'protection' and which might include the following layers (Figure 10-3).

Figure 10-3. Starting with a specific

There may of course be any number of layers in this hierarchy, but the point here is that it is perfectly possible to *start* with the specific task. The significance of the hierarchy is that we would thereafter expect learners to explore up and down it in order to inform their design of the body purse. They would need for example to examine the kinds of personal possessions to be protected, and how this is affected by being on the move, and even ultimately what it might mean to 'protect' them. It might mean *hide* them or *disguise* them or *fix* them. The task is only the entry point to the hierarchy. (Kimbell et al., 1996, pp. 40–41)

The third issue arising from this analysis is one of control. Who has control over the process; the learner or the teacher? In reality it will seldom be quite such a stark either/or matter, but it is inevitably the case that tasks set at a contextual level will make greater demands on learners to pin down some starting point for themselves. By contrast, tasks set specifically can be grasped immediately, even though a proper development process would require the fleshing out of wider contextual issues.

The immediate accessibility of tasks – and the extent to which they provide immediate starting points for activity – is a matter on which we derived a good deal of data from the *APU Design & Technology* and *Understanding Technological Approaches* projects. We shall see in Chapter 13 that the matter has profound consequences for learning.

Before getting to that point however, we must recognise that the task is only a starting point for engaging in the activity. Whilst learners might see this activity as design & technology, teachers should be seeing it differently. For it is also a **learning** activity, and the manner in which it is pursued has a major impact on the effectiveness with which learning can be enabled and empowered. These learning and teaching issues are the focus of Chapter 11.

Chapter 11

LEARNING AND TEACHING

Why you might find this chapter interesting

In this chapter, we take forward the idea (from Chapter 10) of designing as a pedagogic vehicle. We examine in particular the role of design portfolios from the points of view of both the learner and the teacher. Learners will typically see the portfolio as a product development device, whilst the teacher will additionally be looking in on it as evidence of learners' cognitive processes; their proposals, their communication approaches and their decision making. We recognise the need to respect the individuality of learners' approaches to designing and reassert the design-like nature of broader decision-making processes.

We conclude the chapter by analysing the pedagogic power of structuring in design processes. This is not about the task that drives the activity (see Chapter 10) but rather about the steps and sequences of the process through which the activity unfolds. We discuss the autonomy / constraint paradox that has been highlighted in a recent research project, and use it to identify the twin demands of any design challenge.

***

We described in Part One of this book our starting points for grappling with research, and these starting points were principally located in the territory of **learning** and **teaching** towards the goal of building learners' **capability**. In Chapter 15, we discussed the multitudinous descriptions of the activity of designing, and how we took a somewhat different view of that process. We also discussed the nature of design tasks that launch this process. In this chapter, we explore how these two take on particular characteristics when viewed through an educational lens. What does designing look like when the principal purpose of the activity is not to produce an object, but to enhance a learner's capability?

The conceptual framework that we sketched out at the start of this book provides some parameters that give us a starting point. Activities should be based on authentic tasks, with real purposes and users, and they should engage learners with the iterative processes of imaging and modelling, moving progressively towards a resolution of the task. In this chapter, we explore the nature of the **learning** process in design, and how teachers can use the process quite deliberately for pedagogic purposes.

1.   THE PURPOSES OF PORTFOLIOS

We have described in Chapter 10 how we see designing as a dynamic, iterative imaging and modelling process. The resulting portfolio potentially contains all the ideas and thoughts that were part of the evolution of the outcome, and together they tell the story of that evolution. The portfolio becomes an explicit representation of the thinking processes that were involved in the project. And – as a teacher – there are two completely different ways of looking at it.

By reference to the portfolio of drawings, calculations, models and notes left by Edison and Bell, Gorman and Carlson did much more than merely **describe** the development process of the telephone. Additionally, they were able to comment on the state of the science and technology on which Edison and Bell were drawing (what was and was not known at the time). And even more than that, they could comment on the points at which Edison and Bell branch out into new territory – experimenting with ideas that had never before existed; like the 'speaking box' that converted sound waves into a variable electrical current. More even than that, they could comment on what happened with the initiative – how successful it was – and what Edison and Bell deduced from the results of their experiments. Eventually, of course they could describe the final working telephone.

All this is discernible in the portfolio. From Edison and Bell's point of view, the portfolio was a working document that helped them to thrash out how to build a telephone. But this same portfolio becomes something very different when viewed from the standpoint of Gorman and Carlson. For them it is an illuminating lens that shines a light into the minds of the two designers – and into the state of the science and technology that they were using. Gorman and Carlson are not interested in the object – the telephone – they are interested in the process of innovation. The paper they published on the subject was not about how the telephone works. Rather it was entitled 'Interpreting invention as a cognitive process' (Gorman & Carlson, 1990)

They wanted to know why Edison and Bell took this route rather than that one; how they solved that problem; why they used that bit of technology; and what they thought about it at the time. The portfolio – the collection of drawings, notes, models and letters – provided the trail of evidence that enabled them to work it out. Gorman and Carlson behaved like experienced trackers, following the twists and turns of the intricate thought processes of two highly inventive men. It is these tracks that make up the portfolio.

So these are two very different ways of interpreting a portfolio. In the hands of the **designer** it is a development tool to support the evolution of the product. But in the hands of a **skilled tracker** it becomes a diagnostic illuminating lens that tells about the route that the designer took through the task. Just as Gorman and Carlson re-created the process through which Edison and Bell developed their concept, so too can teachers re-create the processes through which learners plot their course towards the achievement of their own design solutions.

In many of our projects, we have engaged in this painstaking process of tracking learners' thinking processes. Using the extensive archive that we created from the *APU* survey, we spent hundreds of hours teasing apart:

- **Proposals** that learners were making
- **Issues** that informed these proposals
- **Concepts** that learners were drawing on
- **Appraisal** strategies that they were using
- **Communication** techniques they used

More importantly however, we spent even longer exploring how these qualities in learners' work **interacted** to make convincing (or not) outcomes. We found many examples of excellent performance in one or more of these qualities, but too often such excellence did not enhance the work overall, because (e.g.) the strength in identifying issues was not reciprocated in the strength to make proposals that did something about those issues. It was this analysis that eventually drew us to focus so strongly on holistic approaches to assessment. Regardless of individual areas of strengths and weakness, is the work making progress? Is it convincing?

Underlying this issue is the question of **motive**. Why are we doing it? Why are we getting learners to engage in designing in the first place? Do we encourage design & technology portfolios so that learners can acquire the skills of becoming a designer? Or are we using the portfolio as a device – a **learning** device – that enables learners to become self-aware and take personal control of their own thinking, decision-making processes.

If the former, then portfolios are only important to the extent that they allow individual learners to get through the task and create convincing outcomes. But if the latter – if we are using the project/portfolio as a device for learners to experience (and **learn** from) designing processes – then the teacher may be justified in structuring the process in order to maximise that learning.

2.   STRUCTURING *LEARNING*

It was during the analysis of data from the *APU Design & Technology* and *Understanding Technological Approaches* projects that we first identified some of the factors affecting the performance of learners. First, tasks themselves can be set at a very open 'contextual' level, or tied down more tightly. We described this issue in Chapter 10, and we shall explore more of its effects on learner performance in Chapter 13.

But second, there is an effect created through the **structure of the activity** itself that also influences learner performance. The activity may be very tightly structured, with many demands and little 'free' opportunity for learners to do what they want to do. Or alternatively the activity might be very loosely structured, with few demands and accordingly far more 'free' development time. We might (as in *Assessing Design Innovation*) break a 6 hour activity into 20 or so **subtasks** of varying length between 5 and 30 min. Or we might just say 'get on with it' and then look at the results in 6 hours time. The former is tightly structured by the demands of the subtasks. The latter provides masses of freedom for learners to do as they choose. We established through *APU* data that these very different approaches had a significant impact on learners' performance – and particularly so with lower ability learners.

With an understanding of these effects, it becomes possible to exploit them quite deliberately to create **optimum effects** for learning. For novice groups one might use **task** (a) or (b) rather than (x) or (y). With experienced, capable groups we might use **structure** (1) and (2) rather than (7) or (8). The combination of task (open/closed) and structure (open/closed) enables the imaginative teacher to create a vast range of activities that are framed so as to support learning by particular groups. We recognise that this may not be the natural **designing** behaviour of every learner. Rather, it is **teaching** behaviour driven by the teachers' pedagogic choices. Its justification lies in our ability as teachers to present the designing activity in ways that best help learners get to grips with it.

3.   'NATURAL' DESIGNING BEHAVIOUR?

We have drawn attention above to the pedagogic potential that exists when design activities are structured to promote learner responses. We recognise, however, that there are dangers in this policy, not least the extent to which this can make the process artificial in the eyes of the learner. Not all learners think and design in the same way. Some (typically girls) are more **reflective** while others (typically boys) are more **active** in their approach. Some prefer to manipulate ideas through models while others prefer operating with words or images. Some will operate holistically, conceiving whole solutions and then working out the consequences for individual elements. Others prefer to work on parts of a solution and gradually build up the whole. Chapter 13 examines some of these differences in detail. Here, we simply acknowledge that any particular structured designing activity will suit some learners better than others. What are we to make of this?

We explored some of these issues in *Wholes and Parts* (see Chapter 7) specifically looking at the cognitive processes involved in designing. Do learners conceive of whole solutions and then work out the details, or do they work out the bits first and gradually assemble a complete solution.

The important point for us in this chapter is not to do with the findings of that project, except to note that there was indeed a lot of evidence to suggest that learners had very different approaches to their design tasks – some operating *very* globally and others in *very* small incremental steps. The essential point here however is that as part of the methodology for that project we created two very different activities; designing a water toy and designing a packed-lunch container. The topics are not important – except to note that they had to appeal to (or at least not repel) the age group involved. The important feature was that we **structured the activity** in two very different ways. The water toy activity began by seeking broad concepts of what such a toy might be like. The packed-lunch container activity began from some highly specific investigating. Not surprisingly, the two activities promoted very different kinds of response and when we analysed the work we were quite able to place it on a two different 4-point scales:

- Is this learner a strong holist?
- Is this learner a strong partist?

Interestingly, having started with the view that these two are ends of the same continuum, the analysis of work illustrated otherwise. We found it necessary to create two different scales since some learners could operate effectively both as holists and partists, some were not strong with either, but most had a bias one way or the other.

This project alone illustrates the unavoidable truth that individual designing styles vary and, as a result, an activity choreographed to suit one group will suit another group less well. But this is no a reason for **not** using activity structures to support pedagogic ends. Rather it is a reason for creating a broad battery of activity structures that collectively enable all learners to succeed.

At one level this is a simple point about fairness, but there is a deeper issue involved. Whilst we acknowledge the tendency for individuals to be drawn to one approach rather than another, we do not believe one is **better** than another. They are just different, as a cox apple is different from a Worcester or a Bramley. All delicious in their own way, and all apples – but different.

But a cox apple has no choice but to be a cox, just as a Worcester does not have the potential to be a Bramley. However, with intelligent young people, whilst designing styles may be **working preferences**, they are not irrevocably genetically programmed. The **learning experience** allows youngsters to explore other ways of working – to experience how it works when I do it like this; or how it works differently when I do it like that. We work from learners' strengths with the aim of enhancing their weaknesses so that – in the end – they possess a rich tapestry of approaches that they can tap into on demand.

When we were reflecting on the data from *APU Design & Technology* and *Understanding Technological Approaches*, we described it in the following terms.

> If a pupil's current tool box of strategies is not adequate to help them work out some aspect of their design, then it needs to be enriched. The issues that we have drawn attention to above about the 'typical' strengths and weaknesses of gender or ability groups are therefore not something about which we just shrug our shoulders. We should not accept these strengths and weaknesses as anything other than starting points. But in order to build from them, we need first to recognise that they are (probably) there and only then can we work *from* existing strengths and *towards* creating new ones. (Kimbell et al., 1996, p. 98)

The *Wholes and Parts* project was based substantially on the work of one of our colleagues, Tony Lawler, who was working towards his research degree. He has subsequently taken the project forward into a new phase building on *Wholes and Parts* and exploring the extent to which the approaches might impact upon an extended programme of teaching. In a longitudinal study a whole Year 7 cohort in one school were assessed diagnostically to identify their designing style. Teachers then adopted a pedagogy that acknowledged the individual designing styles throughout the following 5 years of work in design & technology. At the end of this time there appeared to be clear indications that individual learner 'preferences' still drive their work, but that they have also developed a more rounded capability through the development of other aspects. (Lawler, 2006)

4.   IS IT ALL DESIGNING?

One of the challenges that we were constantly exploring in *Wholes and Parts* was the extent to which we were noting a **designing** phenomenon or a broader **cognitive** phenomenon. Was it about designing styles or cognitive styles? In the same vein, we drew attention in the previous chapter to the power of portfolios to enable learners to become self-aware of their own decision-making processes. But are these just design decision-making processes or might the portfolio approach facilitate awareness and capability in broader decision-making processes?

We have explored this idea in several of our projects, and perhaps most explicitly in the Design Council project '*Decisions by Design*' (see Chapter 8). We hypothesised that the explicitness of the thinking and decision-making process as used by designers might be observable by non-designers. We were specifically interested in school managers; heads and deputy-heads with no direct experience or familiarity with designing. We thought it would be interesting if we could contrast such non-designers' decision-making processes with those of designers. If the non-designers could indeed 'see' that thinking (particularly through the activities that created the portfolio), then how might it influence their own thinking? As we outlined in our proposal:

> We intend to explore the extent to which – and the ways in which – design activity can be used to enhance the decision making of school managers. We are concerned with the *ways in which decisions get made*, rather than the structures that exist in schools or the substance of the decisions that result. Specifically we are interested in the extent to which these decision-making processes reflect design behaviour; and in the consequences for decision making when those responsible for the decisions are made aware of the procedures of design thinking. (Kimbell et al., 1997, p. 2)

What emerged was quite dramatic. Not only were the teacher fellows able, through case studies, to identify their own decision-making trail, but they were fully able to see the differences when observing designers and their portfolios. They could readily identify the explicitness and the public accessibility of what we might call 'designerly' thinking, and in particular they were astonished at the extent to which designers 'model' their ideas for the future. They recognised this modelling (typically using images and two-dimensional [2D] and 3D models) is a highly explicit kind of thinking, and moreover one that can readily be shared with others. They also acknowledged that this was not something that typically featured in their own thinking/decision-making processes.

Once again however, the methodological issue is more important than these specific findings. In order to develop the idea in this project we created a structured **designing** activity and – in parallel – we developed a **management** activity that used exactly the same protocols and procedures. We were then able to explore how the teacher-fellows managed as they undertook the two tasks. The point is an obvious one – but important; designing requires creative decision-making capabilities, but so too does managing schools. The success of the exercise however was dependent on the concreteness of the portfolio structure.

We should never underestimate the flexibility and the power of the portfolio (unpickled or otherwise) in exposing, exploring and developing learners' thinking and decision-making processes.

5.   EXTREME STRUCTURE: FOR INNOVATION

Through many of our projects, including those focused on assessment, we have used the idea of structured activities to promote learners' performance, and not infrequently these projects have involved activities that operate on a short timescale and with paper and pencil modes of response. However, in recent projects, *Assessing Design Innovation* and *e-scape*, we have taken these ideas forward in two particular respects:

1. To embrace material modelling as an idea development process
2. To involve team-based support systems

The specific challenge of *Assessing Design Innovation* is clear in the title; to promote **innovative** performance in such a way that it can be assessed. We have used all kinds of devices within the structure of the activity to encourage and support learners' innovation. As we describe in Chapter 6, the activity has become 6 hours in length and is choreographed through a series of 22 interlinked subtasks, using an activity workbook and making use of a camera to record (every hour) the progress of the modelling. In *e-scape*, the subtasks are done digitally (on a PDA) in a newly created design interface, using the device as a camera, a notebook, a sketchbook and a voice-memo recorder. We examine some of the assessment issues of this project in Chapter 12, but before getting to that, it is worth outlining here some of the issues raised by the way the activity was structured.

In Chapter 6, we show an illustration of the work of one learner – an A2 sheet that comprises the design booklet developed for *Assessing Design Innovation* (Figure 6-7). It shows one learner's response to the task of creating a new form of light bulb packaging that – when no longer needed to store the bulb – can be transformed into a lighting feature in itself (or part of one in combination with other light bulb boxes). The subtasks are very different from those that are typically presented to learners in a design task. Instead of spending the first 3 hours of working time on clarifying the task, generating a brief, or doing some investigations – which would be the conventional starting point – our first 3 hours was spent in a combination of: exploring a handling collection of 'transformation' objects; working in groups of three to rapidly generate and swop design ideas; moving swiftly to 3D modelling using a range of 'rapid' modelling materials; recording regularly through photographing and printing images of their models; and reviewing each other's developing work from the stance of 'critical friend'.

Each of these subtasks, and the ways in which they fitted together to choreograph the whole activity, was trialled in a series of experiments with learners. In total these explorations took about a year, until we evolved a combination of subtasks that seemed to be effective. It helped learners to get into the task quickly and also enabled them to push their ideas ahead quickly.

We asked teachers to note the structural features in the activity that they felt had been supportive of learners innovative performance, and the following issues emerged regularly: the administrator script in association with the folding booklet; the layout and the way it (the worksheet) folds so that the pupils can see what they have done; the handling collection and inspiration table; the teamwork; the photo-storyline. The following comment was typical.

Students enjoyed the challenge. Great atmosphere in the room. Students were totally engaged for the majority of the time. Loved the photographs! (Teacher evaluation database, MH)

We invited learners also to comment on the activity, and they too were vocal on what they saw as the activities strengths.

Working in groups but having the ability to work independently … You can make things you didn't expect … Working in groups helped for inspiration with ideas ,,, I could show people my ability … Starting from scratch to make you think … Being able to make something by myself and what I wanted to make. (Learner evaluation database, AB216, AB219, AB2116, AB2210, AB323)

\In a way there is little that was new about the things we asked learners to do: taking photos, reflecting on their ideas, using a handling collection, and so on. But there were some organisational differences that proved very important in enabling learners to push their activity forward: the use of blocks of time (3 hours at a stretch); the very short, sharp time allocations for subtasks (5 min for this – stop – now 5 min for that); and critically the iteration of these subtasks between an active focus (e.g. generating ideas) and a reflective focus (e.g. red pen reviews)

This approach had been part of our thinking since APU days, where we had originally evolved the idea of unfolding work booklets and the concept of choreography through the administrator script. Perhaps the biggest shift with *Assessing Design Innovation* lay in our approach to the use of materials and modelling. Whilst *APU* activities were largely paper based, we were keen in this project to allow all learners to develop their thinking through modelling. We have explained the centrality of modelling in principle in Chapter 10, but how to make it happen in practice?

Two devices were eventually used. First, we provided a range of interesting, 'soft', quick modelling materials. Second we introduced these materials in a particular way, **after** the first round of early ideas, but **before** learners got into product development mode. In this way we enabled learners who had got the first glimmerings of an idea to try to represent it (model it) for themselves in reality. This proved to be a hugely empowering innovation, seeing modelling not as a way to show your final design, but rather as a way to sort out the ideas as you go along. Once again, the learners told us of the value of the approach.

> Using your own ideas; making models instead of drawing – they work better ... Seeing your idea develop ... It made you think about how you could do things and with different materials (Learner evaluation database, AB314, AB319, AB423)

As it turned out, a significant proportion of the learners (and many boys) used models as the principal means for developing their ideas. Whilst some booklets are rich in graphic explorations elaborated through models, some booklets are almost devoid of drawing and all the product evolution has been through modelling.

In retrospect, we recognised another element that ought to have been built into the booklet. Beside each photo we should have asked learners to explain briefly what they were trying to do. Whilst **drawn** development is typically full of annotated explanations, the model photos are silent on this. We have to interpret and imply meaning from what they have done.

Having come to this realisation, in our subsequent project – *e-scape* – we have modified our approach making use of the new technology. With the PDA as the basic design and development tool for the project, learners had immediate access not just to a digital **sketch-pad** and **notebook**, but also to a **camera** and **voice-memo** recorder. Accordingly, we modified the protocols of the activity, asking learners to take a photograph and then record a 30 second 'sound-bite' that explains the model, what is good and works well and what needs further development. This protocol – repeated six times through the activity – provides a photo-storyline of development, enriched and illuminated with (literally) the 'voice' of the learner.

The combination of devices used in these structured activities was developed essentially for the purpose of assessing levels of design innovation. Accordingly, whilst many of the subtasks within the structure were principally intended to push learners' ideas forward, some of them were intended primarily as ways of making learners' thinking explicit to assessors. Interestingly, sometimes these two imperatives merged in unexpected ways. The photo-storyline is a case in point.

This was intended primarily for the assessor, so that we could get a regular check on learners' thinking processes as expressed through modelling. But as it turned out, it had a hugely empowering effect on learners' ideas. Once they saw the first photo, they knew what was coming next time around and were ready for it, keen to show us where they had got to in their work for photo 2. Moreover, because they had the photo of the model – pasted into the workbook – they were less precious about keeping it and were prepared to rip it apart to modify it as their idea evolved. So what started as a trick to support assessment, turned out to be a device that supported innovation.

We discuss in detail in Chapter 12 how this process plays out in the development of assessment devices.

6. THE AUTONOMY/CONSTRAINT PARADOX

The structured portfolios that have been one of the TERU hallmarks over the last 20+ years have constantly provoked debate between us – both in terms of the development of activities and in the analysis of data flowing from them. As we have indicated in Chapter 6, some particularly tantalising data arose from *Assessing Design Innovation* that bears on the paradoxical relationship between the **constraints** and the **freedoms** offered by these structured activities. On the face of it our structured activities were tightly constrained.

> Students are effectively frog-marched (by the teacher script) through a series of steps that are tightly timed and within which they have to put their thoughts in delineated sections of a pre-printed worksheet. At first glance it might be thought to be a bit like painting-by-numbers. (Kimbell et al., 2004, p. 61)

But this apparent lack of freedom has to be set beside learners' reaction to it.

Being able to use my own ideas how I wanted to ... We got to try out different things, using our ideas ... I liked getting my imagination go wild. (Learner evaluation database, AB119, AB3111, AB411)

So many of their responses testified to their 'own ideas' and their delight in the freedom to innovate. But looking at the teacher script one would hardly imagine that 'freedom' is the right word to use when describing the activity.

The fact is that within a designing activity there are two kinds of learning going on simultaneously.

- First there is **procedural** learning; the 'what am I going to do next' kind of learning. This is the kind of learning that enables learners **to manage themselves** through a task from start to finish.
- Second there is **content/idea** learning; it is going to be a ....; It will be like ....; I want it to do ....; This kind of learning **centres on the content of learners' ideas** and how they can be developed into a solution.

A couple of really important questions arise from this. Is one more important than the other? Is one more generalisable than the other? On the face of it, one of these kinds of learning (the second) is deeply about the **stuff** of design & technology about materials, ideas and modelling. The other is a more generic kind of learning that might be applied in any task-related activity – like a scientific investigation or composing an essay. This task-centred **procedural** learning does have obvious spin-off elsewhere, whereas the product/idea learning might seem to be more subject bound into design & technology. In reality however, the two are usually interwoven, with teachers expecting learners to be able to cope with both.

Either of these kinds of learning can be fostered in a design task. But equally we can choose to prioritise one over the other. In *Assessing Design Innovation* we were primarily concerned with **learners' ideas** and how they could develop them. We were less concerned about their overall project management. We recognise that this is important in design & technology, but it is already well represented in existing project-based assessment and our brief was to prioritise innovation and ideation.

So we tightened down the process; taking most of the responsibility for this management function into the design of the activity – managed by the administration script. We quite deliberately loosened the controls on learners' ideas, and we found ways to encourage learners to experiment and take chances with them. This explains the apparent paradox we outlined above. We were tightly controlling the process – but liberating learners' ideas. We described it in the following terms.

It is a bit like jazz with a rigid 12 or 16 bar rhythm. Within that tight structure, the most outlandish improvisation can be liberated. So too with our activity booklets and the teacher script. By taking away from students the need to think about how they will organise and present their work, they are empowered to **concentrate on the ideas** that drive their designing. (Kimbell et al., 2004, p. 61)

In the *North West Province Technology Education Project* we took a somewhat different position. The priorities there were twofold: first about teamworking to develop technological solutions, and second to focus on the content areas of the experimental technology curriculum. Specifically, the clients were concerned about the extent to which learners could helpfully deploy their understanding about three areas of content. As we described in the report;

> Within this third dimension we were looking to establish the extent to which the technological content identified and taught through the PROTEC materials could be applied to the task in hand. Consequently we structured this aspect of the assessment through the knowledge groupings provided in the project booklets:
>
> • materials and processes (named materials and construction processes, understanding of their properties, application to the task);
> • energy and power (mechanical and electrical sources, understanding of their properties, application to the task);
> • communications (systems communicating with systems and systems communicating with people, understanding the properties of communication systems, application to the task). (Kimbell & Stables, 1999, p. 7)

As we outline in Chapter 9, the task was developed with these **content** requirements in mind, whilst at the same time the structure of the booklets managed the **procedural** elements – including teamworking.

Once again we are drawn to the observation that structured designing activities of the unpickled portfolio kind, linked to the learners' response booklet (or PDA) and teachers' administration script provide a fantastically flexible tool for learning. It can be designed to encourage and develop learners' capability and to assess their performance. It can focus on procedural qualities or target more of the specifics of product development.

Any of these variables can properly be the focus of teaching and can be introduced on sliding scales of demand.

Project A might be only loosely constrained by the teacher in procedural terms, but have lots of scope for learner autonomy with the substantive content and ideas for a solution. Project B might be the reverse of this with very little procedural guidance from the teacher and much more content/ideas guidance. Project C might sit between these two extremes.

The activities would provide the teacher with very different kinds of control and equally different ways of exercising it. **Content** demands are largely decided by the details in the task, and we examined in Chapter 10 how this task might be tightly or loosely constrained. **Procedural** demands are not constrained so much by the task – but by the response mode in the learner booklet and the teachers/administrator script. This procedure might be tightly constrained or relatively loosely managed.

It is important to recognise that these qualities are not reciprocal in the sense that a greater degree of procedural control does not necessarily require a lower degree of content control. They are independent factors – one controlled by the task and the other by the procedural response mode. So it would be possible to have a tightly specified task *and* a tightly controlled procedure, and equally it is possible to have a loosely defined task and a loosely controlled procedure.

One thing you can be absolutely sure about however is that these two extremes would suit very different learners. The evidence of our projects suggests that girls will tend to do better in some tasks/structures and boys with others; high-ability learners will tend to do better with one combination and low ability learners with another. We explore these issues in Chapter 13 and suffice it here to remind ourselves of the message that emerged from our analysis of *APU* data

> One is led to the somewhat sinister conclusion that it would be possible – given an understanding of the nature of these effects – to design activities deliberately to favour any particular nominated group. More positively it would also appear to be possible to design activities that largely eliminate bias or at least balance one sort of bias with another. It must be a matter of great importance for teachers to attain such a lack of bias (or at least a balance of bias) in designing tasks for pupils – or in negotiating them with pupils. (Kimbell et al., 1991, p. 208)

The desirable end point of a learning programme would be that learners can cope with any possibilities that are thrown at them. But getting learners to that point requires careful, self-conscious structuring by teachers both in terms of tasks and activity structures.

Chapter 12

ASSESSING PERFORMANCE

Why you might find this chapter interesting

*It has been our experience that the better we are able to assess learners'
performance, the richer can be our approaches to developing it. This chapter
explores this tight interrelationship of teaching, learning and assessment. We
begin by exploring the **purposes** of assessment, and what happens when there
is confusion or disagreement about those purposes. We reassert the centrality
of **performance** assessment, designed to provide insights into the **capability** of
learners. This capability however is not a single monolithic quality, but can be
flavoured to emphasise particular perspectives on capability. We discuss
frameworks for creating authentic assessment tasks and techniques we have
used for presenting these to learners in convincing ways. We explore the
substructuring of activities and the critical role that this plays in revealing
evidence of learners' capability.*

*Once the activity has been completed, the challenge changes to one of
making judgements about the quality of learners' work. We discuss the role
of (and the relationship between) holistic and atomistic approaches, of
rubrics and approaches to using them effectively, and explore the challenge
of assessing group performance. We then outline a radically different
approach to assessment (differentiated pairs) that does not involve any
'marking' or attributing of scores, but is based rather on multiple direct
comparisons of pieces of work. It is an approach that demands performance
in digital form (web portfolios) and our use of it is currently attracting great
interest from assessment and policy bodies. We conclude the chapter with
some reflections on our whole unpickled portfolio approach to assessment.*

***

Learning and **teaching** processes are two of the key threads running through so much of our work and in both cases have consistently been focused on how we might better understand and promote design & technological **capability**. Inevitably, therefore, we have also continually been drawn to the challenge of assessment – for to **understand** capability and to have a sense of how one might **develop** it, one also needs to be able to get a grip on it – to weigh it – to judge its constituents and its quality. It has been our experience that the better we are able to assess learners' performance, the richer can be our approaches to developing it.

1.   THE CENTRALITY OF PURPOSE

The starting point for considering assessment must be that of purpose, as the nature of the purpose will have profound consequences for the form of assessment that might be most efficacious. Nonetheless, we recognise that there are many examples of systems designed for one purpose, which are then forced into wider service for additional purposes. This multipurposing frequently has damaging repercussions since tools designed for one purpose seldom operate as well when used for a different one. The blood that is frequently spilt when screwdrivers (and even chisels) are used as paint-can openers provides a salutary lesson. In the education world, far too much blood has been spilt using National Curriculum Standard Assessment Task scores (summative motive) for constructing league tables of schools (evaluative motive) – something we witnessed first hand through our involvement with the initial Standard Assessment Task development projects.

This is not to say that a particular assessment tool cannot be exploited for different purposes where the context and assessment intentions can be well serviced by the use of the tool. To illustrate both the problems of purpose and the potential of a multipurpose assessment tool, *APU Design & Technology* provides a useful example. The project was principally an **evaluative** project, designed to enable us to report on the performance of 15-year-old learners in England, Wales and Northern Ireland.

The strength of this light-sampling approach was that it enabled us to develop an extremely comprehensive set of tests that, taken together, reflected a complete perspective on capability in design & technology as described at that time. Because the learner sample was so large, we were able to distribute the tests across the sample, so that no individual learner undertook more than two, i.e. 3 hours of testing. If each learner had taken the whole test battery, it would have taken them 36 hours to complete. But *APU* procedures enabled us to construct a picture of overall national performance by amalgamating the performance of so many individuals, each doing their bit.

In addition, we were able to identify how this was influenced by gender effects, by general ability levels of learners, and by their experience of the design & technology curriculum. It was all done with a 'light' touch, in the sense that only a tiny 2% minority of the cohort was involved. Assessment of Performance Unit assessments (in many subjects in addition to design & technology) were highly efficacious, providing maximum evaluative information about the details of performance in design & technology with minimum disruption of schools and curriculum.

1.1 National Curriculum Standard Assessment Tasks and the Conflict of Purpose

When the National Curriculum was introduced in 1990, the DES abolished the Assessment of Performance Unit, which for the previous 15 years had provided it with these evaluative data. The belief was that such data could be gathered from National Curriculum Standard Assessment Tasks at ages 7, 11 and 14. But these Tasks were designed primarily to provide **summative** data about the performance of individual learners at the end of particular Key Stages of the National Curriculum. Because of that priority, it was essential for **every** learner in the country to be tested, and with approximately half a million learners in each cohort this was a monumental undertaking. Teachers and schools were anxious to ensure that such tasks caused minimum disruption to the curriculum, which put huge pressure on Standard Assessment Task developers to **minimise** the requirements of time, materials and facilities, etc. So every learner in the country at ages 7, 11 and 14 ended up taking a short, sharp, impoverished tests. Of course they all had to take the **same** tests.

When we try to use such data for **evaluative** purposes, all we can say (e.g. about the reading ability of 7-year-olds) is what we can glean from a common, short-sharp test. Previous APU reading surveys – specifically designed to inform the profession about national performance in reading – were able to draw (in the same way as we have described for design & technology) on far richer data from many different subsets of it taken by individual learners, but combining to create a picture of overall performance over 20 hours of testing.

If you want to find out about individuals (what they know and can do) at the end of a programme of study, then design assessments for the individual. If you want to know about design & technology (national levels of performance) then design assessments for that. Assessment schemes that are designed to derive a **summative** view of the capability of an individual learner are very different from those one might use to derive an **evaluative** view of national performance. The procedures for administering them (and who one administers them to) would be totally different. Chisels do not make good paint-can openers, and in the hands of non-experts they are positively dangerous.

But the National Curriculum Standard Assessment Task developments were subjected to all kinds of problems, many of which derived from attempting to address **different** purposes – or from not being clear what the purpose should be – and the history of these developments was somewhat less than happy.

The central problem of purpose is illustrated in a fascinating report by the School Examinations and Assessment Council that includes an illuminating discussion of how to reconcile Standard Assessment Task scores that were emerging from the trials with pre-existing teacher assessment scores.

> If the principal purpose of NCA (National Curriculum Assessment) is to provide summative and evaluative information then it may be appropriate to use a common structure across all subjects …. if however the principal purpose of NCA is formative, then it may be more appropriate to take subject-based decisions…

> The decision about whether to combine scores (i.e. for example by taking the mean of the two scores) also depends upon the principal function desired for NCA. If the main purpose is to provide evaluative information at a class or school level then the 'uncombined' test scores alone may be appropriate. On the other hand for formative use at the individual pupil level then some form of combination is probably appropriate.

> The precise method of combination should also be determined by the purposes of NCA. (SEAC, 1991, paras 157–160)

In short, after 2 years of development, and after countless millions of pounds of expenditure, and after equally countless millions of hours of teacher labour, the School Examinations and Assessment Council had not decided what the principal purpose was for National Curriculum Assessment. For an agency whose whole rationale was assessment and evaluation, these passages represent a quite astonishing admission of incompetence.

The story is told in detail elsewhere (Kimbell, 1997) but the nub of the issue was the inappropriateness of attempting to achieve evaluative information on national levels of performance from the same assessments that were providing feedback on individual learners. Gipps (1992) pinpointed the problem of the incremental shift of the purpose of the Standard Assessment Task from evaluative to summative.

> If the SAT is only an overall moderating device, then it needs only to sample across Attainment Targets. If, however, it is to be used to confirm

teacher assessment for each child then it has to cover every Attainment Target. Thus the problem is that the SAT as originally conceived – i.e. packages of tasks administered through a range of modes, including practical, oral, extended and group tasks, to ensure validity and good curriculum backwash – is simply not appropriate for assessing literally hundreds of assessment points. ... it becomes too time consuming. (Gipps, 1992, pp. 2–3)

For the *CATS KS3 Technology* team the dilemma proved to be that developing assessments that assessed every learner across the full spectrum of Statements of Attainment, could (in the light of our beliefs about capability) only be done reliably and validly through full projects – there were no valid and reliable 'quick fixes'. But such full-scale projects lasting 10–12 hours were seen to present too big an assessment burden – and to be too much under the influence of teachers themselves. The policy makers were looking for short sharp tests. Effectively they wanted to have their cake and eat it. They wanted individual formative and summative learner assessments that could be aggregated up to provide 'evaluative' data on schools. What we witnessed through *CATS KS3 Technology* was a sharp step back towards a system designed to create league tables – feeding a competitive 'market' in schools. Lawton commenting on this shift underscores the political agenda.

TGAT placed emphasis on teacher assessment ... integrated with good established teaching practices, and formative assessment which might also become the first step in the process of diagnosing weaknesses. But ... SATs of the TGAT kind, it was realised, would be difficult to produce and would require plenty of time for trials and teacher preparation; the real timetable was political rather than educational. At the first sign of difficulty the Government has retreated to the ideologically more acceptable solution of short written tests. This intensifies the conflict between professional assessment and tests to be used for market choice. (Lawton, 1992, p. 97)

1.2   Being Clear about Purpose

Interestingly, *CATS KS1 Technology* tells a more positive story – and, once again, the difference comes down to the focus on purpose. The Key Stage 1 tasks were never intended to have an evaluative purpose – as we have outlined in Chapter 6 they were to support teachers in making their own assessment decisions – both formative and summative. The specification we worked to was more centrally in the spirit of the educational underpinning given to the venture through the initial work of the Task Group on Assesment and Testing (DES/WO, 1988a). While superficially appearing very different to the *APU* materials, the tasks were based on the *APU* model – but with activities mediated by the teacher rather than an assessment booklet, a strategy we considered to be more appropriate for young learners. Like *APU*, a suite of activities was developed that between them covered the breadth of design & technology, but unlike *APU*, the aim was for teachers to be able to use any or all of these, across the 2 years of the Key Stage, to support both the teaching and assessment of the full range of Statements of Attainment in different contexts. Teachers were encouraged to enable learners to 'revisit' aspects of the curriculum, rather than treat the Programmes of Study and Statements of Attainment as items to be ticked off on a list. So, freed from the need to produce evaluative performance data, we could adapt the *APU Design & Technology* model, focusing on formative and summative assessments.

The *APU* model, and in particular the 'unpickled portfolio', became a tool whose potential we could exploit for various purposes, so for the *North West Province Technology Education Project*, and *Enriching Literacy through Design & Technology* we used the tool for evaluative purposes. For *Assessing Design Innovation* we adapted it for summative purposes and in *Researching Assessment Approaches* for formative purposes. In each instance the tool was not used as a solitary method – but as part of an interrelated set of tools aimed at that same purpose. Where we used it evaluatively it was combined with interview data; where we used it for summative and formative purposes, it was seen as part of a set of complementary assessment approaches. In *Researching Assessment Approaches* it was intended to be used alongside continuous assessment through portfolios, both approaches working to the same assessment criteria. What these various projects showed is that our unpickled portfolio 'tool' is a generic, neutral tool capable of adaptation to a variety of purposes. It is the details of its adaptation and use, and by extension the understanding of the operator, which determines and constrains its value.

Purpose should be the first consideration when thinking about assessment. While we might do our best to drive a straight and true path in this respect, we have occasionally experienced the uncomfortable intervention of political decision making. After all, assessment is a sensitive matter and sometimes a high-stakes political one.

1.3   The Ethics of Purpose

Interestingly, our current project – *e-scape* – provides another interesting twist to this point. As we have explained in Chapter 6, the project develops the idea of e-assessment, and there is huge political interest in this matter. This is both big P Political interest at Ministerial level (all part of the e-learning and e-assessment National Strategy) and small p political interest at the policy level of the Qualifications and Curriculum Authority and the General Certificate for Secondary Education Awarding Bodies. Our research is based on building an e-assessment system, **not** to produce data on learner performance, but rather to yield data on the nature of the assessment tool that we have developed. So we are testing individual learners, not because we need to know about those individual learners but rather because their performance can tell us about our new system.

This raises some interesting ethical issues, not least that of putting several hundred young learners through an assessment when the data is of no direct help to them or their teachers – but rather is valuable to the research community. Apart from the general point that we only work with willing participants, the wider point is that these assessments are invariably activity-based and deliberately designed to promote good practice. In the process of providing us with data, they also support the growth of learner capability and enhance teachers' understanding of capability and how it might be assessed. In short, whichever way you look at it (from the learner, the teacher or the researcher perspective) they are assessment for learning.

This is all part of our commitment to authentic assessment and to a procedural, capability model of learning and teaching – where learners are engaged in authentic activities for assessment purposes, the information provided has the **potential** to be used both **for** and **of learning**, and both **for** and **of researching**. The problems arise (as we have indicated above) when assessment of learning is removed from a learning climate, and when its primary purpose changes to meet the requirements of instrumental or political purposes.

2. PERFORMANCE ASSESSMENT PRIORITIES

Being clear about the purpose that assessment has to serve is only a first step. We have also argued for the centrality of the concept of '**capability**' in design & technology, and the immediate consequence of this for assessment is that the **process of making judgements** about the design & technology capability of a learner, must be based upon the experience of a learner undertaking a genuine design & technology task.

But the task itself is only one of the key features of an assessment. All our assessment projects have served to underline the tight interrelationship between the **task** that learners undertake, the **activity structure** that steers progress through the task and the **assessment framework** that is used to guide the process of making judgements of the quality of the work. Experience has taught us that these three hang together well when there is a clear focus throughout on what is to be assessed – in our case design & technological **capability**.

2.1   The 'Flavour' of Capability

The detailed nature of this capability varies from project to project according to the priorities of that project. In some instances we have been presented with the constituents that sponsors were keen to have assessed – as we were with *CATS KS1 & KS3 Technology*, the *North West Province Technology Education Project* and *Researching Assessment Approaches*. In the *North West Province Technology Education Project*, for example, the task (transporting medicines across country) undoubtedly enabled learners to demonstrate their technological capability. But the sponsors were interested in the impact of their specific curriculum (concerning energy, materials, etc.) and this 'flavoured' both the task and the subsequent displays of capability.

Recently, we have again been in our preferred position of deriving the constituents empirically, and from within our own research processes. As an example, in *Assessing Design Innovation*, we used an approach that enabled us to diagnose – through interaction with teachers – the qualities of capability that they saw as representing 'innovative' performance. Working closely with these teachers, with General Certificate for Secondary Education senior moderators, and LEA support staff we used learners' own project work as our starting point for analysis, inviting teachers to identify different pieces of work that represented innovative performance or non-innovative. Through analysis of the resulting contrasted piles of work, we teased out the distinguishing features of innovative work that teachers were using, even though at the outset they found it hard to articulate this reasoning. We were able to shed light on their **intuitive** judgements and make them explicit. Through this process we demonstrated how design innovation hinges upon the crucial role of **ideas** in learners work. The resulting **assessment framework** that guided the development of our assessment instruments was focused on **having** ideas, **growing** ideas and **proving** ideas – effectively, a more detailed structure of the generative dimension of our earlier framework.

2.2   Creating Authentic Assessment Activities

From identifying the constituents to be assessed in each of our projects, we typically moved to the challenge of creating performance assessment instruments. We seek to create instruments that have the authenticity of genuine designing but that are capable of operation within tightly limited time frames.

We are well aware that every year in design & technology in England, Wales and Northern Ireland, there are approximately half a million General Certificate for Secondary Education candidates all of whom undertake a major project that purports to provide a measure of their capability. Whilst being broadly supportive of this policy, there are several problems with it:

- It takes (on average) about 30 hours of curriculum time
- Countless hours of non-curriculum time typically on 'folder-work'
- There is variable support from school to school (and teacher to teacher)
- Various 'parts' of design & technology at General Certificate for Secondary Education level (e.g. food, systems and control) produce radically different statistics about the relative performance levels of girls/boys (see Kimbell, 2002a).

Whilst these factors might give pause for reflection about the reliability of extended project work assessment, it does remain warmly supported both by schools and by the Qualifications and Curriculum Authority.

Coursework is also a powerful motivator for many candidates in many subjects, giving them a chance to study an area in greater depth and take more responsibility for their learning .... The benefits of coursework generally outweigh any drawbacks. (QCA, 2005, p. 5)

Our work initially for *APU* focused our attention on the antithesis of this normal situation. We were required to design assessment instruments that could be sent through the post to schools; could be administered in 90 min; in a standard form; to populations all around the country; and demanding standardised resources.

In respect of authenticity, the situation presented three challenges: creating authentic tasks and contexts; creating authentic activity structures; and creating a performance (i.e. procedural) assessment framework. We have discussed some of these elements in relation to particular projects in Chapter 6, and it remains here to draw together the issues.

2.2.1   Authentic Tasks and Contexts

APU Design & Technology alerted us to the importance of context and task structure in developing authentic tasks and promoting capability. There are however a number of further issues that has become progressively clearer since we have undertaken more recent projects. And high on this list is the **cultural significance** of the task.

When we were contacted by the DFID and challenged to create a task for the *North West Province Technology Education Project*, we were thrust right into the heart of this issue. What kinds of task would 'work' in the townships of Johannesburg? Would the same task 'work' in an isolated rural community on the edge of the Kalahari where there is no electricity supply, no telephones, and water is something one has to walk to get. These issues were dealt with regularly by the NGO that we worked with during that project (PROTEC). For example, they had developed a task about soap-making that was popular with learners, but hardly the stuff of mainstream design & technology in the UK.

We settled on the task of transporting medicines – across huge distances, through the bush, by jeeps driving on rough dirt tracks (see Chapter 9). Through the task we pinpointed the need for protection – from the climate, the bumpy journey and from pilfering. We gradually refined the task – and its three principal subtasks through detailed discussions with the NGO and with our colleague Ole, a Botswana Ph.D. student at Goldsmiths. Ole (Olefile Molwane) was important to this project not just as a cultural reference point but also as fieldworker during the trials in South Africa, where his ability to speak directly to the learners in their own language (Tswana) proved immensely helpful. We have always found it necessary to 'trial' tasks with groups of learners to gauge their responses to them, and we did the same with this medicine transportation task. But trialling in South Africa was a luxury we could not afford – we had to take everything with us in its 'ready-to-roll' form. So we trialled the task in London (with the target age group) and we were dependent upon Ole to help us to predict how the real target learners would respond in South Africa.

If the **cultural setting** of tasks was thrown up as a big issue in *North West Province Technology Education Project*, the issue we had to address in *Enriching Literacy Through Design & Technology* was how to create a context and task that would engage a 6-year-old. We had our experience of developing Key Stage 1 Standard Assessment Tasks to draw on, but classroom teachers had managed those activities, effectively as extended projects. Experience had taught us the importance of hands-on experience and of embedding the young learners in the context. The 'what a surprise' activity illustrates how we did this by

- Providing a 'handling collection' of surprise greeting cards
- Providing a range of simple concept models of paper pop-ups
- Using storytelling to help learners grasp the concept of designing for clients

The simple 'concept model' handling collections were drawn on heavily as these very young learners used them to trigger their imagination – for example, the paper coil that evolved into a twisting, turning skateboard track. As we had found in earlier work with this age group, the story was crucial in helping the young children empathise with a design client.

From these starting points they were able to design a surprise card for someone who was special to them, to stay 'on task' through an intensive 75 min assessment period – and to evaluate the experience, telling us quite explicitly how much they had enjoyed the activity.

Assessing Design Innovation provided a very different challenge. Here we were trying to create tasks that would explicitly foster innovative responses. What emerged from our debates and school trials was the importance of **double demand**. If a new product has to do X, then it is relatively uncomplicated, but if it has to do X **and** Y, the complexity escalates dramatically. This complexity throws up the potential for highly innovative work. Double demand was created in the 'light fantastic' activity through the requirement that the prototype had to be **both** a **protective package** for the light bulb **and** transform into a **lighting feature** (Figure 12-1).

Having set the task, it is important to provide the stimulus that makes it possible for learners to grapple with it. We used handling collections, and of two kinds. The first was a set of light bulbs of various kinds and in various forms of packaging. This enables learners to get physical with the bulbs – handling them – debating them – exploring them. The second was set of 'idea objects' that all contained elements of transformation. If the light bulb box is to be made to transform into a lighting feature, then learners need to see what that transformation might be like. The table of idea objects was there to provide inspiration about the double-life of objects: it can be this – or that. The lurid Christmas decoration was a good example: from an uninteresting pile of shiny paper it pulls out to become a very complex 3D form.

Figure 12-1. The handling collection for 'light fantastic'

The twin challenge of the tasks was often too great and learners concentrated on one element of the task to the exclusion of the other. But where both were tackled some outstanding work emerged, an example of which is shown here, where the learner redesigned the light bulb box to a tapering pentagon that could fit with many other identical boxes to build into a hanging sphere. Each box had a letter cut-out with inset lighting film. With a bulb suspended at the centre of the sphere the feature would project the letters onto the wall. The learner created his own strapline for the prototype: 'your name in lights' (Figure 12-2).

Figure 12-2. 'Your name in lights' box unit

In all of the examples given above, the activities were only ever designed to get learners to a developed idea or first working prototype and there is a huge amount of work that remains to be done to bring the design to a proper resolution. This raises a further important point about these activities. They are *not* complete assessments of design & technology capability. Each allowed us to highlight evidence of certain targeted constituents of capability, and, in line with the assessment **purpose** of each, they performed a particular role.

Teachers who have interacted with us through these projects expressed clearly that the real strength of the activities lay in getting design activities up and running really fast, engaging learners with the task, and getting early ideas flowing.

For all learners, the key elements in the success of these assessment activities have been:

- Ownership of the task
- A task rich in design issues
- Real props to inspire and promote ideas
- Concrete, hands-on experience

In Chapter 5, we described the need for double testing to help separate learners procedural capability from their understanding of the details of any given context/body of knowledge. Was the learner who developed 'your name in lights' good at developing innovative ideas, or was he good because of his familiarity with lighting and packaging.

We explored exactly this issue within the project, for each learner undertook two tests with different tasks but set within a common procedural framework. We then compared the variance of holistic marks for each learner across the two tests. We were able to report that

> [T]he general consistency of the data from test 1 to test 2 does suggest that in the vast majority of cases, design innovation is a sufficiently generalised quality of capability that it can consistently be diagnosed through our assessment activities. (Kimbell et al. 2004, p. 44)

2.2.2 Authentic Activity Structures

Authentic tasks are a good starting point, but without a well-constructed activity structure they lose their potency. Based on the original *APU* model, the two key devises we have used have been the administrator's script and the learner response booklet. Both of these devices have been through a number of iterations over the last 20+ years, driven both by the challenge of new research demands and by our increased understanding of the subtleties of the ways the strategies operate. The following general rules have emerged from these numerous modifications of the original.

Concerning the **script**, e.g.:

* Iteration of subtasks between active and reflective.
* Short/sharp timing of subtasks – to drive development forward.
* Timings must be flexible enough to be tuned to the details of each particular school. Normal break and lunch times are important.
* Indicating words that must be said verbatim and words that can be rephrased by the teacher.
  Concerning the **booklet**, e.g.:
* Immediate past work must be visible while working on current subtask
* Space must be **only just** big enough for the drawing time available, since big spaces intimidate and reduce the inclination to 'have a go'
* Including 'thought bubbles' which prompt deeper or broader thinking by not providing answers
* Making the size of the opened booklet comfortable for the learner (typically A3 for younger children and A4 for older) and, for pragmatic reasons, folded down to a size that can be easily filed.

3.   MAKING ASSESSMENTS

The process of creating an assessment instrument is closely tied to the process of creating an assessment framework. They are linked and parallel processes, both derived from our view of capability. This generic view of capability can then be fleshed out (flavoured) with the specific qualities that are sought within individual projects.

So, for example:

- *CATS Key Stages 1* and *3* assessment frameworks were tailored towards the National Curriculum Attainment Targets in design & technology
- *North West Province Technology Education Project* framework was tailored towards performance that reflected the content areas of the experimental curriculum, and group performance
- *Enriching Literacy through Design & Technology* framework was tailored towards assessing literacy as well as design & technology
- *Assessing Design Innovation* framework was tailored towards qualities of innovation

The development of the activity and the tuning of the assessment framework proceed hand-in-hand. If the framework suggests that we need evidence of quality x, we look for ways of promoting evidence of that quality within the activity. We then try it out in schools and see if we really do get evidence of that quality. If not, we try again with a different strategy – or modify somewhat the description of the quality. An aspect of this process that has proved important is providing several opportunities within an activity for evidence of a quality to emerge – and to take note of the evidence, even if it emerges in parts of the activity we had not anticipated it would. This point came home very clearly to the team through an instance where we got it wrong. In *Researching Assessment Approaches* (reported in Chapter 6) we encountered genuine problems reliably assessing the competence 'accessing information' simply because we had not provided multiple opportunities for evidencing the competence.

But generally, what does emerge from this double-ended development process is the **best fit we can achieve** between the qualities we want to assess, and the evidence that the activity can provide. At that point both the activities and the assessment framework emerge from their 'trial' phase. The activities are run 'for real' in schools with the designed learner sample, and the resulting work is then matched up against the assessment framework to evaluate learners' performance.

3.1   The Primacy of Holistic Judgement

When making assessments, we have always encouraged assessors to start by making 'big picture' holistic judgement first. Some judgements are easier to make than others, and we have consistently found that making 'big picture' judgements of **whole** pieces of work is easier (and more reliable) than making small-scale judgements about individual elements. This was fundamental to making assessments in *APU*, again linked back to our view of capability.

> Precisely because of the integrated nature of the activity and the complex interactions of the various aspects of it, holistic assessments of excellence – which allow us to take these interactions into account – have been far more commonplace in design and technology than in many other, more analytic, areas of the curriculum. … In the final analysis, our markers were able to make these holistic judgments of excellence at a level of reliability that was significantly higher than that achieved for the assessment of individual aspects of capability'. (Kimbell et al., 1991, p. 31)

First create an overview of the quality of the work; then drill down into it to unpick the elements of quality that make it up.

3.2   Assessment Rubrics to Support Judgements

We should not underestimate however the difficulty of making such judgements about the work, even when informed by an assessment rubric. Once again our approach has evolved into a two-stage process. Stage 1 involves **identifying evidence** of qualities of performance in learners' scripts/booklets. Stage 2 involves **making judgements of the quality** of the performance.

To assist with the assessment process we have also developed tactics for helping markers delineate qualities, for example by using colour coding. We first developed this approach in *CATS Key Stage 1 Technology*, where we encouraged teachers to keep the activity integrated but to 'put on their pink glasses' to see one dimension, and their 'blue' glasses to look at a second Figure 12-3).

Subsequently, when training the fieldworkers in the *North West Province Technology Education Project*, we took them through a process of (first) identifying the evidence and (second) making judgements.

> Our assessment guide was colour coded (a different colour for each quality) and we required the team to work in pairs over scripts, highlighting evidence using appropriately coloured pens. … In this way the assessors became skilled in *identifying* the evidence before them. (Kimbell and Stables, 1999, p. 9)

Figure 12-3. NWPTEP fieldworker assessment training

We then repeated the process with another script, asking markers to compare with the original one in terms of strengths and weaknesses. We thereby introduced the idea of the relative **quality** of capability evident in the work.

> Through this process we established common understanding of the standards to apply. Initially this standard was based on the exemplars we brought from London, but through the training process we helped assessors to create for themselves their own standardised exemplars of performance based on work from South African students (Kimbell and Stables, 1999, p. 9)

3.3   Assessment and Groups

Readers will have noted the extent to which we use group activities in many of our assessment projects. But it is important to recognise that we use groups principally as a device to support **individual** performance rather than having an explicit focus on **group** performance.

We have established (to our satisfaction at least) that learners improve their performance when they have the opportunity to interact with their peers and discuss their work. Sometimes this collaboration is in 'active' mode; enriching the bank of ideas that learners have access to, and sometimes it is in 'reflective' mode; giving one's work to a teammate to get their reaction to it and their suggestions for what works well and what might need more development.

Our first experience of group activities for assessment was when we created the discussion session in the original *APU Design & Technology* modelling tests. We were genuinely astonished at its impact, both in terms of the way it pushed learners' ideas forward and in the positive way they responded in their evaluation of it.

Recently, in *Assessing Design Innovation*, we have used group collaboration (three learners to a group) in both active and reflective modes at different times in the 6 hours activity. Interestingly – and despite the fact that they know the process is about assessment – not a single learner has ever mentioned the idea that this might be 'cheating'. On the contrary in **every** evaluation of the process that we have undertaken (i.e. in **every** school), the idea of 'team support for my ideas' comes top of their list of good things that learners point to about the activity.

It is important to understand why this is the case. At the outset of the activity (despite all our efforts at contextualising the task and using handling collections to stimulate ideas), when learners have to commit themselves to an idea it is invariably hesitant. At such an early point in the activity, learners almost inevitably lack confidence in whether their first idea is really any good. If at that point the idea is constructively added to and enriched by their teammates, then it gives them far greater confidence to get on with it. Frequently, the ideas contributed by teammates are ignored – but that is not the point. The point is that the idea has acquired more gravitas and substance, it has not been laughed at or ignored. It has rather been taken seriously and teammates have done their best to strengthen it. All this tends to counter the natural uncertainty of a new idea.

We have also used the power of the group to support understanding of the context and task itself, by encouraging small groups to engage in discussion at the start of the activity. We used this tactic, for example, in *Enriching Literacy through Design & Technology* by encouraging discussion of the handling collection provided and in *Researching Assessment Approaches* by encouraging at the start of the task small group discussion about personal experiences related to the context of the task.

It has only been in two of our projects that we have been asked explicitly to assess group performance. For *North West Province Technology Education Project* the experimental technology curriculum in South Africa that we were evaluating had teamwork as one of its core concerns. We therefore had to devise ways of making assessments of it. We have described this process in Chapter 9, and suffice it to report here that the learners were not only familiar with group-based learning, but were also very comfortable with displaying it as they optimised their part-solutions for the medicine transport task during the activity (Figure 12-4).

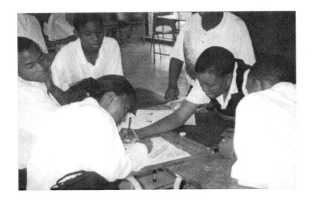

Figure 12-4. Working as a team to optimise a solution

The second project was *Researching Assessment Approaches*, which included assessing competence in 'teamworking'. As described in Chapter 6, we built on the *North West Province Technology Education Project* experience and, in addition, asked the learners to identify and justify their own actual and wished for roles in the team.

It is good to be able to report that group working is becoming more commonplace in schools. When we launched the group discussion in the modelling test for *APU Design & Technology* (in 1987–1988) it was a very rare idea – not just with learners but also with teachers. But with *Assessing Design Innovation* learners and teachers have adopted it very readily and it does not appear to create anything like the shock that it originally was.

3.4   A Brave New World of Judging

It is worth at this point giving brief mention to a completely different approach to assessment that we have been experimenting with for our current project, *e-scape*. As we have described in Chapter 6, this project involves the use of hand-held computers with learners building their design portfolios dynamically in a web space. This web-based facility opens up the possibility of a completely new approach to assessment.

We have been working with General Certificate for Secondary Education Awarding Bodies and have met with Alistair Pollitt, who was at one time the director of assessment research at the University of Cambridge Local Examinations Syndicate. He has drawn our attention to a system of assessment that we might call 'differentiated pairs' since the assessment process involves making a single judgement about which of two scripts is the better.

The fundamental requirement of summative examinations is to judge the overall quality of students' work in some educational domain on a standard ordinal scale. Usually, in Britain, the scale is then divided into bands to indicate relative grades of performance. But while scoring and aggregation seems to suit those examinations composed of many small questions, examiners in some other subjects, where they want to assess created objects or performances, have often used the method only reluctantly, and in design & technology we have consistently argued for the primacy of the holistic judgement.

It is not obviously necessary that exams should be marked. The requirement is to find some way to **judge** the students' performances in order to create the scale that is needed, and an alternative method does exist, in which the examiners are asked to make holistic judgements of the quality of students' work. In a recent book on the psychology of judgement (Laming, 2004) it was pointed out that there is no **absolute** judgement; 'all judgements are comparisons of one thing with another'. In other words, all judgements are relative. Since 1995 almost all (non-statistical) studies of examination comparability in England and Wales have used a method of relative judgement (Pollitt, 2004), in which examiners are asked to compare pairs of 'scripts' from different exam syllabuses, simply reporting which is the 'better' of the two.

The basic approach with differentiated pairs was explored in a trial of 20 pieces of work from *Assessing Design Innovation*. The 20 pieces had been marked (as described above and using a rubric of criteria) on a 12-point scale. The 20 pieces were selected from across that scale. They therefore represented a rank order about which we were confident.

Pollitt then used a software package to decide what pairs of scripts should be compared in the trial. In outline, each piece was compared to at least six other pieces and was judged by at least four judges. There were six judges involved in the trial and we each had 40 judgements to make; i.e. a total of 240 pairs to differentiate. All we had to say (by reference to the same overall criteria of performance) was which of the pair has better performance. We had to read the work on both pieces – understand it – and make a judgement. To make the process quicker, Pollitt created 'chained' pairs

3 and 17
17 and 6
6 and 15
15 and 4

and so on. This ensured that the judges only had to take in one new piece of work to make each pair judgement. The following statistics (based on Rasch analysis) were then prepared by Pollitt from his analysis of the trial data (Figure 12-5).

Two of the pieces (8 and 17) won every pairs judgement, and every judge reported the same. The lowest performer (18) lost every pair judgement and equally, every judge reported the same. As Pollitt reported

> To confirm the results of the analysis the scripts' parameters were plotted against the marks previously assigned to them. As expected, there was a strong but non-linear relationship between the parameters and the marks. (Kimbell et al., 2006, p. 8)

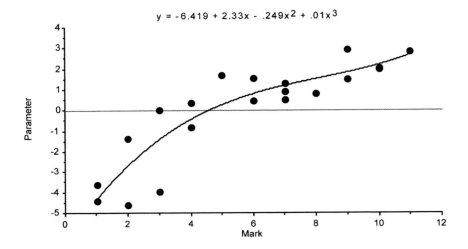

$$y = -6.419 + 2.33x - .249x^2 + .01x^3$$

Figure 12-5. The non-linear relationship between the judging parameter scores and the numerical mark

There are three key measures of the effectiveness of an assessment system. Does it provide **valid** measures of capability? Is the assessment **reliable**, and is it **manageable**? Validity is a measure of the extent to which the resulting number is an authentic way of representing the design & technology capability of the learner. Reliability is a measure of repeatability; do all judges say the same? Manageability is (as the name suggests) about whether the judgements are do-able in a reasonably efficacious way.

We were convinced of the validity of the approach. Using holistic judgements (informed by criteria in the rubric) we were able to make overview judgements that reflect the complex interactions of elements of each learner's work.

The reliability statistic was very good because (unlike normal marking) the work is seen in relation to many other pieces and by many judges. It is therefore – by definition – a 'repeatable' judgement.

The problem was manageability. When judge 1 wanted to see piece 3 and 17, judge 5 was already looking at 17 and comparing it to 10. The logistics of not having the 20 pieces available to all judges all the time proved very time-wasting.

Which explains why Pollitt is so excited about *e-scape*. If all the work is in a web site, it is all available, all the time, to any judge who logs into the system, and from wherever they log in. The differentiated pairs system of judging has been **only** a research tool because of the logistic problems of making it anything bigger. The *e-scape* system provides – for the first time – the opportunity for it to become a front line assessment device.

Imagine a world in which teachers' formative assessment in the classroom is **not** shaped by the demands of summative assessment. If summative assessment were managed by some variant on the differentiated pairs approach, what would formative assessment look like? How would teachers help their students to maximise their performance?

They would **not** be saying:

• You can get 15 marks for 'research' if you do this and that
• You can get 18 marks for 'presentation' if you do this and that

Instead they would have to be saying:

• Your overall performance would be more convincing if …

Would that not be a healthier state of affairs?

The judgements at the end of the day would be a composite of many judges looking at the work. If teachers themselves are the judges (but looking at work from many schools) would this not distribute a wider understanding of standards of capability? (For a fuller account of the judging process see Kimbell (2007).)

4. REFLECTIONS ON THE BOOKLET ACTIVITIES

Choreographed assessment activities in specially designed booklets (and in the *e-scape* case a specially designed PDA screen and web site) have become something of a hallmark of our work in TERU. They enable us to:

• Focus our research data on **performance assessment**
• Collect these data in a much more **compressed timescale** than 'normal' project work
• Structure the activity to **focus on the qualities** that are important to the project in hand
• Force to the surface **evidence** of those qualities for assessment purposes
• Use the learners' own **teacher** as the means for administration of the assessment
• **Standardise** the approach, equitably for all learners across the sample

But perhaps the major advantage of this assessment format is that it derives directly from a description of capability and results in activities that are not usual in the design & technology world. Teachers look at them and see how they might present design & technology projects in a different way. The monolithic 'project', which is slow to start and rumbles painfully along for months is given a blast of fresh air by activities that are fast and furious, and that present very different models of what designing might be. Our reports are peppered with teachers' reactions to this approach, but perhaps the following comment, from a teacher involved in *Assessing Design Innovation*, illustrates this best.

> This trial has had a real effect on my teaching. It has reinforced things I do, reminded me of things that I have done, and prodded me to think of things I have never done. My PGCE student is completely 'gob smacked' with the method of working and is implementing many of the principles in the trial in his teaching. His lessons are showing real pace and focus.

> We found the project to be a very rewarding experience – we have had time to reflect and it will enrich our learning style considerably. (Kimbell et al., 2004, p. 37)

A further issue that it is important for us to acknowledge is that these assessment activities do not confront the harsh realities of making, although in *Assessing Design Innovation* we have recast **making** as **modelling**, with very pleasing results. In this project, many (probably a majority) of the learners chose to do most of their design development work through progressively more sophisticated models – supported by (not led by) sketching. This is *not* the normal approach in schools, which assumes that drawing must precede modelling. However, our approach chimes very closely with practice in the commercial world of design innovation. Myerson (2001) talks to IDEO designers about the centrality of modelling.

> We build lots and lots of imperfect prototypes not because we think we've got the right answer, but to get responses from buyers and users. Then we can fix their complaints. We're into multiple realisations of what the future can be. 'Faking the future' describes the rough and ready IDEO formula of building lots of crude prototypes....Kelley describes this as 'fast fearless prototyping. (Myerson, 2001, p. 32)

In our activities we have liberated learners to create 'multiple realisations of what the future can be through 'fast, fearless, prototyping'. But we accept that learners do not (e.g. within the 6 hour activity) have to face the really harsh decisions that confront them when 'real' making is undertaken. We accept that these short, sharp activities are not a **replacement** for extended design

& development projects where these material and manufacturing realities come to the fore. Rather they are a supplement, shedding light into elements of learners' capability in ways that extended projects tend not to.

These choreographed design & technology projects, and the teacher scripts and learner response booklets that shape them, offer an infinitely adjustable mode of performance assessment. It is as though one has a palette of possibilities, each of which contains numerous options. What capabilities are we interested in; with what learners; in relation to which design & technology settings; and using what timescale? Given the answers to these questions, we can design authentic activities that have meaning to learners and that will provide performance data on their capability. As we have seen from *Researching Assessment Approaches*, this potential extends to other curricula where the focus of assessment is on learners' **performance**.

Across the various projects in which we have utilised our assessment approach, we have amassed quantities of data not just on performance in general, but more particularly of the insights the data have given us into differences between learners: between girls and boys, between those of different ability and different age groups. It has also provided insights into learning style and designing style – and it is to our cumulative understanding of these issues of differentiation that we now turn.

Chapter 13

LEARNER DIFFERENCES

Why you might find this chapter interesting

We begin this chapter by making the somewhat paradoxical point that equality of educational provision can only be achieved when every learner receives an individual – and different – experience. Taking this as a starting point, we examine some of the data from the projects in Part Two to illustrate the varied responses of different subgroups of learners in relation to their performance. We examine the active/reflective emphases of age and gender groups as well as their levels of engagement with tasks. But we are careful not to assume these tendencies are necessary conditions, and rather we explore the power of 'working from strengths to tackle weaknesses'. We discuss the issue of learners 'designing style', that was the explicit focus of one project and a powerful influence of several others. We also explore the interestingly different effects of models of teaching and learning through the years of schooling; very different approaches being used by teachers, e.g. in primary and secondary schools. Finally, we examine the differential effects on learners' performance of the resources and the substructures of the activities (see Chapter 12) that we have used to shape and steer our assessment activities.

*** ***

1. DIFFERENCE AND EQUALITY

Before considering the differences between learners explored through our various research projects, it is important to tease apart issues surrounding learner difference, equal access and differentiation, and to make our position on these matters clear. At the outset of *APU Design & Technology* our understandings of difference were more limited than they have become through the research we and others have conducted since that time. But we recognised the link between difference and equality, our views echoing those expressed by Downey and Kelly.

> equality is not a demand for similarity of treatment at all but for a justification for differential treatment, a justification which must take the form of demonstrating that our reasons for discriminating between people in certain contexts are relevant reasons and, therefore, arguably, fair, just and impartial reasons. Differential treatment of patients, therefore, is justified if they are shown to have different diseases or different constitutions; differences in our treatment of offenders are to be justified by reference to differences in the nature of their offences or the circumstances under which they were committed; and differences of educational provision are to be justified by appealing to differences exhibited by pupils in their ability to profit from education or what appear to be differences in their educational needs. (Downey & Kelly, 1975, p. 175)

We acknowledge that each learner will have strengths and weaknesses, some of which will be generic – such as a strong visualising or verbalising capacity, and some more directly related to design & technology. There are myriad ways in which learners can be different, and, if one is seeking equality for all learners, then teachers must take account of these individual differences in providing equal access to a design & technology curriculum. Downey and Kelly sum up this apparent paradox.

> We have seen some of the inequalities that can result from attempts to fit 'off-the-peg' curricula or programmes to all pupils ... All of this would seem to point to the desirability of individually tailored provision. The paradox of equality in education is that it is only when the educational diet of every child is different from that of every other that we can really hope that we are near to achieving it. (Downey & Kelly, 1975, p. 205)

At first glance this presents a scenario so complex as to make all but a superhuman teacher feel unable to run an effective classroom. But in reality, awareness of a few key differences can have a significant impact on understanding how the development of design & technological capability might be affected. Our own understandings were deepened through *APU* as the whole issue of difference was opened up through our analysis of empirical data, focusing on gender and ability. These understandings have been extended by further projects as we have conducted research with a broader range of age groups, and also to see difference through an additional set of lenses – those of learning style and designing style.

2. PROCESS-BASED QUALITIES

2.1 Starting with Performance

In *APU Design & Technology*, in advance of considering differences between **subgroups** in our sample (such as gender or ability), we explored differences in **performance** emerging from our analysis of work. This analysis we described as 'fingerprinting'

> because, like a fingerprint, each script was unique, but by building up a list of discriminating yes's and no's it became possible to describe the uniqueness in any particular scripts [and] ... to generalize these descriptors by selecting all high scorers and printing out the discriminating characteristics that they did contain and those that they did not contain. (Kimbell et al., 1991, p. 32)

This fingerprinting was undertaken within an assessment framework derived from our model of capability. Not only did it confirm the features of the model, in particular through the emergence in the work of the qualities of **reflection**, **action** and **appraisal**, but it also provided different profiles of performance. At an overarching level, these profiles could be categorised into what we described in Chapter 5 as 'balanced', 'reflective skew' or 'active skew' performance.

2.2 Action, Reflection and Appraisal

Having identified these profiles, we examined the make-up of the subgroups in each profile and, broadly speaking, found a mixed gender group in 'balanced' performance, more girls than boys having a 'reflective skew' and more boys than girls having an 'active skew'. Two things are important to note in relation to this: first, high-level performance was typically balanced and broadly equal in terms of gender; second, where we found the gendered differences in active and reflective skews, the groups were still mixed, albeit with a predominance of either girls and boys. The message we took from this was that teachers needed to be aware of the difference between reflective and active skills, to recognise the value of the iterative relationship between them, and to identify learners with a 'skew' and support them to develop skills that would enable more balanced performance. We took the view that understanding the qualities and skills and how they could be recognised and developed was more significant than attributing, in a stereotypical way, one profile to boys and another to girls.

However, the strengths exhibited by girls in reflective skills and by boys in active skills have been a recurring theme through projects. For example, the position was confirmed in *CATS KS3 Technology*, where girls showed their strength particularly in Attainment Target 1 (Identifying needs and opportunities) and Attainment Target 4 (Evaluating), and boys in Attainment Target 3 (Planning and making). A similar position was found with *Key Stage 1*. With *Understanding Technological Approaches* we were afforded the opportunity to look inside the processes that learners operate, to explore the ways in which active and reflective skills are deployed across the length of full projects. To do this we need to reconcile two quite different sets of data. The first kind (from *APU*) is **assessment** data derived from looking at the results of learners' performance on a series of technology tests. It is 'outcome' data. The second data set (from *UTA*) is based on 'real-time' observation of learners providing '**process**' data through the life of projects. But both projects provided evidence of processes and **sequences** used by learners in tackling design & technological tasks, with data collected in line with the same *APU* model of **thought in action**. As outlined earlier, the overarching position established through the short, focused APU tasks suggested that:

> [G]enerally, girls do far better on the more reflective tests than boys, and boys do somewhat better than girls in the more active tests. In other words, girls appear to be better at identifying tasks, investigating and appraising ideas, whilst boys seem to be better at generating and developing ideas'. (Kimbell et al., 1991, pp. 204–205)

Looking then at data derived from full-length projects one might speculate the following.

1. Boys would be more active and girls more reflective in their response to tasks
2. Given that the start (sorting out the task) and the end (evaluating the outcome) of a project are typically more reflective, girls would be more comfortable at handling these starting and finishing phases of the task
3. Given that the middle of the project (making) is typically very active, boys would be more comfortable at handling this central phase

If we examine the *Understanding Technological Approaches* Key Stage 4 data, i.e. the data that is closest (in age terms) to the *APU Design & Technology* data, these assertions appear to match very closely with the evidence. Using the 'motoring' data (see Chapter 7), girls engage with the early (typically reflective) part of the task far more readily than do boys and the boys only begin to get on terms with them in the middle of the project in the more active making stages (Figure 13-1).

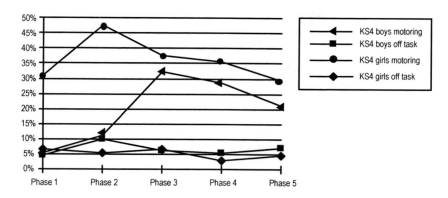

Figure 13-1. UTA – time spent 'motoring' and 'off-task' by KS4 girls and boys

We found it somewhat startling that, on average, the boys in our Key Stage 4 sample spent the first two fifths of their project at a very low level of engagement (a mere 5–10% motoring) when compared to the girls (around 40% motoring). Given that General Certificate for Secondary Education projects range up to 50 hours of timetable time, this represents a prodigious waste of valuable time. It begs the question of what boys were doing with their time – albeit at a 'poddling' level of engagement. The data showed that, in these early stages, the boys are much more likely to be doing 'active' things (e.g. modelling) whereas girls are more likely to be doing 'reflective' things (e.g. investigating or evaluating) (Figure 13-2).

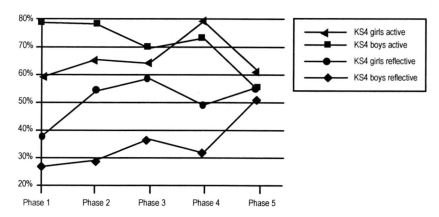

Figure 13-2. UTA – KS4 girls/boys active and reflective activities

Taken together, the data on **engagement** with the task and the data on the **substance** of the activities being pursued suggest that our three speculations (above) are broadly true. But this 'real-time' observation data also showed us the changes in performance **across the phases of the project**. The boys' performance **starts off** with an enormous disparity between the active (79%) and the reflective (26%) modes of response and **ends up** much more balanced (61% and 51%). The girls' is more balanced throughout. This 'real-time' data confirms a significant pedagogic finding from the *APU* data – but one that (at that time) we could only infer from performance on different tests.

> [B]oys are more able to get to grips with reflective aspects of capability when they are practically engaged in developing a solution, and especially so when they are able to do this through more practical modelling activities. Girls on the other hand would appear to be more able ... (to do this) ... without the benefit of such practical engagement. (Kimbell et al., 1991, p. 215)

The boys' engagement in practical activity enables them progressively to gain access to reflective issues. The girls appear more likely to be able to hold a balance throughout the activity. One important question that flows from this, is the extent to which this significant difference in the performance styles of the gender groups is reflected in data from the younger age groups, i.e. from Key Stage 3 (lower secondary) and Key Stage 2 (upper primary). Our *Understanding Technological Approaches* data allowed us to examine these same issues across this wider spectrum of schooling, and three initial differences about active/reflective responses at Key Stage 3 became obvious.

First, there is far less difference between boys and girls than there is at KS4. Broadly, the curves follow each other closely, with reflective activities growing through the project (from 20% to 40%) whilst active activities decline (from 90% to 70%) (Figure 13-3).

Second, the actual levels of active/reflective activity are even more extreme than they were at Key Stage 4. With this age group the averages were 68% active, 37% reflective. At Key Stage 3 the averages are 78%

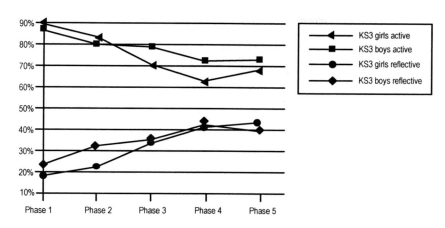

Figure 13-3. UTA – KS3 girls/boys active and reflective activities

active, 32% reflective. Third, the profile of performance (boys **and** girls) is far closer to the boys' profile at Key Stage 4 than it is to the girls' profile. Boys **and** girls at Key Stage 3 respond very like the boys at Key Stage 4.

As we outlined in Chapter 7, the data from *Understanding Technological Approaches* caused us to characterise Key Stage 3 technology as being 'disciplinary' technology in that it is more instructional than any other Key Stage and this instruction is in **the skills and knowledge of the material workshops** at the expense of design skills and experience. In the far more tightly teacher controlled environment of Key Stage 3 technology, it was not surprising that individual learner differences were squeezed out, producing more homogeneous data. Moreover, the focus on skill acquisition – at the expense of designing – created the more extreme active/reflective imbalance of responses.

What then of the position at Key Stage 2? Might one expect performance to be more like that at Key Stages 3 or 4?

The data indicated three important features about the performance of boys and girls at Key Stage 2. First, it is very similar; the boys and girls profiles are almost exactly matching. Second, profiles are significantly different to those at Key Stage 3; there is a better active/reflective balance throughout the project. Third, the Key Stage 2 profiles (girls and boys) match more closely to the **girls** Key Stage 4 profile than to the boys Key Stage 4 profile (Figure 13-4).

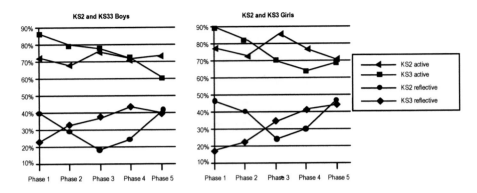

Figure 13-4. UTA – comparing KS2 and KS3 girls/boys active and reflective activities

It would appear that in the sample of learners we observed, the imbalance in action and reflection was imposed through the teaching approach in Key Stage 3 classrooms – and that the boys appear to be more influenced by their Key Stage 3 experiences than the girls. If it is true – as we found in *APU Design & Technology* – that at Key Stage 4 'the boys engagement in practical activity enables them progressively to gain access to reflective issues' then it is as much a comment on KS3 design & technology as it is on the boys themselves. For at Key Stage 2 they were – equally with the girls – quite able to grapple with the reflective as well as the active throughout the task.

Further insight into this issue came, somewhat unexpectedly, through the *Enriching Literacy through Design & Technology* project where we were presented with a fresh opportunity to use the short, focused style of assessment activities developed for *APU* but with much younger children – those in Years 2 and 6. With these groups, we collected performance data on active and reflective skills, and examined the differences between those children who had experienced the curriculum initiative in question and those who had not (see Chapter 9). With the girls, we found that the intervention group (A) significantly outperformed the control group (B) in all assessed areas – reflective and active. With the boys, those in the intervention group also outperformed their counterparts in the control groups, but most interestingly, this was far more marked in the reflective areas (Figures 13-5 and 13-6).

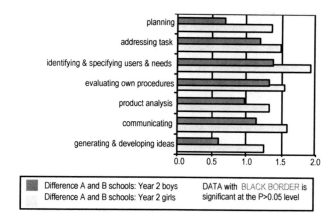

Figure 13-5. Enriching literacy through design & technology – comparing Year 2 A and B schools by gender

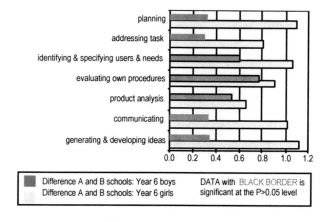

Figure 13-6. Enriching literacy through design & technology – comparing Year 6 A and B schools by gender

As we have outlined in Chapter 9, the curriculum these boys experienced was very much 'hands-on' – engaging with and evaluating real-world products in the course of their design & technology and literacy activities. Through first-hand product analysis activities, the boys appear to have developed reflective skills – echoing the findings of *Understanding*

Technological Approaches. As we remarked at the time, this enhancement of boys' skills was not due to remedial action, but through involving them in sound design & technological learning and teaching practices.

> [T]he activities provided by the project that have created this impact, have been curriculum driven, derived from what has come to be recognised as good practice in design & technology, rather than from the introduction of remedial activities, aimed specifically at compensating a particular gender. (Stables & Rogers, 2001, p. 129)

2.3   Designing Style

As all of the above indicates, the issue of curriculum impact is critical in considering learner differences, but before we turn to this, there is a further dimension to the performance of girls and boys to introduce into the discussion – that of designing **style**. This issue emerged strongly through the *Wholes and Parts Project* (see Chapter 7) where, in conjunction with colleagues from the psychology department at Goldsmiths, a study was conducted that initially set out to explore parallel interests in psychology and design concerning the cognitive operations involved in **seeing** and **designing**.

This project built on the work on cognitive style of Riding and Cheema (1991) and Atkinson (1995), in particular looking at the two continua of 'wholists' to 'analysts' and 'visualisers' to 'verbalisers'. Tony Lawler, a member of the Wholes and Parts team, had used this work in analysing the designing styles of student–teacher designers at Goldsmiths (Lawler, 1996, 1999) and had posited two descriptors of designing style: 'big picture' designers and 'small step' designers.

> 'Big pictures designing' projects into the future, shows complete ideas, focuses on what might be, takes risks, synthesises ideas, is playful, spontaneous, imaginative and intuitive. … Small steps … designing disassembles tasks and ideas by being diagnostic, calculating and weighing conflicting constraints and being systematic but does not take risks and is not predictive. The small steps designer enjoy[s] recording the progress of the designing. (Lawler, 1999, p. 132)

These descriptors were explored further in *Wholes and Parts*. While not being synonymous with descriptors of action and reflection, there is a relationship between the two sets of descriptors. As with action and reflection, the descriptors are not 'either/or', but facets of the way designing is approached. Most learners assessed had a tendency towards the style of one descriptor – typically for boys towards 'big pictures' designing and for girls towards 'small steps. For *Wholes and Parts*, we created *APU* style tests that had a bias towards one or other style and explored the ways in which learners (undertaking both tests) reacted. Adding further and complementary insights to the *APU Design & Technology* and *Understanding Technological Approaches* findings, girls tended to perform better when the bias was towards 'small steps' and boys when it was towards 'big pictures'. The Wholes and Parts study deliberately took primary age children as its focus, in order to avoid the influence of what we described through the *Understanding Technological Approaches* project as the 'disciplinary' tendency in teaching style at Key Stage 3. Reflecting on the findings of the study in the light of the secondary design & technology curriculum, Lawler pondered on the impact of this curriculum.

> These findings are not a result of students having had imposed a design procedure by their teachers but represent the pupils' preferred ways of working at age 11. At present it would seem that the 'preferred' designing procedure adopted by most [secondary] teachers of designing and technology in UK schools, and favoured by examining boards, matches most closely with what I have called 'small steps designing', which I suggest at age 11 favours girls. (Ibid. p. 136)

3.   CURRICULUM IMPACT

So yet another of our projects forced us to confront the issue of equity – and the way the curriculum, teaching (and management) style or assessment regime can (perhaps inadvertently) disadvantage an individual or group of learners. But we also have evidence of the positive impact curriculum can have, as we saw above with the impact on boys reflective skills in *Enriching Literacy through Design & Technology*. In *APU Design & Technology* we explicitly created subgroups within the total survey that came from the 'subjects' that were forerunners of National Curriculum design & technology. Within these curriculum subgroups we witnessed the positive impact on performance, both the greater balance between action and reflection and the range of issues being dealt with. A particular example that illustrates this is the extent to which learners addressed 'user' and 'manufacturing' issues in their response to the tasks set.

In the *full* survey population, these two facets of the task threw up some interesting differences in the balance of concern of the gender groups.

> It would appear to be the case that girls are generally significantly more able at developing products in terms of the user, whilst boys are more able at actively considering the manufacturing dimension. Both the general trend and this gender difference are demonstrably present in test

3iA where girls – of all ability levels – outperform all boys in 'user' developments, whilst boys – of all ability levels – outperform all girls in the 'manufacturing' developments. (Kimbell et al., 1991, p. 217)

However, when we looked more closely at the design & technology-related subgroup, the girls showed far greater evidence of addressing both user *and* manufacturing issues. When we followed this matter up in the *UTA* data we initially made comparisons with the full *APU* survey population – and found to our surprise that the 'real-time' *Understanding Technological Approaches* data suggested that girls are prepared to deal with user issues **and** manufacturing issues at equivalent levels to the boys; indeed often to higher levels. As evidence of this, Figure 13-7 highlights learner performance in this area at Key Stage 3. It shows a clear advantage to the girls **as the project takes its course**.

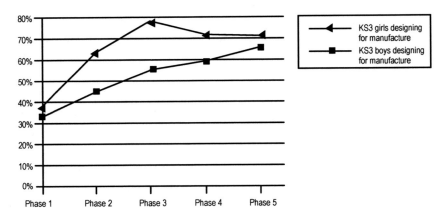

Figure 13-7. UTA – KS3 girls and boys designing for manufacture

At the outset of the project, neither the boys nor the girls take manufacturing issues too seriously, but these form a major concern from the mid-point of the project onwards. Parallel (though not quite such extreme) results emerge at Key Stages 2 and 4. How then are we to interpret this in the context of the *APU* data?

The first point to observe is the extent to which these data relate to the phases of the project, and moreover the phase pattern at each Key Stage creates another pattern. At Key Stage 2, girls concern with manufacturing issues varies across the project (42–57%). But at Key Stage 3 the maximum–minimum span is somewhat bigger (36–77%) and at Key Stage 4 it is bigger still (20 – 77%) (Figure 13-8).

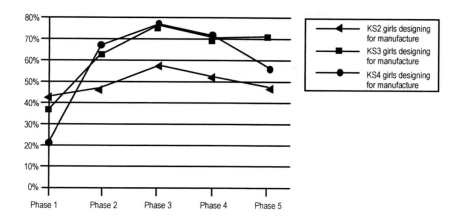

Figure 13-8. UTA – Comparing KS2, 3 and 4 girls designing for manufacture

The girls in our *Understanding Technological Approaches* sample appear to be learning to concentrate their energies on particular things at particular times – and manufacturing concerns are increasingly seen as appropriate in the middle of the project and less appropriate at the start and towards the end. Progression across the Key Stages would appear to be characterised by increasing specialisation and focus and it is very difficult to accommodate this in short-term testing. Incidentally, an exactly reciprocal curve exists in their designing for the user, which starts at a high level – dips through the mid-point of the project – and rises again towards the end (Figure 13-9).

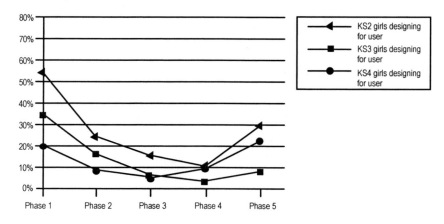

Figure 13-9. UTA – Comparing KS2, 3 and 4 girls designing for user

Engagement with the National Curriculum in this aspect appears to have empowered the girls to deal with a more complete range of issues than their counterparts evidenced in the pre-National Curriculum era.

A further example of a staggeringly positive curriculum impact comes from the *North West Province Technology Education Project* (Chapter 9). Once more the impact was related to gender, and here the difference was evidenced through the confidence, positive attitudes and empowerment that came through the development of technological capability. In Part One, we referred to Sen's view of capability and the way in which, for him, the development of capability links to equality. This issue was immediately observable through the activities enacted in this project. Through the 'attitude' questionnaires and the interviews with the learners, the message came through loud and strong; the girls from the schools where the curriculum had been introduced were more positive about technology generally and about their own capability and what it offered for their futures, than were those from the control schools. Equally importantly, the boys from the project schools also held positive views about the girls, in marked contrast to those expressed by the learners from the control schools. This is illustrated, for example, in the data from the activity questionnaire, in the level of agreement with negative statements about working in teams (mixed gender, three boys and three girls). The learners in control schools agreed more with all statements and when this was split by gender, the girls in control schools agreed most, whereas there was little difference between girls and boys in the project schools (Figure 13-10).

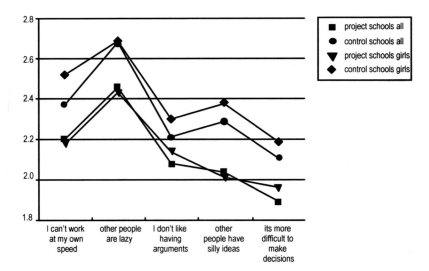

Figure 13-10. NWPTEP – level of agreement with negative statements about teamwork

4.   THE INFLUENCE OF RESOURCES AND STRUCTURES

In the findings from *Understanding Technological Approaches* and *Wholes and Parts*, the implication is that boys are being constrained by a particular approach to design & technology. A rather different story was told when we explored the impact of the introduction of CAD technology into secondary design & technology (Chapter 9), where there were indications that the new technology liberated the boys. The following section from the final project report highlights the data from teacher interviews.

Gender differences were noted by several teachers:

'it's given boys more interest in designing'

'boys used to hate design (folder stuff) and just want to MAKE. Now they love designing'

'they ask so many questions and PLAY with it – they experiment'

'you have to stop them – but girls will wait for the next task'

'boys are not more able – but will jump in with both feet. Girls are conservative, careful, take small steps – and can outstrip the boys with well worked out solutions – same as non-CAD work'

'girls are less willing to lose or change what they have got'.

(Kimbell et al., 2001, p. 8)

The outcome of this spirit of adventure and what closely resembles the approach described as 'big pictures designing' in the previous project was then evident in the performance of the boys in the assessment activity we undertook for this project. The boys' performance was wildly variable, either paying off handsomely, or failing altogether, as opposed to the girls who, generally speaking, neither shone nor failed, but by and large achieved moderate success.

This last example is not just about differences in procedural approaches but also about how this interplays with the resources provided – in the above case the resource of new technology – and the way the task is structured. Our research has identified a range of issues with regard to the context, structure and deployment of resources. In the *APU Design & Technology* tasks we saw how lower ability learners, and particularly girls were supported by tightly structured, concrete tasks and how they were less well supported, even potentially intimidated, by being given too much unstructured time. Other resources have been variously useful to different learners, such as the provision of modelling materials, the opportunity to discuss issues and ideas with other learners, the use of neutral questions and prompts and the provision of handling collections and concept models.

Scanning through these sections, we are reminded of a further feature of learner performance that does not readily fit into any of these sections – because it fits into all of them. In Chapter 10, we drew attention to the effects of the **context** of tasks, and the need to make tasks real and believable for learners. Moreover, contexts are not all equally comfortable for all learners. *APU* data demonstrated how industry-rich contexts are more accessible to some subgroups, whilst people-rich contexts are more accessible to other subgroups.

We also drew attention to the role of **tasks** in making activities do-able for learners. A task might be very open and broad-ranging and in fact little more than a context (e.g. 'security'). But conversely tasks might be far more precisely defined – and may even have performance requirements built into them (e.g. a disguised 'safe' to be designed into a bedroom to store objects up to x size). Different subgroups of learners will respond differently to these very contrasted kinds of task.

In Chapter 11, we drew attention to the ways in which learners' response can be affected by the **procedural structure** that is used to manage the learning activity – specifically through the use of subtasks. Essentially, if an activity has long, unstructured blocks of time it presents a very different challenge to one that has many short, targeted subtasks. Different subgroups of learners will respond differently. In this chapter we have looked at these issues from a different viewpoint – exploring active and reflective skills; different designing styles (big pictures/small steps); and the general effects of this on gender groups.

It is important to recognise that these effects on learner performance do not operate singly. Just as doctors need to understand the overlapping and compounding effects of prescribed medication, so too must teachers understand the compounding effects of all these overlapping influences on learner performance. This was first drawn to our attention through the analysis of data from *APU Design & Technology*. We identified girls as doing far better than boys in one of our tests. Was this a context effect? Or was it a task effect? Or was it a procedural structure effect? In reality, it was all three – operating in harmony to dramatically elevate the performance of one subset of learners.

Wherever the effects that we have described above overlap and operate to the advantage of the same group, then we must expect that group significantly to outperform other groups. Only occasionally of course, do the effects all operate in the same direction. More often, if one effect operates in favour of one group this is balanced by a different effect favouring other groups, and a good example of this is test 3iA. Here, the fact that it is in context A (designing a moving toy for babies and toddlers) appears generally to favour girls, but it is also one of the more 'active' and procedurally 'open' test structures, that generally appear to favour boys. The total effect is to reduce the gender bias in the results, and there is no significant difference in holistic performance between girls and boys. (Kimbell et al., 1991, p. 208)

As we remarked at the time, with an understanding of these effects it is possible to create activities that deliberately favoured one or other group. But more importantly, the understanding can also be used to good effect – making sure an activity is equally accessible and supportive to all learners, whatever their learning or designing style. It is to this challenge that we have sought to respond in many of our research projects. Increasingly, we have explored not just whether or not to launch a task in this way or that way, or whether some particular kinds of props should be provided. Rather we have sought to find ways of working that enable all learners to access what best helps them take their ideas forward. The culmination of these understandings has enabled us to facilitate increasing measures of success in *Assessing Design Innovation* and *e-scape*.

The further we have explored the dimensions of learner difference, the more we have been able to find ways of facilitating learner performance from the various standpoints represented in these differences. It is just as Downey and Kelly pointed out; only when all learners are treated individually (and differently) can we claim to be offering them an equal opportunity to succeed and to excel. Our increasing understanding of supporting learners differentially has identified a range of ways of addressing issues of learning, teaching and assessment – and we have explored these in this chapter and in those immediately preceding it.

But equally the issues of difference throw up a number of methodological considerations that we have had to grapple with during these projects. It is to these matters that we now turn, throwing the focus onto the methodological challenges that have influenced the development of our understandings, approaches and repertoires.

Chapter 14

RESEARCH METHODOLOGY

Why you might find this chapter interesting

This methodological end piece for the book draws together many of the priorities and 'rules of thumb' that we have developed and lived by through the projects in Part Two. We begin by exploring the 'fit' between the values of researchers and their clients. Whilst a degree of disinterested objectivity is required of us as researchers, we inevitably (as experienced professionals) hold to sets of values that shape our world. If these values prove to be in conflict with those of the client / sponsor, some hard choices are inevitable.

    Thereafter, in the chapter we explore the lessons we have learned about the effective conduct of research projects. About the critical role of research design, about instrument design, and about the many facets of being an effective observer of classroom activities. Once the data have been captured, we explore some of the approaches we have used for bringing it to life both for ourselves and for others; making it understandable, meaningful and immediate (particularly through data compression and graphic approaches). We conclude with the point we made in Chapter 4 of Part One that researching is a very design-like activity.

***

We were emboldened to get into research in the first place in part because we saw it as a designerly kind of activity. Once inside it we felt free to exercise our creative talents. This does not mean that we assumed a licence to be dilettante, but rather that, given a specific research challenge, we developed all kinds of tools (sometimes very unusual ones) to give us some purchase on the issue in hand. Sometimes these tools have empowered us to **gather** data more effectively, sometimes to **organise** those data in new ways, sometimes to **analyse** data and sometimes in the **presentation** of data both to ourselves (to aid our understanding of the issues in the data) and to our clients and stakeholders (to get messages across).

As we have worked through projects over the last 20+ years, we have therefore developed a set of understandings that are manifested in a range of approaches that we have introduced to generations of research students at Goldsmiths. It seems appropriate to outline some of these approaches here as a methodological end piece for this book.

1.   THE CHALLENGE OF VALUES

Any research methods guide will underline the importance of getting a clear starting point, and we would absolutely agree with that. Teasing out the questions that one is trying to answer through the research is a necessary and sometimes complex process. The more precise the questions are, the easier it is to decide what will count as data to enable us to answer them.

Part of the complexity in this process of elucidating research questions derives from the common occurrence that the clients/sponsors of research are unclear themselves about exactly what they want. It frequently takes a good deal of negotiating to dig out what they **really** want to know. The process is just the same as when a lay person commissions a designer or architect or gardener to generate a new product/living space/garden. The lay person will typically have some vague notions of what they want. They might have cut out pictures from magazines or (in rare cases) sketched for themselves what is in their head.

But it then remains the job of the designer/architect/gardener to bring their expertise to the task. This is 'what-if' time. What if it was like this? What if it did that? Would it be good if? Would you like it to do that? In doing this, the creator is not throwing **solutions** at the client, but is rather trying to tease out their response to see what excites or interests them. The process is all about digging out the **values** that the client is trying to embody in the work. Are we after a peaceful/tranquil garden space; or a formal architectural space; or a space of light and movement; or; or; or.

It is precisely the same with research clients. We offer up tentative solution types to gauge reaction and thereby get a better grip on what is really wanted. Are they looking for a **statistic** that will convince a policy body or a collection of case study examples to **illuminate practice**? Or do they seek **to shape that practice** in particular ways? Not infrequently the client will say 'yes' 'yes' and 'yes'... we will have all of that. At which point it is our turn to point out that **everything** is not an option unless there is lots of time and money. So we help them to prioritise what they **really** want, and what might be a nice added extra. These underlying value debates then directly shape what we might do in the research.

But teasing out the clients' priorities is only part of the complexity of finding a starting point. For overlaying them are the priorities that we ourselves bring to the task. We are not just jobbing researchers looking to earn a crust by doing anyone's bidding. We have our own set of priorities – typically concerning designing and learning – that we are always interested to understand better. Since we are reasonably well known in research circles, most of the clients that approach us do so knowing that these are our concerns. It is therefore not difficult to find research questions that are appropriate for the client and of interest to us. But there have been some cataclysmic fallings-out over this matter, and *CATS KS3 Technology* (Chapter 6) provides an interesting case.

This was a hugely valuable project that we obviously wished to be a success. But this eventually proved impossible because of the conflict in values between what the client (the School Examinations and Assessment Council) wanted and what we were prepared to do. The first round of development was possible because the looseness of the brief enabled us to bridge the divide (or perhaps fudge the conflict) in values. But as we moved towards the second round of development, the terms were drawn far more starkly. We were not prepared to develop an assessment device that would operate as required. We judged it to be completely wrong at every level; for schools, for teachers, for learners and for design & technology more widely. So we did not do it and we were removed from the development process. We lost a huge amount of money. This one case brought home to us very clearly that client values and researcher values have to be aligned before any research venture can succeed.

2. RESEARCH DESIGN

Assuming that a clear set of questions has emerged from the negotiations establishing a project, the research design becomes a critical aspect, and moreover a part that offers great opportunities for creative thinking. From the priorities identified at the outset we have to create a **design** for the research that stands some chance of achieving the desired outcome. What are we going to do? How are we going to do it? Central to the answer to both these questions is another one: what will count as data?

Think yourself into our shoes at the outset of the *Decisions by Design* project for the Design Council (Chapter 8). We had an absolute alignment of their values and priorities with our own. They were interested (and so were we) to see how the lay person's everyday decision-making process might be the same as, or different from designerly decision making. How might we do that?

The context of the project lay in schools (the Design Council's 'Total Schools Design' initiative) so it made sense to us to think about lay people in schools. Since we would need cooperation at a reasonably high level, it also made sense to target the school management team. We also wanted to have both primary and secondary schools involved. But how many? And from which schools?

We already recognised that if we were to get at their decision-making processes, we would need some significant blocks of time working with them to allow them to develop sufficient trust in us (and what we were doing) and equally to allow us to get inside their thinking processes. So case study methods seemed sensible, and, since their time and our budget were limited, they would need to be drawn from London schools. We also wanted to be able to sit around a table with them all at one time. Using these thought processes we settled on the idea of six teacher fellows (three primary and three secondary) each selected from the schools management team, and committed to giving 12 days of their time to the project over a year. But that is only half the problem, for where would we get the contrasted designerly decision makers – and how would we get them together?

Goldsmiths has a flourishing PGCE programme of teacher education, and each year we take in 40 or so fresh young design graduates who have an interest in becoming teachers. So we had a captive audience of design thinkers who were also sympathetic to thinking about schools. Maybe we could use them?

In the end, we operated a double procedure. First – mostly in their own schools and in their own time – the teacher fellows were asked to draft a 'fly on the wall' description of what had happened in their school when an important decision gets made; e.g. about school development planning, budget making, timing for a new school day, or disciplinary procedures of a member of staff. We asked them for a 'cradle to grave' account of one decision, recording all the things that might have contributed to that specific decision making process. The aim was to gain a comprehensive account of why and how the decision got made in the way that it did.

Then, through the subsequent term, the teacher fellows observed our PGCE designers at work on a group-based design project. Four sessions were dedicated to working with students who were asked to work as they would normally do in design activities. Each group had a teacher fellow assigned to follow their development. Throughout the term the teacher fellows took on the roles of observers and participants in these design activities, and moreover they were required to reflect upon their experiences:

- Analysing the design techniques used
- Debating their strengths and limitations
- Reflecting on the transferability to other problems and settings

- Speculating upon their applicability to specific problems faced by the Senior Management Teams in their schools

In the end, the teacher fellows were astonishingly lucid about the differences between their own and the design students' decision-making processes.

This research design – as with all research designs – was in part based on debates of principle. But at the same time it was also based in part on the pragmatics of what can be done in the time available and with the resource at our disposal.

We could have done something very different. We might have sent questionnaires to thousands of people (some designers and some not) inviting them to tell us about their decision-making processes. We might then have analysed the differences and (possibly) derived some statistically solid data. We judged however – as a point of principle – that we had to put our 'subjects' into decision-making mode and ask them to observe and reflect upon what happened. This is far more demanding and time consuming, but (in our judgement) far more likely to reveal the realities of decision making. Having made that research design decision of principle, we then had to manage the pragmatic consequences of who, when, where and how. Perhaps we should note here that we have never – ever – used blanket questionnaire techniques. We believe that questionnaires can be useful when administered in person to get particular bits of information from people we have worked with and who understand what we are doing and why we are doing it. But our own response to 'blind' questionnaires through the post or on the High Street makes us vary wary indeed of attaching any significance at all to any resulting 'findings' from such blunderbuss techniques. We also recognise, however, that this instinct is informed by our basic philosophy of research, which, as we explained in Chapter 4, is to lean more towards interpretive than positivist models.

The challenge of research design frequently rests on the trade-off we have illustrated here from *Decisions by Design*. What we would like to do in principle – set against what we have the resources (time/money/expertise) to bring to the task. The end result has to be convincing and worthwhile, but equally it has to be do-able.

3.   INSTRUMENT DESIGN

It has frequently been the case that our projects have involved the development of new instruments for promoting learner performance or for collecting data of one kind or another. Once again it is our designer instincts that pop to the surface when faced with these challenges.

We have already explained – in Chapters 5 and 6 – how we evolved the *APU* response booklets for learners to work through over a 90 min task. We have outlined how this 'unpickled portfolio' approach has been modified and used subsequently on many occasions, right up to the current *e-scape* project in which the booklet disappears to be replaced by a digital PDA. These are cases of instrument design where the priority is to find ways of promoting design performance in a short time (i.e. appropriate for a 'test') but without losing the integrity of real designing behaviour. In fact, in these cases, the booklet has to be seen alongside the administrator script and the assessment rubric. Together they comprise the 'instrument' and a huge amount of time, experimentation, trialling and modifying was involved in the original and subsequent versions.

But a very different challenge arose in the *Understanding Technological Approaches* project (Chapter 7) that we undertook immediately after the *APU* experience. We were very aware of the limitations of the *APU* activities (and the single-minded concern with 15-year-old learners) and we determined to investigate 'real' project work, over 'real' time, and with all year groups from Year 1 to Year 11. This was 1992 and the National Curriculum had made design & technology compulsory for all learners throughout these compulsory years of schooling. So what went on in these projects? Did teachers do the same kinds of things in all these years? The research design issues were interesting and essentially we settled on an approach that required us to be **observers** of activity in the classroom.

But as any research manual will testify, being an 'observer' is far from straightforward. Do we intervene and ask questions of the learners or not (participant or non-participant observers). Do we record the process with audio or video? Do we explain who we are and what we are doing – or do we pretend to be wallpaper?

For the immediate purpose of this section, the question that dominated our thinking was 'what is it we are going to observe'? A class full of learners and a teacher over a period of 48 hours (which one KS4 project ran to) can generate a prodigious amount of 'stuff' to be observed. Are they smiling or frowning? Talking or silent? Working in groups or alone? With numbers or drawings or words? Engaged or off-task? Undertaking interesting or banal work? Mechanical or visual or digital? And so on ad infinitum.

Moreover, the research design was based on using a small team of researcher-observers, each taking a set of schools and somehow observing the **same things**. We had to decide what **was** to be observed and what was **not**. We had to develop an instrument that would allow casual (but specific) observations to be transformed into recorded data. It was, by some distance, the most comprehensive observation-based project we have undertaken, and the instrument we developed for it had a number of interesting features.

3.1 Designing Effective Observation

The first challenge arose from the fact that we were, in each school, attempting to observe a **process** in action; a process of design & development by learners, managed by teachers. But whilst processes are continuous, observations represent a moment in time. So how many moments need to be observed in order to gain a 'true' record of the evolving process? This is a bit like plotting points on a graph. How many data points are needed to render a valid representation of the curve?

The question is informed by how long it takes to make the observation. Is it an instant thing or does it take 30 seconds, or 1 min or 2 min? As an example, if we were really trying to observe how much of a lesson the learners were smiling and how much they were frowning, then that is pretty well an instant decision and the observer can just hit a tick/cross list. But there are 25 learners in the class, and 25 ticks/crosses will take (maybe) 1 min in total. So for any one learner we end up with **episodic** data – every 1 min. But we still get (say) 90 bits of data per learner per double lesson, and in reality of course we need FAR more data than this to make sense of their activity.

3.1.1 What and Who to Observe?

All kinds of data might inform our understanding of what is going on. We would like to know about the **task** they are undertaking; about the specific **subtask** that they are doing at this moment; about whether they are doing it alone or in a **group**; about whether the teacher is **interacting** with them or not; about what **kind** of interaction it is; about their **engagement** with the task (motivated or disenchanted) and so on. All this takes a significant amount of time (say 1 min). But there are 25 of them in the class – so now we have episodic data every 25 min on an individual. This is clearly not adequate to reflect the evolving activity. We were forced by this process to focus our observation not just on specific things but on specific learners; and we chose four learners in each group to follow in detail. The choice of these four was done very carefully in discussion with the teacher. We asked to follow:

- Very best designer
- Two middle of the road designers (ideally one male/one female)
- A low ability learner who was nonetheless making progress with design & technology.

All four needed to be good attenders as there was little point collecting a huge quantity of data on learners who were frequently absent. The decision to follow four learners was made in association with three related decisions and involved a difficult optimising process:

- How many observations do we want to make?
- How long does it take to make them?
- How many learners can we follow?
- How episodic does the data therefore become?

In the end we evolved a system with an episodic cycle time of 5 min. In that time we could observe the detailed behaviour of four learners across a rich variety of data. But our decision might have been different. It might have been more data on less individuals; or more data on more individuals with a longer episodic cycle. This is the hard stuff of design decision making in research.

3.1.2   Transforming Text Notes into Tick-Lists

To an extent we were able to speed up the process of data capture. Initially, we just had an A4 pages with lines ruled across it leaving us with 50 mm of space for each 5 min in which we scribbled as furiously as we could to capture what was going on. We had a time box in each slot and could fill that in before the lesson started (e.g. 9.05, 9.10, 9.15, etc.), and we then used the empty space to make notes on what was happening. We had four sheets – one for each learner.

Through a series of school trials we gradually derived a list of things that we believed were more important than other things and that were happening all the time – like communicating. So we evolved a tick box to identify whether there was a teacher/learner interaction at the moment of observation. More than that we were able to identify what **kind of interaction** it was, at least in terms of who initiated the interaction. Was it initiated by the teacher (providing guidance/instruction to the whole class or to a subgroup containing our observed learner) or to the individual learner? Or was the interaction initiated by the learner (seeking specific support from the teacher)? Two ticks in related boxes could now represent a complex interaction, the noting of which had previously taken a lot of free text.

3.1.3   Pace

Having observed only a few lessons it became obvious to us that we needed some measure of the learners' engagement with the task. We wanted to distinguish between learners who were disenchanted or disengaged or just off-task, from those that were fully engaged, crashing ahead purposefully and at pace. In trying to record these data we identified a middle category who were in what might be termed 'tick-over' mode; doing enough to be seen (by the teacher) to be working, but more going through the motions than making real progress. We evolved a categorisation of these behaviours into a three point tick box:

- **Stationary** – going nowhere/off-task
- **Poddling** – in tick-over mode
- **Motoring** – fully engaged, making real dynamic progress

With intervening categories (e.g. between poddling and motoring) we had a 5-point scale to capture this level of engagement. It proved very easy and reliable to note and the resulting data rendered really valuable insights into learning and teaching practices (Figure 14-1).

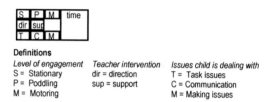

Definitions

Level of engagement	Teacher intervention	Issues child is dealing with
S = Stationary	dir = direction	T = Task issues
P = Poddling	sup = support	C = Communication
M = Motoring		M = Making issues

Figure 14-1. UTA – coding pace, interaction and focus of work

3.1.4   Behaviour or Intention?

One of the problems of observation data is that some of the important things that are happening in a classroom are not observable. This is not because the learners are hidden behind a cupboard or facing the wrong way – but because the important thing is literally not externalised as behaviour. Rather it is going on at an inner level of cognitive processing. One of these inner levels that interested us a great deal was learners' **intentions**. You cannot **observe** intention. It is not a **what** thing or a **how** thing, but a *why* thing. As a result of repeated trials we had created a list of observable behaviours enabling us to capture (with a simple tick) all kinds of workshop-related activity – are learners measuring, cutting, filing, shaping, drawing, etc. The lists initially got longer and then shortened as we categorised and streamlined them. But designing is **purposive** behaviour and the more we collected the behavioural data the less important it seemed to be. Does it matter if a learner is filing a shape out of a piece of acrylic sheet or whether they are hammering a piece of metal? What matters is why they are doing it.

- Is the acrylic filing in order to produce a finished **object** or **component**?
- Or is it to produce a **template** that can be marked around to produce standard components?
- Or is it to produce a **transparent template** that can be marked around at the same time as seeing something important through it?

These different ways of thinking that might inform the edge-filing of a piece of acrylic might reflect significantly different levels of designerly behaviour. Even though the behaviour is the same.

The only person who knows what the intention is of a piece of behaviour, is the person exhibiting that behaviour. So we were committed to talking to learners about what they were doing in order that we could understand why they were doing it. It was for this reason – amongst others – that we chose to be **quasi-participants** in the observed lessons; rather than pretending to be wallpaper. However, our questioning always remained 'neutral' seeking out why they were doing something, rather than commenting on whether we thought it a good thing to do, or suggesting other things they might consider doing. The learners became accustomed to us constantly moving around the room noting things on pads, and that we might occasionally wander over to them to see (and ask about) how they were getting on.

We acknowledge that this observation process will also have changed to some extent the behaviour being observed. This is the perennial dilemma of the observer. The more you get involved the more you find out. But the more you get involved the more you influence what happens, when what you really want to know is what would be happening if you were not there. There are difficult trade-offs to be made here, but the importance of **intention** in design behaviour is so overwhelming that we were obliged to gather it. Often we felt confident in **inferring** an intention from the combination of behaviours we had noted. But occasionally we had no alternative but to ask. Noting the intentions behind the behaviours and the way the behaviours were manifest, gave a rich picture of the different ways learners approached their designing (Figure 14-2; see Chapter 7 for full framework)

Intentions	Manifestations	
generating	discussing	making
mod exploring	thinking aloud	-cut
developing	looking	- join
modify	drawing	- fit
detailing	reading	- mould
constructing	writing	- mix
planning	listening	- finish
organising	waiting	- base
investigating	arranging	- add
receiving	selecting	preparing
evaluating	measuring	testing
reviewing	marking out	cleaning up
recording		off task
explaining		
presenting		
seeking help		
intentionless		

Figure 14-2. UTA – coding data on design intentions and manifestations

3.2   Bringing Data Alive; The Art of Data Compression

The *Understanding Technological Approaches* project generated oodles of data collected from countless hours of observation. *APU Design & Technology*, that preceded it, had generated even more. How should be set about making sense of it all?

Our general approach to data analysis has typically involved a search for patterns in the data and (being designerly folk) we work better with visual patterns than with any other kind. So wherever possible we find ways to represent the data graphically so that trends and anomalies stand out as visual signposts to something interesting that might be happening.

This approach was one we developed during *APU Design & Technology*, very much supported by the team's decision to buy its first Apple Macintosh computer. Up till this time we relied on posing a research 'hunch' to the team's statistician who went and ran a very time consuming data analysis process on the College mainframe computer, producing for us (often 24 hours later) the answer to a question we were no longer interested in. With the introduction of our first 'Mac', we could suddenly explore the data, ably supported by the statistician, for ourselves – and utilise the Mac's simple graphics software to visualise our findings. The following examples illustrate this approach.

First, when exploring data on the comparative analysis of girls of different abilities, we noted that sometimes the lower ability girls did considerably worse than the mid-ability girls, whilst sometimes they were almost on a par with them. Our hunch was that this had something to do with the way the tests were structured, and so presented the data in such a way that the most loosely structured tests were at one end of a continuum, the most tightly structured at the other. As can be seen from Figure 14-3, the more tightly structured the test, the better the performance of the lower ability girls – and equally interesting – the apparent lack of importance this has for high ability girls.

Using graphics helped us make sense of the data for ourselves – and also when communicating this with others. Figure 14-4 shows the raw composite data for holistic performance for girls and boys across the three contexts tests were set in. To the naked eye, what an unintelligible set of figures it is.

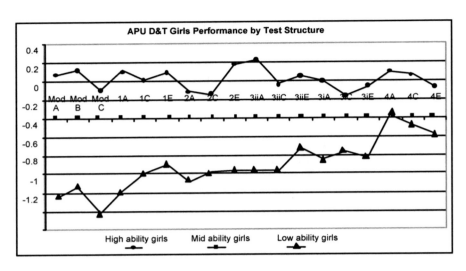

Figure 14-3. Test structure influence in girls' performance

APU holistic performance by context (A, C & E) and gender

	People	Environment	Industry
T.1 Boys	2.19	2.03	1.71
T.1 Girls	2.42 *	2	1.95*
T.2 Boys	1.89	1.77	1.99
T.2 Girls	2.02	1.85	2.21**
T.3i Boys	1.97	2.23	1.87**
T.3i Girls	2.06	2.19	1.58
T.3ii Boys	1.96	1.8	2.41
T.3ii Girls	2.08	1.77	2.29
T.4 Boys	2.15	2.09	1.96
T.4 Girls	2.5**	2.40**	2.29**
Mod Boys	2.29	2.55	2.65*
Mod Girls	2.38	2.37	2.38

* indicates 5% sig.
** indicates 1% sig.

Figure 14-4. APU – raw composite data on holistic performance

As we considered this data we were conscious of a gender effect related to the context of the test – girls tending to outperform boys when the context focused heavily on people, more mixed effects when the focus was on industry and virtually no effect when the emphasis was on the environment. Presenting the data in Figure 14-4 in a graphic form makes this effect far more visible (Figure 14-5).

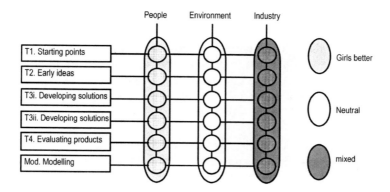

Figure 14-5. APU – context effect on the performance of girls and boys

Giving further consideration to the 'mixed messages' of the industry-focused test, we became aware that there were two effects in the data – context **and** test structure. At times these effects were working in the same way for a gender group, at times they were working in opposition. So once again, using the same raw data from Figure 14-4, we could show these different effects graphically, as in Figure 14-6.

Figure 14-6. APU – context and test structure effect on performance of girls and boys

UTA also provided several classic examples of how this pattern-seeking approach yielded interesting interpretations of the work that learners were undertaking. As we outlined in Chapter 7, the starting point involved developing approaches that make it possible to compress huge quantities of data into relatively simple data sets. First, we entered all the observations as raw data in a spreadsheet. So, taking the example of **interaction** between teacher and learner, we had a column in the data record showing (for every 5 min period) whether the learner was interacting with the teacher and – if so what kind of interaction it was (e.g. **directive** from the teacher or **supportive** sought by the learner). These data were represented in a single code within the column, and the column ran for the entire duration of the project. A typical case was a KS3 project that ran for 485 min, with 97 units of coded data.

From this data we could see, over the life of a project, what percentage of time the learner was seeking support from the teacher, and conversely what percentage of time teachers were being directive. Since we had identical data across all 11 years, it was then a simple matter to represent it graphically (Figure 14-7). With startling consequences, for immediately it became obvious that something odd happens in the transition from Year 6 to Year 7.

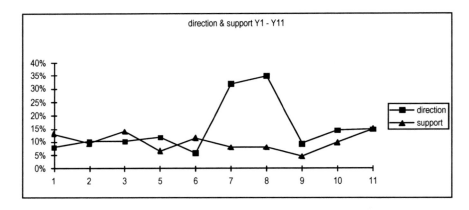

Figure 14-7. UTA – percentage of time with directive and supportive actions

However, whilst charts of this kind are highly informative of generic data, they also tend to hide **trends** in data because of the averaging effect across the life of the project. Since we were concerned with designing as a real-time rolling process, we were equally interested to look at **phases** of data through the life of the project.

As we describe in Chapter 7, to create these working 'pictures', we clustered the data into five project phases, created simply by taking the first 20% of project time, then the second 20% and so on. The resulting data-maps were **condensations** of the data. We referred to these condensations as

data-maps since they enabled us to take huge amounts of data and reduce it down to a form in which we could create simple graphic representations of the trends that lay within it. The illustration of pace data given in Chapter 7 (Figure 7-2) demonstrates how clearly the trends can be seen when presented in this way.

3.3   Gathering Data from Different Perspectives

As has been clear throughout the projects, we have been equally comfortable with combining research approaches – qualitative and quantitative, and different tools – if we judged they would provide us with rich data to inform our research questions. This has involved us, for example, developing parallel interview structures, where effectively the same question is being asked to different stakeholders. A clear example of this was in the *North West Province Technology Education Project* where we used the same question structure to interview teachers involved in the project, their school principals, provincial and NGO officers, and through group interviews, the learners themselves. We have used this approach in a number of projects and typically in the evaluation projects described in Chapter 9, as the approach helps us to gain insight into an issue or situation from a range of perspectives.

A further approach to gaining a rounded, fuller picture of an issue has been to gather linked qualitative and quantitative data, the former allowing us to explore patterns and trends in the data, the latter to illuminate the data and speculate on its meaning. The *North West Province Technology Education Project* provides an example of how we collected a range of data that helped us to explore gender differences in and between the learners from schools involved in the initiative and those from the control schools. Figure 14-8 illustrates different types of data we collected: demographic data (the gender of the respondent and who they worked with); quantitative data about whether they worked well together and what their attitude to gender-related aspects of technology were; and qualitative data through a 'free response' question on the 'best things' about working with boys and girls. The composite insights provided allowed us, for example, to examine in detail the collaborative dimension developed through the initiative (Stables, 2000) and the capability and attitudes it enhanced (Stables & Kimbell, 2001).

From the Activity Evaluation Questionnaire ...

ABOUT GIRLS AND BOYS WORKING TOGETHER

		boy	girl		
4.	Was the partner you worked with today a boy or girl?	☐	☐		

		very well	well	OK	poor
5.	Do you think you worked well together?	☐	☐	☐	☐

6.   What are the best things about working with BOYS?

_____

_____

7.   What are the best things about working with GIRLS?

_____

_____

From the Attitude Questionnaire ...

		strongly agree	agree	disagree	strongly disagree
14.	Girls think technology is difficult	○	○	○	○
18.	Technology is only for girls	○	○	○	○
22.	Boys and girls should learn about technology	○	○	○	○
35.	Girls' attitudes to technology are different from those of boys	○	○	○	○

Figure 14-8. NWPTEP – gathering gender data

3.4   Visualisation to Support Data Capture

The process of rendering abstract ideas into visual form is something that we have consistently sought to do, and not just for analysis and interpretation purposes. Two other instances are worth a brief reference.

We have explained in Chapter 9 how, in *North West Province Technology Education Project*, we had used the unpickled portfolio approach to create activities for the learners to operate on design tasks. The resulting work was to be assessed by the research team in Mafikeng and we decided to operate this through a two-stage process. First, using the assessment rubric, we worked through the learners' responses looking for evidence of the qualities identified in the rubric. Second, having identified the evidence, we sought to attach values to it, enabling us to assess all the work consistently.

It was in the first of these processes that we used a very simple, but effective, visualisation tool. We provided 'high-lighter' pens for the assessor team, using different colours for different qualities in the rubric. This highlighting process – done in pairs – then led to a group debate about the qualities concerned. Is this an example of quality X … and if so does it reflect high level performance or poor performance? Do you agree that that is an example of quality Y … and so on.

This sharing process – based on highlighted evidence – proved very helpful to assessors who were then moving on to value the work.

A different kind of visual approach was used for data capture in *Attitudes of Potential Teachers*. We were interviewing graduates from design, engineering and related degree programmes to tell us about their experience of design & technology in schools. Rather than merely present them with a bald list of bullet points to complete, we sought to appeal to more graphic/designerly instincts, and created the thumbs up/thumbs down images (Figure 14-9). They wrote their keywords inside these two images. We cannot say that it worked better than bald listing, but it did create an impression and it did work.

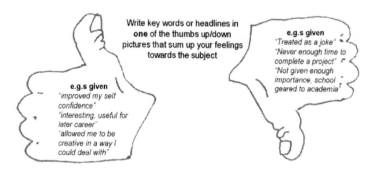

Figure 14-9. Attitudes of potential teachers – thumbs up/thumbs down keyword response

In both these cases the techniques might be thought to be barely noteworthy. But data capture is often a delicate and difficult exercise. In the first case (assessors colour coding) the learner responses are highly complex with many kinds of qualities interlinked and overlapping. The colour coding was a do-able task that simplified the process of assessment. Perhaps not by a lot, but maybe by just enough to make a difference. In the second case, we can sympathise with those who find filling in forms a tedious process. So anything that we can do to lighten the task – and maybe raise a smile – is worth doing. It might just make the difference between engagement and disengagement. It is also an approach we have increasingly used with learners – as young as 8 years old – where the symbol of the thumbs give more instantaneous meaning than words could.

This latter technique also exemplifies how we have typically used everyday, and often vernacular, language to create metaphors for concepts we wish to share with research participants – as we did with the use of **stationary**, **poddling** and **motoring** as metaphors for learner engagement and pace and the **wow** ◇ **yawn** continuum for assessing creativity.

3.5   **Research as Design, Design as Research**

We recognise that the form of this chapter has implied a degree of linearity to the process of research. **First**, sort out your research questions; **then** resolve the research design; **then** design the data capture system ... and so on. We tried several ways to organise the story of our research approach, and in the end it seemed best to do it this way. But we would like to enter a caveat here that cautions against a too sequential view of the research process.

Whilst it is broadly true that sorting out research questions is a primary task, and that it leads into questions about research design, as soon as we get inside a task we have found it helpful – and even necessary – to model what the data might look like and how we might capture it. This modelling process typically involves not only mock-ups of instruments of one kind or another – but also trials to see what happens when they get used. Sometimes this process reveals other features of the research task that we (perhaps belatedly) come to see as important and decide to find out about – so we modify the research design, redesign the instruments and trial it all again.

As we identified in Chapter 4, the process is iterative; starting with a view of how we think the research task will shape up and what it involves, and then moving forward through a series of iterative steps (innovation–modelling–trialling, reviewing: innovation–modelling–trialling–reviewing) until we get to the point at which we think enough of the confusion is ironed out and the instruments work sufficiently well and reveal enough of the things we are interested in. Because at some point we have to draw a line under these iterations, cross our fingers, and just press the 'go' button.

The whole researching process is, as we keep saying, just like designing.

Chapter 15

CONCLUDING REFLECTIONS

Throughout any designing process – and not least at the end – there are some questions that it is always worth asking of the designer. In schools, learners are familiar with this process, including on occasions presenting their work to their peers for critical review. When we have been responsible for choreographing such sessions, the hardest question we often ask is 'so what?' In fact we have elevated this somewhat crude question into a formal research tool.

'Doing a 'so-what'' is a nice shorthand way of probing into the questions that lie beneath the surface. OK so you have developed a new chair/calendar/baby-feeder. So what? How is the world changed? For whom is life better and richer? Who ends up worse off? And why? Such questions challenge budding designers to think of themselves as something more than merely developers of more stuff.

Throughout this book we have repeatedly drawn attention to the similarity that we see between designing and researching, so perhaps we should turn our question on ourselves. 20+ years of research in TERU: so what? How is the world changed? For whom is life better and richer?

We might offer all sorts of answers to this challenge, and – on reflection – they might be seen to fall into three categories that, taken together, act as a satisfactory conclusion to this work.

The superficial answer would be to claim that, since we have always managed to answer the research questions we set ourselves (or the ones that were set for us), we now know a lot more – about designing, learning, pedagogy, capability, assessment and the rest – than we did when we started. Moreover, the fact that this research is frequently cited elsewhere might be taken as evidence that the work has some value in the educational world. But that is to take a somewhat limited view of things – not unlike the designer pointing to the new chair as if that – by itself – is sufficient justification for all the hours, weeks and months of labour. Nonetheless, we would not wish to diminish the importance of these practical extensions to the stock of knowledge and understanding that collectively informs the educational game.

Perhaps a more significant 'so-what' argument might be made for the impact we have had on others' work. We point out at the end of Chapter 5 that one of the biggest impacts of the *APU* research that started us off, lies in the huge circle of people that were directly and indirectly touched by the project. The research team of course, and also the very eminent Steering Group and the team of civil servants who oversaw the process; the teachers who administered the tests; the team of markers and so on. We have frequently bumped into them in the subsequent years – in various parts of the world – and they often point to the significance of the experience for them as growing professionals. What goes for *APU* has subsequently applied in equal measure to all the projects, and for all the colleagues that we have interacted with in the process. We do not exclude from this circle the learners themselves, who so often find themselves at the uncomfortable cutting edge of one of our experiments. In describing (in Part One) the values that underpin our work, one of them has always been that the outcomes should be such as to empower and enliven learners and their lot in school. It has been one of our greatest sources of satisfaction to see these learners – sometimes the strugglers rather than the stars – enjoying themselves and growing in confidence and capability. A comment that will live with us from the *Assessing Design Innovation* project was made by a teacher in South Wales as she handed us the evaluation sheets from her group who had taken part in the first version of the 6 hour activity.

> One of the remarks that I recall from the project review sheet was '… it shows what I can do in a positive way'. – This was written by a pupil who is school phobic and finds school work difficult. (Teacher Database A.M-J)

Another group that has inevitably been touched by our work has been the research students we have supervised or otherwise interacted with. Sometimes they found themselves recruited as researchers, but more frequently they were there as a critical sounding board partly for our benefit but also partly so that they could view their own work through a different lens. But sounding boards are not inert – they vibrate at the same frequency as the sound and their creative vibration is sustained beyond the life of the original stimulus. They have all gone their various ways – sometimes within and sometimes not within research-like jobs – but they carry with them more than just their thesis and their beautiful robes. We would like to believe that they also carry some of the values and beliefs that we discussed in Part One, welded to some of the skills and understandings that we have articulated in Part Three.

This second category therefore amounts to a rather bigger and more significant 'so-what', for quite beyond the substance of the research we have conducted and the findings we have published, our effects on the multiple circles of people with whom we have interacted could probably, justifiably, be described as substantial.

Which brings us to the third and final category of 'so-what', and it is personal. Through the research projects outlined in this book we have tackled some tricky problems and dealt with some tricky clients; we have floated some whacky ideas and sweated to get them to work; we have argued endlessly with ourselves and with many others; we have run short of money on some projects and been grateful for the 'beer-float' that was gradually accumulating in TERU from the small surpluses on others; we have shared our ideas with others throughout the world and sought to understand its significance for them as well as for us.

In the process (which has for the most part been hugely pleasurable and satisfying) we have ourselves grown. So that is the final 'so-what'. It was great fun.

References

Allen, M. G. (1993). *Improving the personal skills of graduates; a conceptual model of transferable personal skills*. Sheffield: Sheffield Employment Department.

Angoff, W. H. (1974). Criterion-referencing, norm-referencing and the SAT. *College Board Review*, 92.

Archer, B. & Roberts, P. (1992). Design and technological awareness in education. In P. Roberts, B. Archer & K. Baynes (eds), *Design Occasional Paper No. 1, Modelling: the language of designing* (pp. 3–4). Loughborough: Loughborough University of Technology.

Archer, L. B. (1980). The mind's eye. *The designer*. Chichester: Wiley.

Archer, L. B., Baynes, K. & Langdon, R. (1976). *Design in general education: part one summary of findings*. London: Royal College of Art, Department of Design Research.

Assessment of Performance Unit (1981). *Understanding design and technology*. London: APU/DES.

Assessment of Performance Unit (1983). *Report of the survey of design & technological activities in the school curriculum*. Nottingham: National Centre for School Technology, Trent Polytechnic.

Atkinson, S. (1995). Approaches to designing at key stage 4. In J. S. Smith (ed.), *IDATER 95 International Conference on Design and Technology Educational Research and Curriculum Development* (pp. 36–47). Loughborough: Loughborough University of Technology.

Baillargeon, R., Pascual-Leone, J. & Roncadin, C. (1998). Mental-attentional capacity: does cognitive style make a difference. *Journal of Experimental Child Psychology*, 70, 143–166.

Bain, J. (2005). Photo-stories from Durham: a case study on assessing design innovation. In E. W. L. Norman, D. Spendlove & P. Grover (eds), *Inspire and educate: DATA International Research Conference 2005* (pp. 19–34). Wellesbourne: DATA.

Barlex, D. (2003). *Building on success: the unique contribution of design and technology – a report to Ministers from the Design and Technology Strategy Group*. London: Department for Education and Skills.

Barnett, C. (1986). The organizational failure. In T. Burgess (ed.), *Education for capability*. Windsor: NFER-Nelson.

Bayliss, V. (1999). *Opening minds: education for the 21st century*. London: RSA.

Berlyne, E. (1960). *Conflict, arousal and curiosity*. New York: McGraw-Hill.

Black, P. (1998). *Testing: friend or foe? Theory and practice of assessment and testing*. London: Falmer Press.

Black, P. & Harrison, G. (1985). *In place of confusion: technology and science in the curriculum*. London & Nottingham: Nuffield-Chelsea Curriculum Trust/National Centre for School Technology.

Bronowski, J. (1973). *The ascent of man*. London: British Broadcasting Corporation.

Brown, M. (1992). Elaborate nonsense? The muddled tale of Standard Assessment Tasks in mathematics at Key Stage 3. In C. Gipps (ed.), *Developing assessment for the National Curriculum* (pp. 6–19). London: Kogan Page.

Bruner, J. (1966). *Towards a theory of instruction*. Cambridge, MA: Harvard University Press.

Buchanan, R. (1995). Wicked problems in design thinking. In V. Margolin & R. Buchanan (eds), *The idea of design* (pp. 3–20). Cambridge, MA/London/England: MIT Press.

Burgess, T. (ed.) (1986). *Education for capability*. Windsor: NFER-Nelson.

Burghes, D. (1996). *MEP Demonstration Project: Report of the 2nd Gatsby Seminar on Mathematics Education*. London: The Gatsby Charitable Foundation.

Burghes, D. & Blum, W. (1995). *The Exeter-Kasel comparative project: a review of year 1 and year 2 results*. Paper presented at the Proceedings of a seminar on mathematics education, Gatsby Charitable Foundation, London.

Burghes, D., Jennings, S., Price, N. & Twyford, J. (1994). Trends in and their relevance to employers *Mathematics and its applications*, 13(3) 101–111.

Burghes, D., Price, N. & Twyford, J. (1996). The interface between mathematics and design & technology in secondary schools. *The Curriculum Journal*, 7(1) 35–50.

Cambridge, D., Smythe, C. & Heath, A. (2005). *IMS ePortfolio best practice and implementation guide*. Retrieved 25th April 2006, from http://www.imsglobal.org/ep/-epv1p0/imsep_bestv1p0.html

Christiaans, H. & Venselaar, K. (2005). Creativity in design engineering and the role of knowledge: modelling the expert. *International Journal of Technology and Design Education*, 15(3), 217–236.

Cognition and Technology Group at Vanderbilt (1990). Anchored instruction and its relationship to situated cognition. *Educational Researcher*, 19(6), 2–10.

Coyne, R., Park, H. & Wiszniewski, D. (2002). Design devices: digital drawing and the pursuit of difference. *Design Studies*, 23(3), 263–286.

Cross, N. (1990). The nature and nurture of design ability. *Design Studies*, 11(3), 127–140.

Crowther, G. (1959). *15–18: a report. Vol. 1*: Central Advisory Council for Education, England.

Csikszentmihalyi, M. (1996). *Creativity: flow and the psychology of discovery and invention*. New York: Harper Collins.

Darke, J. (1979). The primary generator and the design process. *Design Studies*, 1(1), 36–44.

Davidoff, J. & Donnelly, N. (1990). Object superiority: a comparison of complete and part probes. *Acta Psychologica*, 73, 225–243.

Davidoff, J. & Warrington, E. K. (1999). The bare bones of object recognition: implications from a case of object recognition impairment. *Neuropsychologia*, 37, 279–292.

Davis, D. (2001). *Student teachers' beliefs about science, design & technology: influences on planning for activities in the primary classroom*. , London: University of London.

DES (1981). *Understanding design and technology*. London: Department of Education and Science, HMSO.

DES (1991). *Circular 14/91The Education Reform Act 1988: the Education National Curriculum (assessment arrangements for English, maths and science) (key stage 1) Order 1991.* London: Department for Education and Science.

DES (1992). *Technology – Key Stages 1, 2 &3. A Report by HMInspectorate on the First Year 1990–91.* London: Department of Education and Science, HMSO.

DES/WO (1988a). *National Curriculum: Task Group on Assessment and Testing: a report.* London: Department of Education and Science and the Welsh Office.

DES/WO (1988b*). National Curriculum Design and Technology Working Group Interim Report.* London: Department of Education and Science and the Welsh Office.

DES/WO (1989). *Design and Technology for ages 5–16.* London: Department for Education and Science, HMSO.

Design Council. (1980). *Design education at secondary level: a Design Council report.* London: Design Council.

Design Council (1996). *Maths by design.* London: Design Council.

Design Council (1999). *Design in Britain 1998–99: facts figures and quotable quotes.* London: Design Council.

Dewey, J. (1991). *How we think.* New York: Prometheus Books.

DfEE/QCA (1999). *Design and technology: National Curriculum for England.* In DfES (ed.) (p. 50). London: DfES.

Donnelly, N. & Davidoff, J. (1998). The mental representations of faces and houses: issues concerning parts and wholes. *Visual Cognition,* 28, 118–139.

Donovan, M. S., Bransford, J. D. & Pellegrino, J. W. (1999). *How people learn: bridging research and practice.* Washington, DC: National Academy Press.

Downey, M. E. & Kelly, A. V. (1975). *Theory and practice of education: an introduction.* London: Harper & Row Publishers.

Eastman, C. M. (2001). New directions in design cognition: studies of representation and recall. In C. M. Eastman, W. M. McCracken & W. C. Newstetter (eds), *Design knowing and learning: cognition in design education* (pp. 147–198). Oxford: Elsevier Science.

Eisner, E. (1993). The emergence of new paradigms for educational research. *Art Education,* 46(6).

Eisner, E., W. (2002). *The arts and the creation of mind.* New Haven/London: Yale University Press.

Eysenck, H. J. (1976). *The measurement of personality/readings selected and comments written by H.J. Eysenck.* Lancaster: MTP Press.

Freebody, P. (2003). *Qualitative research in education: interaction and practice* (2004 re-print edn.). London: Sage.

Gardner, H. (1983). *Frames of mind: the theory of multiple intelligences.* London: Heinemann.

Garmire, E. & Pearson, G. (2006). *Tech tally: approaches to assessing technological literacy.* Washington, DC: National Academy Press.

Gipps, C. (ed.) (1992). *Developing assessment for the National Curriculum.* London: Kogan Page.

Glaser, R. (1992). Education and thinking: the role of knowledge. In R. McCormick, P. Murphy & M. Harrison (eds), *Teaching and learning technology* (pp. 91–111). Wokingham, UK: Addison-Wesley.

Gorard, S. & Taylor, C. (2004). *Combining methods in educational and social research.* Maidenhead: Open University Press.

Gorman & Carlson (1990). Interpreting invention as a cognitive process: the case of Alexander Graham Bell, Thomas Edison and the telephone. *Science, Technology and Human Values*, 15(2).

Hargreaves, D. (2001). Towards education for innovation. In D. Council (ed.), *Changing behaviours*. London: Design Council/Campaign for Learning.

Herschbach, D. R. (1995). Technology as Knowledge: implications for Instruction. *Journal of Technology Education*, 7(1), 31–42.

Hicks, G. (1983). Another step forward for design and technology. *APU Newsletter*, 4. London: DES.

Hirst, P. (1974). *Knowledge and the curriculum: a collection of philosophical papers*. London: Routledge & Kegan Paul.

Hope, G. (2004a). *Drawing as a tool for thought: the development of the ability to use drawing as a design tool amongst children aged*. London: University of London.

Hope, G. (2004b). *Teaching design and technology 3–11: the essential guide for teachers*. London: Continuum.

ITEA (2000). *Standards for technological literacy: content for the study of technology*. Reston, Virginia: International Technology Education Association.

Jensen, A. R. (1981). *Straight talk about mental tests*. New York: Free Press.

Johnson, S. (1989). *National Assessment: the APU Science approach*. London: Her Majesty's Stationery Office.

Kelly, A. (2003). Research as design. *Educational Researcher*, 31(1), 3–4.

Kelly, A. V., Kimbell, R. A., Patterson, V. J., Saxton, J. & Stables, K. (1987). *Design and technology: a framework for assessment*. London: HMSO.

Kelly, A. V. (1992). Concepts of assessment: an overview. In G. M. Blenkin & A. V. Kelly (eds), *Assessment in early childhood education* (pp. 1–23). London: Paul Chapman Publishing.

Kimbell, R. (1982). *Design education: the foundation years*. London: Routledge & Kegan Paul.

Kimbell, R. (1994). Progression in learning and the assessment of children's attainments. In D. Layton (ed.), *Innovations in science & technology education (Vol. 5: Emergence of technology education as a subject in the school curriculum)*. Paris: UNESCO.

Kimbell, R. (1997). *Assessing technology: international trends in curriculum and assessment*. Buckingham, UK: Open University Press.

Kimbell, R. (2000). *Creativity in crisis?* Wellesbourne: DATA/Nuffield Design and Technology.

Kimbell, R. (2002). Behind the headlines. *The Journal of Design and Technology Education*, 7(3), 155–156.

Kimbell, R. (2007). The challenge of holism: where criteria meet norms. *Design and Technology Education: An International Journal*, 12(2), 66–77.

Kimbell, R. & Green, R. (1996). *Technological maths: a research project for the Technology Enhancement Programme (TEP)*. London: Technology Education Research Unit, Goldsmiths University of London.

Kimbell, R. & Miller, S. (1999). *Design skills for work: fieldwork report*. London: Design Council.

Kimbell, R. & Perry, D. (2001). *Design and technology in a knowledge economy*. London: Engineering Council.

Kimbell, R. & Stables, K. (1999). *South Africa: North West Province Technology Education Project – an evaluation*. London: TERU, Goldsmiths College University of London.

Kimbell, R., Stables, K., Wheeler, T., Wozniak, A. & Kelly, A. V. (1991). *The assessment of performance in design and technology*. London: SEAC/HMSO.

Kimbell, R., Stables, K. & Green, R. (1996). *Understanding practice in design and technology*. Buckingham UK: Open University Press.

Kimbell, R., Mahoney, P., Miller, S. & Saxton, J. (1997a). *Decisions by Design: a research project commissioned by the Design Council* (March 1995–April 1997). Final Report. London: Goldsmiths College/Roehampton Institute.

Kimbell, R., Saxton, J., Miller, S., Liddament, T. & Stables, K. (1997b). *Design skills for work: an exploration of transferability*. London: Design Council.

Kimbell, R., Lawler, T., Stables, K. & Balchin, T. (2001). *ProDESKTOP in schools: a pilot study of its impact on design & technology*. London: TERU.

Kimbell, R., Balchin, T. & Stables, K. (2002a). *Energy and the environment: an evaluation of a NESTA LEGO collaborative design & technology project*. London: Technology Education Research Unit, Goldsmiths University of London.

Kimbell, R., Stables, K. & Sprake, J. (2002b). *Design Museum: an evaluation of 'Designers In Action' programme*. London: Technology Education Research Unit, Goldsmiths University of London.

Kimbell, R., Bain, J., Miller, S., Stables, K., Wheeler, T. & Wright, R. (2004a). *Assessing design innovation*. London: Goldsmiths College University of London.

Kimbell, R., McLaren, S., Hamilton, W. & Clewes, P. (2004b). *Roboteers in residence: an evaluation for NESTA and the BBC*. London: Technology Education Research Unit, Goldsmiths University of London.

Kimbell, R., Wheeler, T. & Nast, C. (2006). *e-scape Phase 2 interim report to SEAC*. London: Technology Education Research Unit, Goldsmiths University of London.

Kimbell, R., Wheeler, T., Miller, S. & Pollitt, A. (2007*). e-scape portfolio assessment: a research and development project for the Department for Education & Skills (DfES) and the Qualifications and Curriculum Authority (QCA), phase 2 report*. London: Technology Education Research Unit, Goldsmiths, University of London.

Kosslyn, S. M. (1979). Imaging and cognitive development: a teleological approach. In R. S. Siegler (ed.), *Children's thinking: what develops*? Hillsdale, NJ: Erlbaum.

Laming, D. (2004). *Human judgement: the eye of the beholder*. London: Thomson.

LaPorte, J. (2004). Procedural knowledge, storm doors, and ragged edges of metal. *Journal of Technology Education*, 16(1), 2–6.

Lawler, T. (1996). The use of cognitive style analysis and the APU Design and Technology assessment strategy as means of clarifying and describing student design work. *The Journal of Design and Technology Education*, 1(1), 4–11.

Lawler, T. (1999). Exposing the gender effects of design and technology project work by comparing strategies for presenting and managing pupils' work. In P. H. Roberts & E. W. L. Norman (eds), *IDATER 99: International Conference on Design and Technology Educational Research and Curriculum Development*. Loughborough: Loughborough University of Technology.

Lawler, T. (2006a). Design styles and teaching styles: a longitudinal study of pupils' ways of doing designing following complementary re-grouping and teaching. Paper presented at the *TERC 2006: Values in Technology Education* Gold Coast, Australia.

Lawler, T. (2006b). Design styles and teaching styles: a longitudinal study of pupils' ways of doing designing following complementary re-grouping and teaching. Paper presented at the *TERC 2006: Values in Technology Education* Gold Coast, Australia.

Lawson, B. (2004). *What designers know*. Oxford: Elsevier.

Lawton, D. (1992). Whatever happened to the TGAT Report? In C. Gipps (ed.), *Developing assessment for the National Curriculum* (pp. 95–103). London: Kogan Page.

Lewis, T. (1996). Accommodating border crossings. *Journal of Industrial Teacher Education*, 33(2), 7–28.

Lewis, T. (1999). Content or process as approaches to technology curriculum: does it matter come Monday morning? *Journal of Technology Education*, 11(1), 45–59.

MacLeod, R. M. (1982). *Days of judgement: science, examinations and the organization of knowledge in late Victorian England*. Driffield: Nafferton Books.

Margolin, V. (1989). *Design discourse*. Chicago: University of Chicago Press.

McCormick, R. (1999a). Capability lost and found? *The Journal of Design and Technology Education*, 4(1), 5–14.

McCormick, R. (1999b). Practical knowledge: a view from the snooker tables. In R. McCormick & C. Paechter (eds), *Learning and knowledge* (pp. 254). London: Paul Chapman Publishing.

McCormick, R., Murphy, P. & Davidson, M. (1994). Design and technology as revelation and ritual. In J. S. Smith (ed.), *International Conference on Design and Technology Educational Research and Curriculum Development* (pp. 38–42). Loughborough: University of Loughborough.

McLaren, S. V., Stables, K. & Bain, J. (2006). *Creativity and Progression in transition through Assessment for Learning in Design and Technology Education (CAPITTAL-DT): A pilot project Report to Determined to Succeed Division*. Glasgow: University of Strathclyde.

Millett, A. (1997). TTA Perspective. In *DATA Research Paper 9: Invitation conference on teacher supply in design and technology – Report and findings*. Wellesbourne: DATA.

Munn, P. (1995). What do children know about reading before they go to school? In P. Owen & P. Pumfrey (eds), *Emergent and developing reading: messages for teachers*. London: Falmer Press.

Myerson, J. (2001). *IDEO: masters of innovation*. London: Laurence King Publishing.

Nelson, H. G. & Stolterman, E. (2003). *The design way: intentional change in an unpredictable world*. Englewood Cliffs, NJ: Educational Technology Publications.

Nuttgens, P. (1986). The educational failure. In T. Burgess (ed.), *Education for capability*. Windsor: NFER-Nelson.

Ofsted (2001). *Ofsted subject reports 1999 – 00: primary design and technology*. London: Department for Education and Employment.

Ofsted (2002). *Secondary subject reports 2000/01: design and technology (No. HMI 373)*. London: Department for Education and Employment.

Oxman, R. (2001). The mind in design: a conceptual framework for cognition in design education. In C. M. Eastman, W. M. McCracken & W. C. Newstetter (eds), *Design knowing and learning: cognition in design education* (pp. 269–295). Oxford: Elsevier Science.

Papanek, V. (1995). *The green imperative: ecology and ethics in design and architecture*. London: Thames & Hudson.

Papert, S. (1991). Situated constructionism. In I. Harel & S. Papert (Eds.), *Constructionism: Research reports and essays 1985-1990/by the Epistemology & Learning Research Group, the Media Laboratory, Massachusetts Institute of Technology* (pp. 518). Norwood, N.J.: Ablex Publishing Corporation.

Pearson, G. & Young, A. T. (2002). *Technically speaking: why all Americans need to know more about technology*. Washington, DC: National Academy Press.

Penfold, J. (1988). *Craft design & technology: past present and future*. Stoke-on-Trent: Trentham Books.

Pessant, J. R. & McMahon, B. J. (1979). Participant observation of a major design decision in industry. *Design Studies*, 1(1), 21–26.

Plowden, B. H. (1967). *Children and their primary schools: a report of the Central Advisory Council for Education (England) (Vol. 1: the report)*. London: HMSO.

Polanyi, M. (1958). *Personal knowledge: towards a post-critical philosophy*. London: Routledge & Kegan Paul.

Pollitt, A. (2004). Let's stop marking exams. Paper presented at the *IAEA Conference*, Philadelphia.

Powney, J. & Watts, M. (1987). *Interviewing in educational research*. London: Routledge & Kegan Paul.

Prest, D. (2002). *An analysis of the attainment target level descriptors and associated programme of study in relation to the design and technology mission statement*. London: Department for Education and Skills, Design and Technology Strategy Group.

QCA (2005). *A review of GCE and GCSE coursework arrangements*. London: Qualifications and Curriculum Authority.

Raat, J. H., de Klerk Wolters, F. & de Vries, M. J. (1987). *Report PATT-conference; Vol 1 proceedings* (Vol. 1). Eindhoven: Eindhoven University of Technology.

Ridgway, J., McCusker, S. & Pead, D. (2005). *Report 10: Literature review of e-assessment*. Bristol: Nesta Futurelab.

Riding, R. J. & Cheema, I. (1991). Cognitive styles: an overview and integration. *Educational Psychology*, 11(3), 193–215.

Riding, R. J. & Pearson, R. D. (1981). The Relationship between Personality Dimensions of Extroversion and Field Independence and Art Performance in 13 year old Children. *Educational Review*, 33(3).

Roberts, P. H. (Ed.). (1979). *Design in general education: The report of an enquiry conducted by the Royal College of Art for the Secretary of State for Education and Science*. London: Royal College of Art.

Rogoff, B. (1990). *Apprenticeship in thinking: cognitive development in social context*. Oxford: Oxford University Press.

Sage, J. (1996). Developing capability in technology through collaborative approaches with mathematics and science. *The Journal of Design and Technology Education*, 1(1), 66–73.

Schön, D. (1983). *The reflective practitioner: how professionals think in action*. New York: Basic Books.

Schön, D. (1987). *Educating the reflective practitioner: towards a new design for teaching and learning in the professions*. San Francisco: Jossey-Bass.

School Examinations and Assessment Council (1991). *National Curriculum Assessment at Key Stage 3: a review of the 1991 pilots with implications for 1992*. London: SEAC.

Schools Council (1970). *Schools Council Project Technology: the next two years*. London: Schools Council.

Schools Council (1975). *Education through design and craft: Schools Council Design and Craft Education project*. London: Edward Arnold.

Schwandt, T. (1994). 'Constructivist interpretive approaches to human enquiry'. In N. K. Denzin & Y. S. Lincoln (eds), *Handbook of qualitative research*. Thousand Oaks: Sage.

Secondary Examinations Council (SEC) (1985). *Craft, Design & Technology GCSE: A guide for teachers*. Milton Keynes: Open University Press.

Seltzer, K. & Bentley, T. (1999). *The creative age: knowledge and skills for the new economy*. London: Demos.

Sen, A., K. (1984*). Resources, values and development*. Oxford: Basil Blackwell.

Sen, A. (1992). *Inequality reexamined*. New York: Russell Sage Foundation.

Shavelson, R. J., Baxter, G. P. & Pine, J. (1991). Performance assessment in science. *Applied Measurement in Education*, 4(4), 347–362.

Shaw, G. (1996). *Design into practice: Teachers Training Pack*. London: Design Museum.

Skogh, I.-B. (2005). Innovative performance – how can it be assessed? In E. W. L. Norman, D. Spendlove & P. Grover (eds), *Inspire and educate: DATA International research conference 2005* (pp. 161–166). Wellesbourne: DATA.

Stables, K. (1992a). Issues surrounding the development of technological capability in children in their first years of schools (ages 5–7). In D. Blandow & M. Dyrenfurth (eds), *Technological literacy, competence and innovation in human resource development: proceedings of the first International Conference on Technology Education* (pp. 372–379). Erfurt: WOCATE.

Stables, K. (1992b). *Phase 2 Evaluation Report: Key Stage 1 Technology Standard Assessment Task Development*. London: Consortium for Assessment and Testing in Schools/Goldsmiths College.

Stables, K. (1992c). The assessment of technology at key stage 1. In C. Gipps (ed.), *Developing assessment for the National Curriculum* (pp. 42–50). London: Kogan Page.

Stables, K. (1995). Discontinuity in transition: pupils' experience of technology in Year 6 and Year 7. *International Journal of Technology and Design Education*, 5(2), 157–169.

Stables, K. (2000). Learning technology through collaboration: examining the impact on learners in South Africa of introducing technology education through using collaborative design processes. Paper presented at the *International Conference of Scholars on Technology Education*, Braunschweig.

Stables, K. (2001). Exploring mystery products to develop design and technology skills: case studies from the Design Museum's Outreach Project. *The Journal of Design and Technology Education*, 6(2), 109–115.

Stables, K. & Kimbell, R. (2000). The unpickled portfolio: pioneering performance assessment in design and technology. In R. Kimbell (ed.), *Design and Technology International Millennium Conference* (pp. 195–202). Wellesbourne: DATA.

Stables, K. & Kimbell, R. (2001). Technology education in South Africa: evaluating an innovative pilot project. *Research in Science Education*, 31(1), 71–90.

Stables, K. & Kimbell, R. (2006). Unorthodox methodologies: approaches to understanding design and technology. In M. J. d. Vries & I. Mottier (eds), *International handbook of technology education: Reviewing the past twenty years* (pp. 313–330). Rotterdam: Sense Publishers.

Stables, K. & Rogers, M. (2001). Reflective and literate boys: can design and technology make a difference? Paper presented at the *IDATER 2001: International Conference on Design and Technology Educational Research and Curriculum Development*. Loughborough: Loughborough University.

Stables, K., Kendall, S. & Parker, S. (1991). *Phase 1 Evaluation Report: Key Stage 1 Technology Standard Assessment Task Development*. London: Consortium for Assessment and Testing in Schools/Goldsmiths College.

Stephenson, J. (1992). Capability and quality in higher education. In J. Stephenson & S. Weil (eds), *Quality in learning: a capability approach in higher education* (pp. 208). London: Kogan Page.

Strauss, A. & Corbin, J. (1994). Grounded theory methodology. In N. K. Denzin & Y. S. Lincoln (eds), *Handbook of qualitative research*. Thousand Oaks: Sage.

Temple, S. & Morris, L. (1995). Design degrees. *An investigation into the teaching and learning of the design process in higher education.* London: Design Council.

Threlfall, P. M. (1980). *A level design & technology: the identification of a core syllabus. A report* Council for National Academic Awards/Standing Conference on University Entrance CNAA/SCUE.

Thurstone, L. L. (1927). A law of comparative judgement. *Psychological Review*, 34, 273–286.

Tufnell, R. (2000). The introduction of criterion-referenced assessment to design and technology. In J. Eggleston (ed.), *Teaching and learning design and technology: a guide to recent research and its applications* (pp. 104–115). London: Continuum.

Vygotsky, L. S. (1978). *Mind in society: the development of higher psychological processes.* Cambridge, MA: Harvard University Press.

Waks, L. J. (2001). Donald Schön's Philosophy of Design and Design Education. *International Journal of Technology and Design Education*, 11(1), 37–51.

Weaver, T. (1986). Education for what? In T. Burgess (ed.), *Education for capability.* Windsor: NFER-Nelson.

Wiggins, G. (1990). The case for authentic assessment (Vol. ERIC Digest 073): *Education Resources Information Centre ED328611.*

Williams, P. J. (2000). Design: the only methodology of technology? *Journal of Technology Education*, 11(2), 48–60.

Williams, R. (1965). *The long revolution.* London: Penguin.

Witkin, H. A., Goodenough, D. R. & Karp, S. A. (1967). Stability of cognitive style from childhood to young adulthood. *Journal of Personality and Social Psychology*, 7, 291–300.

Witte, M. H., Kerwin, A., Witte, C. L. & Scadron, A. (1989). A curriculum on medical ignorance. *Medical Education*, 23(1), 24–29.

Index

Printed in the United Kingdom
by Lightning Source UK Ltd.
134474UK00003B/112/P